Value Creation and Branding in Television's Digital Age

Value Creation and Branding in Television's Digital Age

TIMOTHY M. TODREAS

QUORUM BOOKS
Westport, Connecticut • London

Library of Congress Cataloging-in-Publication Data

Todreas, Timothy M., 1961–
 Value creation and branding in television's digital age / Timothy
M. Todreas.
  p. cm.
 Includes bibliographical references and index.
 ISBN 1–56720–272–1 (alk. paper)
 1. Television supplies industry—Forecasting. 2. Digital
television—Forecasting. I. Title.
 HD9696.T462T63 1999
 338.4'7621388—dc21   98–51663

British Library Cataloguing in Publication Data is available.

Library of Congress Catalog Card Number: 98–51663
ISBN: 1–56720–272–1

First published in 1999

Quorum Books, 88 Post Road West, Westport, CT 06881
An imprint of Greenwood Publishing Group, Inc.
www.quorumbooks.com

Printed in the United States of America

The paper used in this book complies with the
Permanent Paper Standard issued by the National
Information Standards Organization (Z39.48–1984).

10 9 8 7 6 5 4 3 2 1

Copyright Acknowledgment

Every reasonable effort has been made to trace the owners of copyright
materials in this book, but in some instances this has proven impossible.
The author and publisher will be glad to receive information leading to
more complete acknowledgments in subsequent printings of the book,
and in the meantime extend their apologies for any omissions.

To my family

Contents

Part I

The Distribution Bottleneck

Introduction:
Value Migrates Upstream

The story of how television programming evolved from its Golden Age origins of Milton Berle in the living room to its post-MTV pastiche is a familiar one. No one who has lived through the last few decades of the twentieth century would fail a basic test on television that contained questions like "name a network news anchorman or a famous television pet." In fact, more people probably know the names of Jerry Seinfeld's friends than the name of their senator or representative.

However, ask whether a television producer or a local station makes more money and you will probably draw a blank. This book tells the story of the business of television. It traces the history of profitability in the television business from the Tiffany network through the hegemony of John Malone, the "Darth Vader of the cable kabal," and into the digital future of cable modems, direct broadcast satellites, and digital terrestrial television. The book is about who makes money, why they make it, and whether they will continue to make it.

The best way to understand the industry and its economics is to think about it in terms of a supply chain (Exhibit 1). In its simplest terms, the industry consists of content and conduit. Content consists of the upstream suppliers: the producers and packagers of programming. Think of packagers as networks that buy and produce programming and put it into schedules. The conduit consists of the downstream distributors: the local television stations, the cable operators, and television manufacturers. The dominant firms in the business are household names. Firms like Paramount, Disney, and Viacom are predominantly suppliers of content—they produce programming like "a Paramount film," the Disney Channel, and MTV—while Belo, Cablevision, and Zenith are conduit

Exhibit 1
The Television Industry Supply Chain

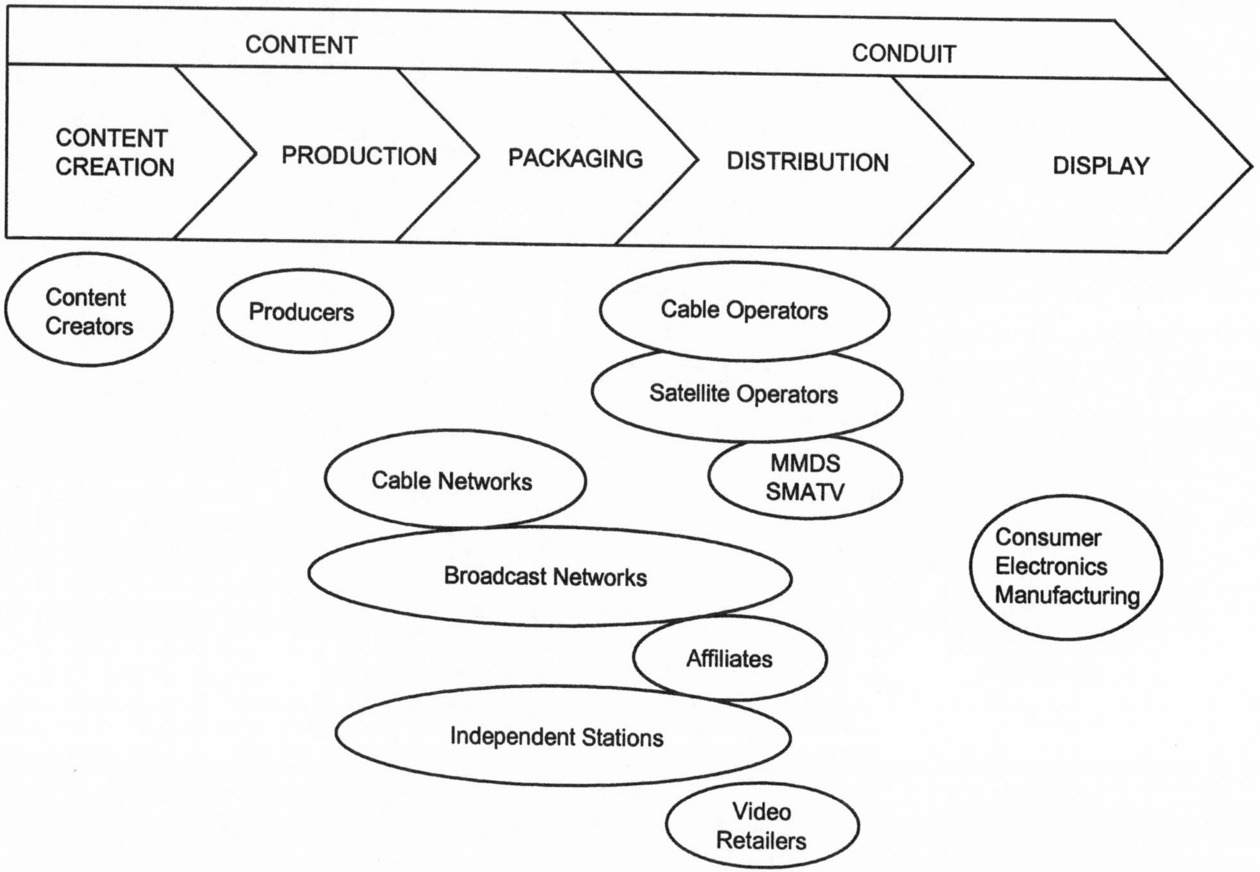

players—they own local stations or cable systems that distribute television signals or, in Zenith's case, they produce the television sets themselves.

A firm's position within this supply chain is the key determinant of profitability. Whether a firm is in content or conduit—upstream or downstream—will matter more in predicting profits than whether it is in one of the traditional categories, like broadcast or cable, used to describe the industry.

Until now the communications industry has been divided into categories; each had its own economic logic as well as its own regulatory framework. The telephone business had nothing to do with television, television was distinct from radio, and radio was unlike print. Even within television, the traditional broadcast side of the business operated under an economic and regulatory framework separate from the cable side of the business.

Technology is now sweeping these distinctions into the dustbin of history. We are on the cusp of a Digital Era in which content will be deliverable in digital form to viewers through no fewer than five conduits into the home. When the technology first appeared that made television possible via satellite, telephone wire, or microwave, these conduits were initially treated like separate businesses. However, all the technologies capable of delivering television are converging into a single video business and are moving closer to being treated identically by regulators. From a business perspective, since all of the conduits for television will be as similar to each other as one wire is to the next, it will not matter which conduit a firm uses or owns.

The more important question will be whether a firm is in the content or conduit business. Systematic differences in profitability have started to emerge between firms positioned upstream and those positioned downstream in the supply chain. These differences will widen as technology changes the nature of the business relationships up and down the supply chain.

WHERE IS THE MONEY? CONTENT OR CONDUIT?

The history of the industry can be divided into three distinct eras (Exhibit 2). In the Broadcast Era, which lasted from the birth of television in the late 1940s to the 1970s, the business was dominated by the broadcast networks and local television stations. The next era began when a group of entrepreneurs began laying an infrastructure of coaxial cable and supplying viewers, for a fee, with a collection of new cable networks. Today, we are entering a new Digital Era of satellites, digital television, and the Internet.

Throughout the industry's first two eras, the money stopped at the

Exhibit 2
The Three Eras of the Television Industry

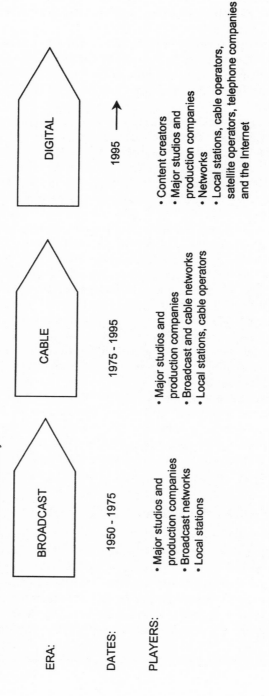

	BROADCAST	CABLE	DIGITAL
ERA:			
DATES:	1950 - 1975	1975 - 1995	1995 →
PLAYERS:	• Major studios and production companies • Broadcast networks • Local stations	• Major studios and production companies • Broadcast and cable networks • Local stations, cable operators	• Content creators • Major studios and production companies • Networks • Local stations, cable operators, satellite operators, telephone companies and the Internet
STRATEGIC PARADIGM:	The "distribution bottleneck" controlled by stations	The "distribution bottleneck" controlled by stations and cable operators	The "Great Value Shift" from distribution to digital brands and content creators

conduit (Exhibit 3). The distribution of television signals was an extraordinarily lucrative entreprise. In fact, it has been one of the most profitable industries in the economic history of America.

The reason? Until recently, distributors had little or no competition. There were only a handful of stations in any one town and, later, only one cable operator. The lucky owners of these businesses had the government to thank. In the "interests" of viewers, policy makers decreed that there would only be a few broadcast licenses in any given market. Later, during the Cable Era, city officials typically granted only a single cable license for each municipality. The broadcast and cable incumbents were further protected by technology and economics that enforced these policies.

Clearly these firms competed with each other, but in the same way that two cellular providers or two large soft-drink makers might compete: with padded gloves. Prices escalate upward, competition occurs in the form of changes to the product, margins stay fat, and the profits roll in.

The 1990s are bringing a new Digital Era. In this new era, the nature of the conduit is undergoing a fundamental shift. The effect of this is to introduce new players into the distribution business and new ways of transporting content. These new players will increase competitive intensity, put pressure on margins, and reduce profits.

At the same time that this shift is destroying value in the conduit, it will create value in content. Technology will not change the process of content creation: the method of making a football game, a Beethoven sonata, or a one-hour drama is still going to be the same. However, content will benefit from the digital revolution in several ways. First, as conduits multiply, they will have to compete with each other to buy and transmit the best content. That means that they will offer more money to content providers at the expense of their own margins.

Second, content can now be sold repeatedly into multiple conduits. While broadcasting was the dominant delivery mechanism, a theatrical film, for example, was sold to broadcasters after it had been exhibited in theatres and was then shelved. Only the most popular films were exhibited once again either on television or in theatres. In the new era of multiple conduits, that same theatrical film can be sold to cable operators, videocassette retailers, satellite distributors, and telephone companies, not to mention non-video media such as print, retailing, and audio. Furthermore, instead of being shelved, films can be sold back to conduits desperate for programming, at a later time, for repeated use.

However, saying that content will win is like predicting that one of the teams that makes the playoffs will win the championship. The content business is multifaceted: it consists of several different stages, each with its own skill requirements and market conditions. Businessmen and

Exhibit 3
The Changing Flows of Profit in the Supply Chain: Operating Profit

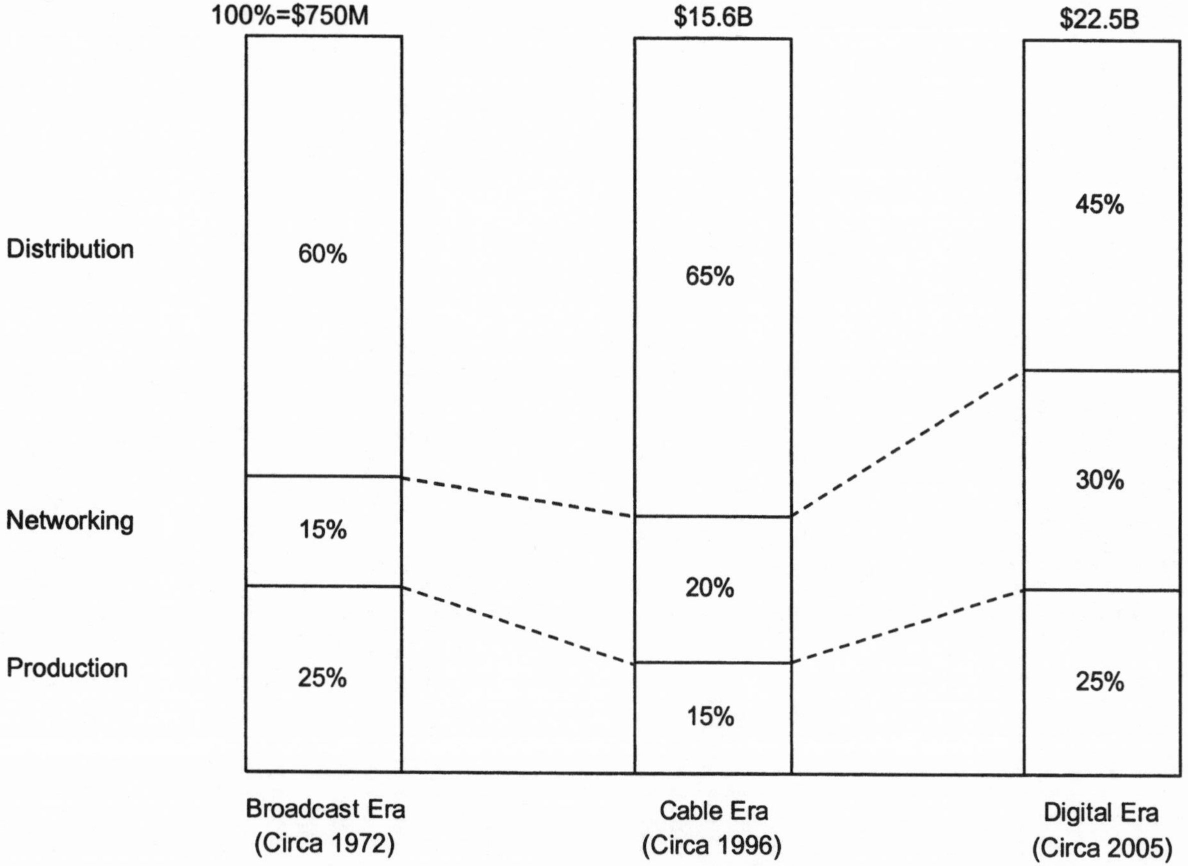

	Broadcast Era (Circa 1972)	Cable Era (Circa 1996)	Digital Era (Circa 2005)
	100%=$750M	$15.6B	$22.5B
Distribution	60%	65%	45%
Networking	15%	20%	30%
Production	25%	15%	25%

investors need to know which part of the content business is best positioned to create shareholder value.

Only content creators and packagers will see large profits. In other words, athletes in the National Football League, band members of U2, or star actors like Harrison Ford will continue to earn spectacular rewards. Established packagers like MTV and NBC will also reap the content bonanza. As we saw in Exhibit 3, the packaging function was already increasing its share of the profits in television during the Cable Era. These packagers are brands that viewers recognize and value in the vast expanse of available programming choices. Established brands are, and will continue to be, the dominant networks. Margins may come under pressure as networks spend to improve their product, but they will remain comfortable.

Rushing into the studio to produce a half-hour sitcom will not generate profits anymore than sitting down and trying to write next year's bestseller ever did. Tastes are too difficult to predict and the business of trying to predict them is simply too competitive and too difficult to manage for the content production business ever to become more profitable than its risk justifies.

Even new distribution and new search tools like the Internet and the next generation of intelligent agents will not change this pattern of profitability. Content ownership and packaging will continue to be the best source of value because viewers will continue to be attracted to good content and because branded packaging will remain the best way to organize content.

Part I of the book begins with a chapter introducing the television industry and tracing its history from its roots in the Golden Age of broadcasting through the era of John Malone and the dominance of the cable operator. The story begins with the defining structural feature in the television industry, the "distribution bottleneck." The distribution bottleneck is the stranglehold that stations and cable operators have had in the television business. Ownership of the bottleneck allowed the distributors of video to capture most of the profits available to the industry.

Distributors did their best to protect the bottleneck, but technological forces were at work. The digital revolution would not change the way a Verdi opera was produced; it would, however, wreak havoc on the way that the production would be distributed. In Chapter 2, the book explains how technology broke the distribution bottleneck.

In Part II, the book goes on to describe the future of television. It starts with the fate of distribution. Chapter 3 describes the "Great Value Shift" with the bottleneck broken, and the migration of profits from distributors. The party will be over for distribution in the new Digital Era.

Where will profits migrate? As Chapter 4 demonstrates, the answer is not obvious. Media giants seem set on two strategies that are unlikely to end with profits. Some chase a set-top box monopoly like a holy grail while others build massive content/conduit combines. Both strategies will not reproduce the sought-after bottleneck.

Profits will be made in the content business. But, Chapter 5 will show that all firms will not win. While stars and sluggers will grow ever richer and a few packagers will emerge as profitable digital brands, the best way to make a large fortune as a producer will still be to start with a small one.

In the Epilogue, we wrestle with the outcome of the "Great Media Free-for-All." Not only will the Digital Era shatter the distribution bottleneck, but it will destroy the walls protecting media from each other. In the Digital Era television will compete against radio, print, and new all digital formats. As exciting as the new world of interactive content is, it will not, in the end, replace television. Television has two big advantages in the Digital Era. First, video is, and will remain, the central part of the consumer's media experience. Second, television has built powerful and enduring brands.

Television can capitalize on these twin advantages by following three strategic imperatives: it must (1) leverage its core competency in video production to make "super" content, (2) take advantage of the new interactive functionality that digital television offers, and (3) extend its brands onto the Internet.

Chapter 1

The Distribution
Bottleneck Strategy

There are three distinct eras in the history of the television industry: the Broadcast Era, the Cable Era, and the Digital Era (Exhibit 2). The fundamental distinguishing feature between each of these eras is the nature of distribution. While the content of television has remained relatively constant—substitute Paul Reiser for Dick Van Dyke to update the situation comedy—the distribution of television has undergone a revolution. Content that reached viewers via three over-the-air signals in the Broadcast Era could also be distributed over coaxial cable in the Cable Era and via broadcast, cable, microwave, satellite, telephone, and utility lines in the Digital Era.

This revolution in television distribution has changed the process of value creation and the patterns of profitability in the industry. Historically, the most profitable part of the industry was distribution. In both the Broadcast and Cable eras, distributors were the bottleneck in the supply chain. Owning distribution was like having a liquor license—except that many fewer television distribution licenses than liquor licenses were awarded. Distributors used their privileged position to build one of the country's most profitable industries. Content was a poor cousin. It was more competitive and less profitable.

As the years have passed and the industry matured, the distribution bottleneck has loosened. With the loss of their bottleneck, distributors are facing a new era with lower profits. Content can begin to imagine the prospect of better times.

This chapter introduces the television industry in its historical context. It describes the Broadcast and Cable eras and sets the stage for the discussion of the Digital Era that is to follow.

THE BROADCAST ERA

Television was not the first technology to bring video to audiences around the world. That distinction belongs to motion pictures. At the dawn of the Broadcast Era, the movies were a vital industry. They drew Americans out of their houses for a day or an evening at the theatre. At the time, these theatres and the pictures shown at them were controlled by an oligopoly of major studios and exhibitors. They constituted video's first distribution bottleneck, and they used it to generate great wealth for their shareholders.

Although the film industry did not realize it at the time, television would break the existing bottleneck of video distribution. The bottleneck would be broken by a new medium that could bypass the theatres and deliver a video signal to viewers in the comfort of their living rooms.

However, television ended up replacing one bottleneck with another. Television doomed the film industry, but replaced it with the tyranny of the local television station. The source of the television station's bottleneck was the electromagnetic spectrum, the "airwaves" through which television signals are propagated, and the spectrum management policies of the federal government.

How did this happen? And, once it happened, who were the winners and losers in the television supply chain?

The Creation of the Distribution Bottleneck

The Broadcast Era officially began in the 1920s with three discoveries—Vladimir Zworykin's iconoscope and kinescope, Philo Farnsworth's electronic camera, and Allen B. Dumont's receiving tube—that together made television possible. They were assembled into the first regular television station by General Electric in 1928. This station, WGY in Schenectady, New York, was joined by about 20 other stations by the late 1930s. In the 1930s and 1940s, television made its first national impact by broadcasting the New York World's Fair, the political conventions of 1940, and a speech by President Franklin Roosevelt.

The basic technology of broadcast television was basically the same as it is today. Programs are recorded using cameras in studios. The programs, prerecorded or live, are then converted into electronic signals of a certain size, or frequency. Transmitters, owned and operated by local stations, send these signals through the air, or terrestrially. Individual households purchase television receivers equipped to receive the signals and convert them into images.

From the beginning of the Broadcast Era, the industry would shoulder significant regulatory oversight. Having some experience from the development of radio, the government knew that television broadcasting would require a licensing system to keep local stations from interfering with each other. The Federal Radio Commission, replaced by the Federal Communications Commission (FCC) in 1934, was established to manage the electromagnetic spectrum.

With the number of television stations growing rapidly to about 100 in 1948, the FCC imposed a "freeze" on further licensing to develop an allocation policy for television. The FCC lifted the freeze in 1952 with its celebrated Sixth Report and Order. With this decision, the commission developed spectrum management procedures that licensed the airwaves and solved the problem of interference. On the other hand, it would also create the "distribution bottleneck."

To be sure, a distribution bottleneck existed even before the FCC got started in its deliberations in 1948: There is only so much spectrum through which television signals could be sent and, therefore, room for only so many television stations. However, in its Sixth Report and Order, the FCC made three basic decisions that would tighten the distribution bottleneck even further. First, the FCC allocated only a limited amount of the very-high-frequency (VHF) and ultra-high-frequency (UHF) bands[1] to television while reserving the rest for other uses. Second, the FCC followed the principal of "localism" and assigned at least one station to each community in the country. In order to accomplish this, each community could have two or three local stations instead of six or seven regional or national stations. Third, the FCC put both the twelve-channel VHF allocation and the technologically inferior[2] 70-channel UHF allocation in the same market. In this part of the decision, the only competition that the FCC allowed was between two very unequal services. The FCC could just as easily have expanded the VHF band or replaced it with an all-UHF system. With these three decisions, the FCC limited the amount of spectrum it would allocate for television, limited the number of stations even further in order to achieve the goal of "localism," and created an unequal playing field for what competition it did allow.

The distribution bottleneck was firmly established. During the Broadcast Era, thousands of stations were broadcasting. However, in any one locality there are still only a handful of stations: typically two to five of the more powerful VHF stations and up to five or ten of the weaker UHF stations.

The "Qwertyness" of Networks

The FCC set up local stations, but where did their programming come from? Of course, each station could have developed its own schedule of programming and transmitted it. Such programming is just what the FCC wanted to encourage with its policy of localism. However, that would not be as efficient as making programming centrally and spreading its costs over a group of stations. It did not take long before the television industry developed a system that circumvented the FCC's rules and took advantage of economies of scale. It was called the network system.

The network paradigm grew to dominate the Broadcast Era, and it continues to thrive today. From an economic perspective, networking makes good sense. Since the cost of programming is fixed regardless of the number of viewers, by joining a group of local stations across the country to show a program, each station could increase its returns to scale from a fixed investment in programming. How did this system work in practice?

The idea was simple. If you could not make programming for a single national station, why not make it for a group of local stations? This is all networking really is: a group of stations getting together and making large-scale programming that none would be able to afford individually. The network can be seen as a vehicle to achieving greater station profitability.

At the dawn of the Broadcast Era, only two VHF stations were consistently available in cities and towns in the United States. This meant that there was only room for two national station groups, or networks; a third or fourth would suffer by having to use less powerful UHF stations in certain localities. The first two national networks to take advantage of this opportunity, NBC and CBS, were radio broadcasters that made the transition quickly into television. ABC would emerge in the 1970s as the third major broadcast network in the era.

These networks performed three essential functions: they (1) made programming or bought it from television production companies, (2) packaged it into a schedule that got delivered to local stations, and (3) marketed and sold time slots on their schedules to advertisers.

Worried that these station groups would become too powerful by owning all of the stations in their vast networks, the FCC limited networks to owning five stations around the country by the 5-5-5 Rule. This rule has been subsequently extended twice: first, to the 12-12-12 Rule, which allowed each network to own up to 12 local stations, not to exceed 25 percent of the national market, and later, to 35 percent of the national market. The networks have consistently bought stations, known as owned-and-operated stations, or O&O's, up to their limits and are among the largest groups of station owners in the country.

Since O&O's did not cover the entire country, the networks had to find another way of gaining national coverage. After all, once the programming was made, distribution to other stations would provide pure marginal revenue. Naturally the networks took the largest markets for their O&O's. For the rest of the country, the networks built up a group of affiliated stations. These stations were bound to the network by an

affiliation agreement that stipulated the amount and terms of the programming that they would receive from the network.

In a network-affiliate relationship, as it has come to be called, the network provides the affiliate with programming, a minute or two of time
during each hour of this programming in which the affiliate can insert
local advertising, and a cash payment, known as affiliate compensation,
which today averages 3 percent of total local station revenue.[3] In return,
the affiliate promises to transmit this programming, complete with inserted network advertising.

The issues that emerged in any network-affiliate negotiation were at
the level of compensation, the length of commercial time given to affiliates, and the quality and type of programming that each party offered.
This last point is important because viewers tend to keep tuned to a
channel. If the local news is popular, network programming that follows
will be popular and vice versa. If networks do not provide good programming, affiliates can try to "pre-empt" it—replace it—with their own
choice of programming that they believe would be more popular locally.

FCC regulations promulgated over the years have tended to protect
the affiliates from the networks by prohibiting such things as all-or-
nothing contracts, compensation schemes that are segmented more finely
than by day-part, contracts made for longer than two years, or network
affiliation with more than one station in a market. In the end, the terms
of the contract tend to hinge on structural factors like the relative concentration of the two sides, in a market: If there are more local stations
than networks, the networks have the upper hand; if there are more
networks than local stations, the local stations have a stronger position.[4]
Once made, the relationships are relatively stable since the costs of
switching are significant; they involve promoting entirely new schedules
of programming.

Not all stations were lucky enough to be affiliated with networks during the Broadcast Era. For the most part, the weaker UHF stations were
left unaffiliated and became independents. Without the network to rely
on for programming, these independent stations had to survive on their
own. They filled their schedule with programs that they produced themselves, like news and sports, purchased "off-network" programs,[5] and
purchased "syndicated" programming.[6] In general, this programming
was more expensive and less popular than the network fare that was
available to the affiliates.

The network-affiliate system was generally considered to be a good
deal for affiliates since they got terrific programming, valuable time to
sell a few local spots, and some cash to top it off. The networks were
happy since they kept the best local stations for themselves and used the
larger affiliate group as a means to obtain scale to develop good programming.

Networks evolved during the era of broadcast television and are now an established fixture in the landscape of television. However, they need not have become so. A view of the economy based on the notion of positive feedback has been developed recently that helps explain how this happened and why it could have happened very differently. This view, called path dependency, suggests that chance events can get combined with positive feedback to determine economic developments. For example, the "qwerty" keyboard for computers, so named after the first six keys on the upper left corner of the keyboard, was originally developed with the first typewriters so that the keys would not get stuck when the typist struck them at high speeds. The keyboard has remained dominant long after the demise of the technology for which it was developed because of the near universal knowledge of the keyboard today and the costs that would have to be incurred to learn a new format. Similarly, the VHS format for VCRs and the twelve-hour "clockwise" design of clockfaces owe their universal acceptance to events that occurred at the beginning of their diffusion and the subsequent positive feedback that took place once they were given a slight edge over the alternatives.[7]

In our industry, had certain events not taken place at the dawn of the Broadcast Era, the networks might not have been in the position they are in today. Networks evolved in order to take advantage of scale economies in the distribution of programming: by producing and distributing national programming to an affiliated group of local stations, networks were able to earn national revenues for the cost of a program while local stations could earn only local revenues for the cost of the same program.

However, there could have been other ways to achieve scale economies. For example, the FCC could have licensed spectrum such that a few national television stations were created. If this had been the FCC's policy, there would have been no need for networks, as the stations could have distributed programming nationally themselves. Or, after the FCC had settled on its licensing scheme, advertisers themselves could have sponsored national programming and distributed it. In fact, at the beginning of the broadcast television era, this was the model for achieving scale in program production: the Goodyear Playhouse was one early example of the sponsorship model. It makes economic sense. Advertisers themselves sponsor national programming and distribute it to stations for free in return for the chance to air commercials for their products. The problem of the limited range of local stations is circumvented and advertisers avoid paying for a middleman, like a network, to distribute programming for them. The power of the model can be seen in the fact that variations still exist today. In the barter syndication market, program producers sell time to advertisers and then sell programming directly to stations, thus avoiding networks; in the cable market, advertisers sponsor programming directly.

Why isn't the advertiser-sponsor model the dominant one today? One of the main reasons why this model disappeared has more to do with "qwertyness," or path dependency, than reason. In the 1950s, a sponsor was discovered to have fixed the results of a popular quiz show. Because of the popularity of the show and Charles van Doren, the contestant whose answers were fixed, the investigation grew larger and the public became more interested. What started as a legal attempt to improve the ratings of a single program became a national scandal that brought on cries to get advertisers out of the program production process. As sponsors withdrew, networks took the opportunity to take their place as a distributor of national programming.

As the networking paradigm developed, it became clear that in addition to providing scale in production, networks could also capture several other efficiencies. Not only does program production have high fixed costs, it also has high risk. Many programs will end without ever catching on with audiences. These programs have to be cancelled and replaced with others until successes are found. By building a full schedule, networks can spread program production risks over a series of programs: A failure or two will not wipe them out as it would a producer of a single program.

Networks also had advantages in planning their schedules. Since viewers tend to remain tuned to the same channel and watch "adjacent" programs, networks could coordinate program schedules to maximize viewing. This concept may be familiar to viewers today of NBC's "Must See TV" schedule for a Tuesday or Thursday night. NBC has built whole schedules around mega-hits like *Friends*, *Mad about You*, and *ER*.

Networks have other advantages over the producer of a single program. They can spread the operating costs of sending their programming to stations across multiple programs during a weeklong schedule. Also, they can offer one-stop shopping to advertisers. By buying a package of advertisements on a network, advertisers can efficiently spread their advertising budgets over several programs.

The Winning Formula of the Distribution Bottleneck

With this new invention occupying a prominent place in the living room, television viewing grew to several hours per day. Since there was not much choice—the only substitute for television was movie theatres—viewing was concentrated on a few channels during the Broadcast Era. The networks consistently took over 70 percent of viewing, with the independent stations dividing up the rest.

This made for a comfortable competitive environment. Stations were not concerned about cable or satellite operators being able to deliver television or about digital compression making it possible to increase the number of stations. The networks did not have to worry about enterprising independents, upstart broadcast networks, or MTV. They were protected by the spectrum policy of the FCC and stagnant technology.

Broadcast networks and local stations earned all of their revenues from advertisers. Demand for advertising was buoyant as consumer goods companies experimented with television—a novel way of accessing large and attentive markets. Since advertising time is a perishable commodity, valueless if not used by broadcast time, the networks tried to sell as much of it as they could "up-front," well before the time would actually be used. What was left over was sold in the "scatter" market, on a first-come, first-served basis up until the actual broadcast time itself.

During the heyday of the Broadcast Era, there were three networks selling national advertising and a few local stations selling national and local spots. No one will ever know whether collusion occurred, but it seems safe to suggest that the market was not characterized by the kind of intense competition one finds in commodity markets or even in industries like computer hardware or air transportation. As one observer noted during the Broadcast Era:

No oligopolists could possibly be more aware than these of their interdependence. The evidence for the networks' recognition of their interdependence includes these facts: they pay thousands of dollars for overnight ratings of their own and their rivals' program audiences; they are all located within a few blocks of each other in New York; they all participate in NAB code decisions about advertising practices (including the number of commercial minutes in prime time), discuss the role of sex and violence on television, rotate coverage of such affairs as the Watergate and impeachment hearings, jockey over the fall schedule and midseason changes, and constantly trade personnel.[8]

Because of this interdependence, most observers have concluded that networks were able to collude in areas that were visible, easily monitored, and in which cheaters could be punished.[9] There were conventions in areas like the terms of the affiliate agreement,[10] the formula for advertising pricing[11] if not the price itself, quantity of advertising to be sold per hour, and even the quantity of original programming produced.[12]

With this kind of gentle competitive environment it is not surprising that the Broadcast Era was truly a golden age. All stemmed from that defining structural feature of the industry, the distribution bottleneck. Government policy combined with the technology of the day, analog transmission, to limit the number of distributors of television. These distributors, the local stations, protected by barriers to entry, banded together into network groups to take advantage of massive scale economies. Fueled by buoyant advertiser demand, they prospered on an unprecedented scale. Pre-tax profit margins for the O&O stations averaged above 38 percent between 1959 and 1976, with network margins

Exhibit 4
Performance in the Broadcast Era: Average EBIT, 1959–1976

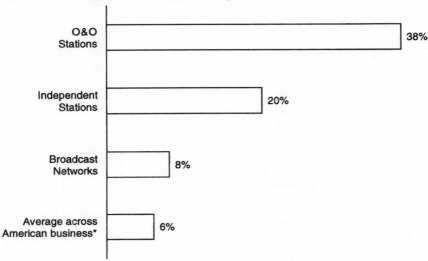

*1959–1970 only.
Source: Christopher H. Sterling and Timothy R. Haight, *The Mass Media: Aspen Institute Guide to Communication Industry Trends* (New York: Praeger, 1978), pp. 208–211. Copyright © 1978 by Christopher H. Sterling and Timothy R. Haight. Reproduced with permission of Greenwood Publishing Group, Inc., Westport, CT.

above 8 percent in the period (Exhibit 4). Network margins are deceptively low; they were treated as a vehicle to improve the profitability of their station groups and purposely understated to give networks an advantage in negotiating with affiliates. Non-O&O stations averaged margins of just under 20 percent. While still above national averages across all industry, this lower average reflects the lower profitability of independents that were forced to program and package for themselves.

Returns on capital were also high for distributors during the Broadcast Era. Litman calculates the rates of return of these earnings on depreciated capital in the mid-1970s to be 60 percent and 102 percent for non-O&O stations, between 310 percent and 379 percent for O&O stations, and between 179 percent and 221 percent for networks.[13]

In addition to rates of return, distribution also took a high absolute amount of the profit that was available to the industry. This can be measured by following the flow of dollars spent by consumers and advertisers up the supply chain and asking, What parts of the chain have the largest amounts of absolute operating profits? In 1972, the height of the Broadcast Era, local stations had operating profits of $441 million, or 59 percent of the total operating profits available to the industry. Production garnered 25 percent, and the networks were left with 15 percent (Exhibit 5).

Exhibit 5
Flows of Operating Profit through the Supply Chain: Broadcast Era, circa 1972

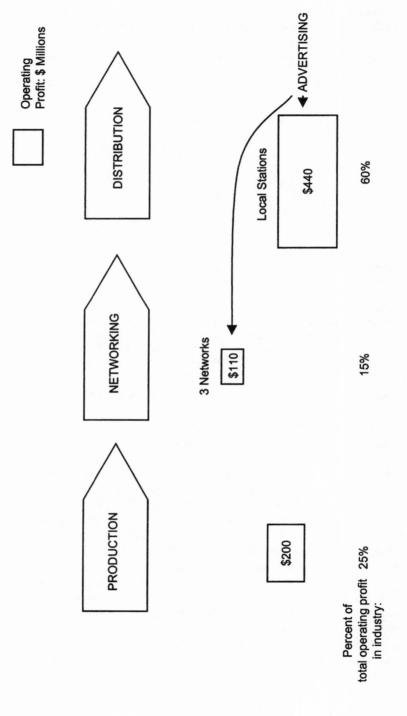

Operating Profit: $ Millions

PRODUCTION

NETWORKING

DISTRIBUTION

3 Networks

$110

Local Stations

$440

ADVERTISING

$200

Percent of total operating profit in industry: 25%   15%   60%

The Problem of Production

The distribution bottleneck limited, but did not stifle, competition. Certainly there was rivalry between the station groups, but it took the form of competition on the basis of product quality. This was expensive, but it proved much less damaging to the bottom line than price competition. Networks and stations spent huge sums of money to make and buy better programming than their rivals. The networks more than doubled the $450 million they spent on programming in 1961, to $975 million, by 1970.[14] To feed this hunger for programming, a television production industry was born.

At the outset of the Broadcast Era, the radio production companies tried to make television programming. However, it was not long before firms grew up that specialized in television production. Eventually, the major film studios realized that by ignoring television and making movies for theatrical exhibition, they were missing out on a new and potentially vast distribution channel. Before long, they had all created groups that specialized in television production.

Networks have always done some program production themselves. They produced their own news, for example, in order to take advantage of the enormous scale economies of production and distribution.[15] They might have produced more but for the Prime-Time Access Rules and the Financial Interest and Syndication Rule, implemented by the FCC in 1970, which limited the hours that the networks could program on their affiliates and also limited the amount of programming that networks could own and sell in the syndication market. Rolled back recently, these rules curtailed integration between networks and program producers throughout the Broadcast Era and much of the Cable Era.

The production business is straightforward. Production companies generate concepts, write scripts, hire talent, design sets and wardrobes, shoot scenes, and edit the tape. Producers range from one man in an office with a telephone to the major studio operations in Hollywood.

It all sounds very glamorous, but it was—and remains—a very difficult part of the business. The problem with this part of the content business was that demand was difficult to predict, buyers were savvy, and costs were high and nearly impossible to control. Despite these drawbacks, there was no shortage of new producers entering the business. Blockbuster hits of the era like *The Mary Tyler Moore Show*, *M*A*S*H*, and *Cheers* did provide windfall profits, but they were few and far between. In the end, these windfall profits only served to provide financing for the thousands of shows that never made it to the networks or that made it only to be cancelled after a season or two. What were the chief characteristics of the production business? The five principal characteristics of the business have changed little since the Broadcast Era: high risk, high cost, low entry barriers, savvy buyers, and difficulty in differentiation. Together, they created the problem of production. It is a problem that continues today.

Each time that television producers attempt to make a new program, they have to predict viewer reaction to the program in order to gauge demand. It should not be surprising that very few producers could do this accurately and consistently. Despite elaborate procedures for screening programming concepts and testing programs through "pilots," taped shows exhibited before real audiences, it is impossible to know whether a show will be a success before it goes on the air. Sometimes the ultimate appeal of a program is not known for several seasons: The mega-hit *Seinfeld* was actually a mediocre performer in its early seasons.

This difficulty creates odds for producers that even casino gamblers would shy from. Of the thousands of concepts, only a handful get made into pilots. Just a few pilots actually are taken by the networks and put into the schedules. Only about a quarter of these series are renewed after their first season. Even if a series makes this cut, it may not make it to television immortality. About a quarter of older series are also dropped from network schedules from one year to the next.[16]

To roll the dice and produce a television program is very expensive. Program producers manage a process that involves many people and much equipment. Any budget contains literally thousands of line items. Nevertheless, these items can be divided into two essential categories: talent and everything else. *Talent* refers to actors, musicians, athletes, writers, or directors who are irreplaceable and unique to the production process. Talent (or "content creators") is the creative force that makes a program special.

The cost of talent can be an extremely large component of total costs, particularly in situations in which talent is closely enough associated with the success of a program to command a percentage of revenues or profit. In the case of a one-half-hour situation comedy, for example, talent profit participations are approximately one-third of the total cost per episode, a cost that includes other fees to talent.[17]

The reason that compensation levels are so high is that talent is in short supply: A particular writer or baseball pitcher may have such unique talents that the producer may not be able to find a replacement. Such specialized labor can present producers with a "hold-up" problem.[18] The talent's absence from the production process can hold up the completion of the program. Other labor that opts to walk out will simply be replaced by producers without any delay in the production process. In this way, truly differentiating talent, the content creators—"stars," top athletes, directors, a few writers—can demand surprisingly high compensation.

In addition to talent, producers need to assemble all of the other personnel and equipment necessary to make a television program: set designers, makeup artists, photographers, cameras, lights, props, and the like. These people and equipment can be hired or rented easily on the market. Television personnel are plentiful: If one actor, writer, baseball player, hair stylist, set designer, or makeup artist demands too much, another can be found to take his place. Generally the market tends to have excess supply and high unemployment at any given point in time due to the glamour associated with performance on stage and screen.[19] Equipment is easily available in a highly developed rental market.

Although the necessary inputs are available to producers, costs are notoriously difficult to control. Unlike in the widget business, it is nearly impossible to link the spending of an additional dollar to an improved product capable of generating an additional dollar in revenue. Will the antique desk on the set or the beautiful braid of the star's hair attract enough additional viewers to justify its costs? A shareholder venturing an opinion will have little justification for his views and likely lose the argument with a renowned director, whose views may or may not be correct.

Costs for programming have been high and getting higher ever since the Broadcast Era began. Cost inflation for programming in the mid-1960s alone was at least triple the consumer price index (Exhibit 6). Prices for a half-hour comedy have gone from $65,500 in the mid-1960s to approximately $750,000 to $1 million in the mid-1990s, and for an hour-long drama from $130,000 to about $1.5 to $2 million. But, programming produced in the first-run syndication market[20] is typically lower in cost than network programming. Most first-run syndication programming is star-driven talk shows, game shows, children's programming, or magazine shows. The cost structure of these shows is similar to network programming in its relationship between fixed and variable costs. The absolute costs are simply lower: in the late 1980s five game shows could be produced for under $250,000.[21]

News programming can be extremely expensive. Producers of network news do not have the flexibility that producers of non-news have. Rather, they must maintain a national and even international organization of news bureaus to cover constantly breaking stories around the country and the world. These bureaus must be staffed with journalists, editors, and camera crews and have access to editing and satellite up-link facilities. Finally, these far-flung newsgathering operations must be coordinated and directed by a central office. These costs are essentially independent of the number of viewers that watch the news programming, the number of distribution channels that carry the programming, and even, although to a lesser extent, the number of hours of news programming broadcast.

Since markets for labor and equipment are open and since most pro-

Exhibit 6
Programming Inflation, 1960–1969

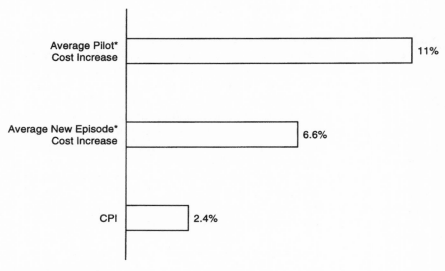

*half-hour program.
Source: B. M. Owen, J. H. Beebe, and W. G. Manning, Jr., *Television Economics* (Lexington, Mass.: Lexington Books, D.C. Heath, 1974).

gramming fails, barriers to entry are low. Open markets allowed small producers to maintain "shell" operations during slow periods and to ramp-up quickly when they win a project approval from a buyer. The high failure rate ensured that there would always be demand from new producers willing to take the plunge into programming.

Low entry barriers and open markets produced a fragmented market: no one or two players dominate. In Exhibit 7, suppliers of network programming are listed by their share of programming in prime-time hours, a proxy for share of market. The exhibit shows the relatively low level of concentration in the industry: The major suppliers account for between 30 and 50 percent of the market. Other measures used by the antitrust agencies to analyze firms do not point to anticompetitive behavior.

Not only is the market fragmented, but the positions of the producers are unstable. From year to year, producers jockey for market share, their ups and downs reflective of the difficulty of maintaining hit programs over the long term (Exhibit 8).

Still, despite the high fragmentation, high costs, and all the hassles of production, it could all be worth it if the buyers will pay handsomely for programming. Unfortunately, they do not. Transactions between programmers and networks developed in the Broadcast Era into a no-

Exhibit 7
Market Shares of Prime-Time Series Sales in the Broadcast Era, 1964–1972

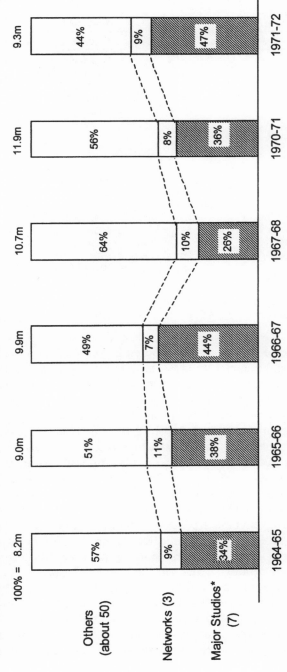

*Universal (includes Revue, MCA), Warner Bros., Paramount, Screen Gems, MGM, United Artists, 20th Century Fox.
Source: B. M. Owen, J. H. Beebe, and W. G. Manning, Jr., Television Economics (Lexington, Mass.: Lexington Books, D.C. Heath, 1974).

Exhibit 8
Market Shares of Top Five Sellers of Prime-Time Series, 1964–1968

1984-1985		1985-1986	
Producer	Share (%)	Producer	Share (%)
1. Universal	14	1. Universal	11
2. MGM	6	2. 20th Century Fox	9
3. CBS	5	3. CBS	7
4. 20th Century Fox	4	4. Screen Gems	6
5. NBC	3	5. MGM	5
Paramount	3		
Screen Gems	3		
Four Star	3		

1986-1987		1987-1988	
Producer	Share (%)	Producer	Share (%)
1. 20th Century Fox	12	1. 20th Century Fox	8
2. Universal	11	2. MGM	7
3. MGM	7	3. Desilu	6
4. Screen Gems	7	4. CBS	5
5. Desilu	4	5. Screen Gems	5
CBS	4	Universal	5

Source: B. M. Owen, J. H. Beebe, and W. G. Manning, Jr., *Television Economics* (Lexington, Mass.: Lexington Books, D.C. Heath, 1974).

toriously complex system. Constrained in their ability to make programming by the Financial Interest and Syndication Rule, the networks became savvy buyers of programming. As producers of some programming themselves and students of viewing behavior, the networks knew as well as anyone what viewers wanted and how much it should cost. Production companies were put into the unenviable position of selling to customers that knew more than they did about their product.

As a result of this buyer power, the impossibility of predicting the ultimate profitability of a program under development, and their legal prohibition from owning programming that might become very successful, the network buyers would pay only some 75 to 85 percent of the cost of the program before production commenced.[22] Should a series fail, this would be the only revenue that a producer would ever receive. Should a series last three years or more, however, the producer would have a proven product that could be sold in the syndication market to independent stations around the country. These revenues would enable the producer to cover the 15 to 25 percent production costs that the buyer did not pay, as well as distribution costs, any residuals, and, finally, a profit. Since most programs, about four out of five,[23] do not survive long enough to go into syndication, the occasional hit must cover their production costs as well—not to mention the overheads involving in running the production company and developing the programs (Exhibit 9).

It has been very difficult for a program producer to break out of the pack and differentiate its programming. Of course, every individual program, sporting event, or musical performance is unique. But, just being different does not mean that programs are differentiated. For a program to be differentiated, its producers and buyers must agree that it has features that set its price apart from other competitive products. The problem from the perspective of program producers is that there is no firm linkage between specific product attributes and viewing share. In other words, just because a program might have differentiating features, its producer is hard put to show the value of these features ex ante.

Clearly, we can list the product attributes that program producers and advertisers *think* differentiates programming:

- genre of program (situation comedy, soap opera, drama, children's programming, news, sports, etc.)
- length of program
- quality and attractiveness of program (actors, lavishness of sets, locations, action sequences, etc.)
- originality, creativity, and appeal of story and writing
- age and prior ratings (for off-network syndication programming).

However, in practice, program producers have a hard time differentiating among their products. Many product attributes do not have a measurable or predictable effect on the size of the viewing audience. In other words, a show with beautiful sets, a creative script, a new format, or a big star will not necessarily draw a larger audience than a low budget rehash of a familiar theme. A case in point is the failure of the expensively produced series *Cop Rock* in the mid-1990s. What happens is that program genres fall into well-accepted price ranges: An hour of drama was expected to cost about $1,500,000 in the mid-1990s, and a network will pay about 80 percent of the production costs. Similar conventions exist for several other attributes like program length and prior ratings.

These five market characteristics—high risk, high costs, low entry barriers, savvy buyers, and difficulty in differentiation—created a very competitive business. Producers will scramble for the opportunity to get a series into a prime-time network schedule even if that means reducing price or investing more in the program itself.

Since transactions between producers and networks are so complex and the products are unique, price competition is difficult to observe. Nevertheless, prices seem to be pinned down, by industry convention,

Exhibit 9
The Long Odds of Producing Hit Programming

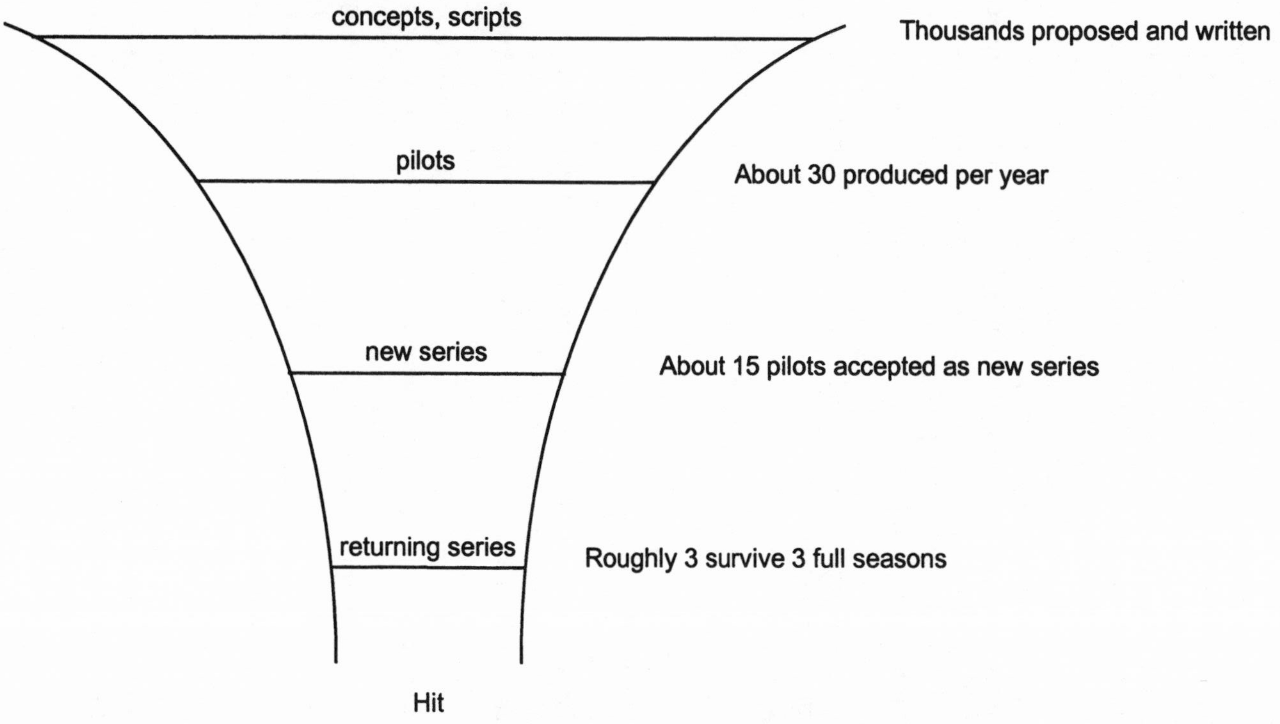

Thousands proposed and written

concepts, scripts

About 30 produced per year

pilots

About 15 pilots accepted as new series

new series

Roughly 3 survive 3 full seasons

returning series

Hit

to low levels relative to cost. As we noticed, the prices that networks are willing to pay are not enough to cover production costs. The production deficit that remains must be covered with syndication fees and earnings from foreign markets. Not only have production deficits remained an accepted part of the business, but their size has increased (Exhibit 10). Producers are taking lower "prices" from networks and larger production deficits—in effect, competing on the basis of price—in order to gain a time slot for their programs that they hope will become a hit.

Occasionally, a program producer is able to compete on price with the development of a new, lower-cost format. *America's Funniest Home Videos* is an example of a low-cost format that enabled its producer to underprice alternative programming. This price-cutting is not debilitating, as production deficits on a percentage basis are not larger.

Further evidence of price competition exists in intense quasi-price bargaining over such issues as spin-off rights, syndication rights, options to do new pilots, and options for cable rights. Networks have increasingly persuaded producers to give these rights up as part of the sale.

Clearly, program producers also engage in product competition. Program producers compete for talent in an effort to make their programming more attractive to viewers. This can be seen in the average annual increase of 10 percent in production costs of television programming throughout the Broadcast Era and into the Cable Era. This has bid up the prices of those unique content creators whose supply is limited— famous actors and directors—and driven up the availability of inputs for which supply can be increased—most actors, production assistants, studio executives, and special effects people.

In the syndication market, for sales to local stations, competition is also intense. Game shows vie to offer larger prize money and more interesting formats; talk shows seek out ever more titillating topics for discussions, to the point of drawing the attention of the right-wing politicians who want to limit their transmission; and the occasional syndicated drama programs are subject to the same forces as their network counterparts.

Given the intense competition of the program production business, it should come as no surprise that the returns were relatively lower than for distribution.[24] This often surprises casual observers who wonder how shareholders can have such low returns when production companies are producing blockbuster hits.

The answer is that for every hit that gets produced, so do a large number of flops. Moreover, product and price competition is so intense that all of these efforts, hits and flops, require larger and larger production budgets and get sold at lower and lower prices relative to costs. In the end, the profit from the hits barely covers the losses from the flops. Exhibit 11 shows the results of modeling a 20-year profit history for a

Exhibit 10
Production Deficits for Network Programming, 1982–1987

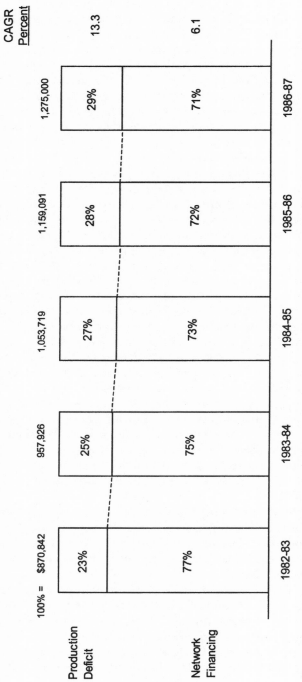

Source: Derived from data presented in Harold L. Vogel, *Entertainment Industry Economics*, 3rd ed. (Cambridge: Cambridge University Press, 1994).

Exhibit 11
The Difficult Economics of Production

$M

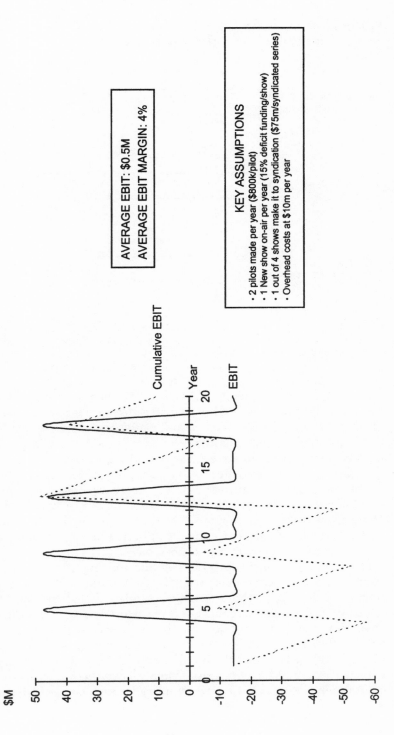

AVERAGE EBIT: $0.5M
AVERAGE EBIT MARGIN: 4%

KEY ASSUMPTIONS
· 2 pilots made per year ($800k/pilot)
· 1 New show on-air per year (15% deficit funding/show)
· 1 out of 4 shows make it to syndication ($75m/syndicated series)
· Overhead costs at $10m per year

Exhibit 12
Average Annual Wage and Cost Increases, 1962–1971

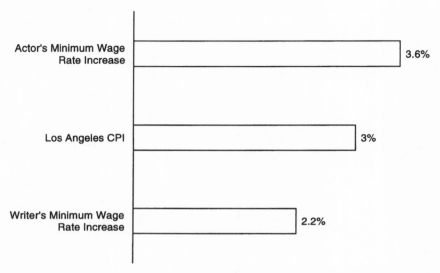

Sources: B. M. Owen, J. H. Beebe, and W. G. Manning, Jr., *Television Economics* (Lexington, Mass.: Lexington Books, D.C. Heath, 1974); A. C. Jacobs, *Handbook of US Labor Statistics* (Lanham, Md.: Bernan Press, 1997).

typical production company. While the EBIT line (earnings before interest and tax) is punctuated with dramatic spikes from the profits of selling hit shows in syndication, the overall results are not spectacular: Average EBIT is only $500,000, average EBIT margin is 4 percent, and it takes thirteen years for cumulative EBIT to finally go positive.

It may be that with tighter cost controls, bigger profits could be made in the programming business. However, as we noted, it is extremely difficult for shareholders to control costs in such a creative business. There are plenty of shareholders who do not even make the attempt. The entertainment industry has a long tradition of attracting starry-eyed investors unable or unwilling to control costs.

Not only did program producers suffer in comparison to the distributors, but content creators as well. The union pay scales for actors and writers in the era barely kept up with inflation (Exhibit 12). This may not come as a shock, since most of these actors and writers were replaceable. However, compensation for the stars was also relatively low, at least in the sense that they were not in the league of the superrich, as they are today. Consider the highly popular 1960s show *Bonanza*. When it began in the 1959–1960 season, total above-the-line costs—costs for supervision, scripts, music, and all miscellaneous talent-related items as well as the compensation for the entire cast—were only $36,700. By the show's close at the end of the decade, that figure had risen to $98,000,[25] a small fortune compared to the $8,800 that the average auto and auto parts worker made at the time, but only by a multiple of 11, which was relatively small compared to what we will observe for later years.[26]

The Broadcast Era, the so-called Golden Age of television, saw the emergence of a distribution bottleneck that would economically define the era. Prior to the invention of the television, we were at the mercy of cinema owners for access to moving pictures. With television, we were freed from their tyranny and could enjoy video in the comfort of living rooms. But, since the FCC licensed only a handful of stations to broadcast television signals, these stations ended up with a distribution bottleneck. A system of network groups grew up to supply programming to these stations. By originating programming centrally and distributing it to stations around the country, these network groups could take advantage of economies of scale. Combining these economic forces with the fact that viewers and advertisers had only a few choices and the broadcasters themselves had only a few competitors created a recipe for an extremely profitable business.

While the distributors of television signals were reaping high returns, content was not king. Program production may have been sexy, but profitable it was not. The production business was highly competitive, with new players entering often and further fragmenting the market. Content creators—the stars, writers, and directors whom the production companies depended on to create programming—were not in the ranks of the highest-paid individuals of their time. But that would change. The Golden Age would not last forever. In fact, from its beginning, forces were in motion that would transform the industry completely.

THE CABLE ERA

Sometime in the mid-1970s, the industry left the Broadcast Era and entered the Cable Era. In the span of about 20 years, from the mid-1970s to the mid-1990s, cable operators built a coaxial cable distribution plant that would become one of the critical parts of the nation's infrastructure. It would deliver the broadcast networks and a plethora of new cable networks to over 90 percent of all households in the United States. With roughly two-thirds of these households subscribing to the service, cable transformed the television industry.

Cable was not the liberating force that it seemed to be in its early years. It did not relieve the distribution bottleneck. Clearly cable allowed new networks, like CNN and The Nashville Network, access to viewers. But most towns were served by only one cable operator. That one operator was the gatekeeper: it selected all new cable networks for carriage on its system, and it built a customer database and collected all of the subscriber fees. As the distribution bottleneck strategy was still viable in the Cable Era, returns to distributors remained high.

The Cable Era was a period of important changes in the structure of the television industry. The paradigm of this book is that the video industry is organized around a supply chain consisting of content and conduit. In the Broadcast Era, no one thought about the industry in these terms. Instead, it was an industry of networks and stations.

The Cable Era was a transition from the Broadcast Era to the Digital Era. During the Cable Era, most people thought of the industry as consisting of two separate segments, the broadcast segment and the cable segment. What was really going on was that the industry was breaking up into a supply chain consisting of content creation, production, packaging, and distribution segments. Call it the disintermediation of the television industry. What was happening was that the content functions were being torn apart from the conduit. Technology was advancing to create several new conduits, and independent content players were emerging to supply these conduits, whatever technology they belonged to.

These changes began a process being played out today in the Digital Era. It is a process that I call the Great Value Shift. In the Great Value Shift, profits in the industry migrate from downstream to upstream. After the Great Value Shift, it will be relatively harder to create value in the conduit, or distribution, business and relatively easier to create value in content. The conduit will come to resemble a commodity while content will have the opportunity to create branded, high-value-added products. It will amount to nothing less than a complete reversal of the economics as we knew them in the Broadcast Era. Let me explain how it began.

In the Cable Era, a new phenomenon emerged: cable networks. These entities were packagers and occasionally producers of programming. Unlike their broadcast network counterparts, they did not exist solely to supply programming to a group of stations. Cable networks were certainly created to feed content to cable distributors, but they now provide their product to distributors of video more generally.

These networks have been phenomenally successful. They have taken viewership as well as advertising from the established broadcast networks. While sometimes owned by cable operators, cable networks have become powerful entities in their own right. The top ten networks have strong bargaining position in the supply chain: They are needed by distributors who want to attract viewers. With a formula of low costs and subscriber fees as well as advertising revenues, they have become very profitable. Moreover, they are forcing the broadcast networks to think about themselves as competing packagers rather than simply as suppliers to station groups.

In financing the cable networks from their humble beginnings, the cable operators may have created a monster. They may have created entities that will be more important to viewers than the cable operators themselves. Cable networks may be entities that outlast the Cable Era: cable operators will become just another conduit in the Digital Era, but cable networks will be valuable to each and every new conduit.

The Cable Era ushered in a second major change. In the Cable Era, compensation increased for content creators, the first link in the supply chain. As viewing fragmented across an increasing number of channels, broadcast and cable networks moved to improve their programming. They realized that the best guarantee for higher viewership was recognizable talent. Competition intensified the number of true content creators.

As in the Broadcast Era, owning a production company was not the key to making money. The real demand was for those genuine stars, brilliant writers, or gifted athletes who attracted audiences. Content creators who were irreplaceable saw their compensation soar.

The Cable Era, then, serves as a critical bridge between the Broadcast and Digital eras. While the distribution bottleneck survived, changes were taking shape that would give the industry its character in the Digital Era. This chapter will examine the changes in distribution, the cable phenomenon, and the rise of content creators.

The Distribution Bottleneck Redux

The broadcast networks and stations had about 20 years to enjoy their oligopoly before a development took place that would transform their industry again. Technology would alter the distribution link of the supply chain. It began on a very small scale at the beginning of the Broadcast Era in Mahony City, Pennsylvania, in 1948, when appliance dealer John Watson wondered why his newly arrived television sets were not selling well. He reckoned that the problem was bad reception caused by the hills that surrounded his valley community. If he could bring better reception to his community, he could spur sales of television sets.[27] To do this, he mounted a television antenna on top of a nearby mountain and allowed his customers to connect their television sets. Sales increased; Watson charged a small fee to hook up; and cable, or community antenna television (CATV) as it was then known, was born.

From these humble beginnings, cable now covers over 90 percent of the country and has 65 million subscribing households. It has grown to be a $30 billion industry. Most of its revenue is fee-based, but an increasing portion is from advertising. As can be seen in Exhibit 13, cable operators have surpassed local stations in terms of revenue.

For most of the Cable Era, cable operators were the only game in town. In most communities, the local cable operator was the only option for

Exhibit 13
Total Distributor Revenue, in $ Billions

Cable Operators

Local Stations*

*Excluding affiliate compensation.
**Preliminary numbers for local stations.
Sources: National Cable Television Association, *Cable Television Developments* (Washington, D.C.: NCTA, 1997); Robert J. Coen and McCann-Erickson, *Annual U.S. Advertising Expenditures* (New York: Advertising Age, 1997).

viewers who were interested in subscription television. And, in 99 percent of all communities, there was only one cable operator.

There were alternative delivery mechanisms during the 1980s. Satellite Master Antennae Television (SMATV), multichannel multipoint distribution (MMDS), and satellite television were available to consumers who wanted to see the same menu of multichannel video programming that was available on cable. However, these multichannel alternatives were only successful in isolated pockets. Their importance was exaggerated by cable operators as a propaganda device to suggest that there was competition. In mid-1994, there were estimated to be only 1.775 million authorized backyard satellite dish (TVRO) subscribers, 492,000 wireless cable, or MMDS subscribers, and about one million SMATV subscribers—compared to about 60 million cable television subscribers.[28]

To be fair, at least one strong competitor to cable operators served to ease the pain of the distribution bottleneck. The rise of videocassettes during the 1980s was a low-tech portent of the digital future. It showed that one way to ease to the distribution bottleneck was to rent or sell tapes to viewers, who could then play tapes at their leisure on their own videocassette recorders.

Of course, the limitations of the technology are severe, as anyone knows who has gone out on a rainy night to a video store only to find that a preferred title is not available. Nevertheless, this distribution outlet is enormous. With $17 billion in revenues in 1992, revenue to videocassette retailers rivals revenue to local stations. The business, however, is very different from the cable or broadcast businesses. With low barriers to entry, it is fragmented, with many small retailers sharing the market. Although large chains have emerged in the 1990s, the business remains considerably more fragmented than either cable or broadcast television. For this reason, profitability has been lower for this distribution outlet than for the others.

Thus, the arrival of cable on the scene added a second major pipeline for distribution for television, but it did not break the distribution bottleneck. Rather, in the Cable Era, cable and broadcast were separate bottlenecks; they may have competed for viewers, but they did not compete with each other for paying subscribers. They were two products with different product attributes and separate demand curves. For a fee, cable offered better reception of broadcast channels and new cable-only channels. Viewers who were heavy television consumers or viewers who had enough money to spare for the service became its subscribers. The "free" signals available over the air constrained the price that cable operators could charge. Broadcasters, of course, could not charge, but they knew that cable subscribers still watched their networks—now through a coaxial cable.

What explained the persistence of the distribution bottleneck through the Cable Era? Why were the cable operators the only game in town? The answer is that they were protected by a set of high barriers to entry. Some of these barriers remain in existence today, while others are being eliminated or circumvented.

The first set of barriers was regulatory. There has been a de facto regulatory barrier to a second wireline competitor "overbuilding" an existing cable operator.[29] In most municipalities cable operators were given a franchise as a result of a bidding process; second franchises were rarely awarded. Hazlett has argued that this happened because municipalities sought to impede competition in order to protect their franchise fee.[30] The 1992 Cable Act clarified the ban on exclusive franchises and required franchising authorities not to "unreasonably refuse" to award an additional franchise. However, this provision is unlikely to settle the question since the problem was never in de jure exclusion but in the interpretation of what is "unreasonable."[31]

Furthermore, both cable operators and broadcasters were, and in many cases still are, protected by regulation from entrants using new technologies. For example, regulatory barriers protected the incumbents against Direct Broadcast Satellite (DBS) and the telephone companies. As we will see, regulation played an important role in delaying the introduction of DBS. It was not until spectrum was licensed in the Ku-band, defining frequencies in the range of 12 GHz to 14 GHz versus the 4 GHz to 6 GHz range of the previously licensed C-band, that satellites could be spaced closer together and high-power DBS could be launched. The video operations of telephone companies are still treated differently from cable companies: they were regulated as common carriers and not allowed to own programming transmitted on their system until the passage of the 1996 Telecommunications Act; today, they are allowed to operate as cable operators, as "open systems," or as common carriers.

The second set of entry barriers was economic. The costs to build a cable system, regardless of whether it wins one subscriber or 100,000, are high and fixed: the capital costs of building a system are estimated at between $600 and $900 per subscriber for an average community of 50,000 inhabitants.[32] With revenues at $350 per year per subscriber, even with an operating margin of 40 percent, it would take over five years just to pay back the investment. This fixed cost structure may not preclude multiple operators from competing, but it clearly gives the incumbent an advantage in its market. Cable overbuilders and telephone companies have cost structures similar to cable operators with high fixed costs. Therefore, they will have higher unit costs if they enter and serve only a few customers. If the incumbent, upon learning of the entry plans of a newcomer, cuts prices to just cover variable costs, the new competitor would be hard put to recover its costs for fixed assets and would likely be deterred from entering.[33] Of course, this barrier is less important for a DBS system. Since its coverage is national, cable operators would have to cut prices nationally instead of in one locality to discourage entry.

The Winning Formula Sustained

During the Cable Era, cable operators held a distribution bottleneck. They were constrained only by the presence of imperfect substitutes, broadcast television and videocassettes, perhaps by the distant threat of the new technologies, and by the on-again off-again imposition of rate regulation by Congress. Economic theory predicts that cable operators would have exercised their market power to the extent that substitute producers and potential new entrants allow. In fact, theory coincided with reality. Cable operators were able to exercise a degree of market power by steadily increasing prices.

In municipalities in which a single cable operator provided service, prices have gone steadily upward, pausing only just prior to re-regulation and subsequent to re-regulation (Exhibit 14).[34] This in itself is not evidence of monopoly power, as cost increases may have been responsible for the increase. Nevertheless, compared to other industries in which prices are more responsive to market forces, the steady and relatively uniform increase of cable prices, at a time when the quality of broadcast television was improving, VCRs were spreading, and the overall economy went through several cycles, does indicate that the industry exerted unusual market power.

Certainly occasional promotions designed to attract new subscribers came in the form of discounts on installation and discounts on premium services for new subscribers. But, these quasi-price competition policies are limited to use in signing up new subscribers and introducing them to a new and sometimes unfamiliar product.

If anything kept cable operators in check during the Cable Era, it was the threat of the entrance of alternative multichannel providers like cable overbuilders, SMATV, MMDS, and, further in the future, DBS, the telephone companies, and the Internet. Cable operators appeared to do the best they could to make life difficult for these alternatives and keep control of the distribution bottleneck. In economic terms, this is called entry deterrence.

Overbuilders, for example, were attacked with ferocity. Incumbent cable operators often cut prices only to those homes that could replace their service with those of the overbuilder.[35] Even if operators have to cut prices over the entire franchise area, they are protected because many cable systems operate multiple systems across the country and could reduce prices for any one system faced with competitive entry while not hurting performance in their other systems. This behavior serves to deter

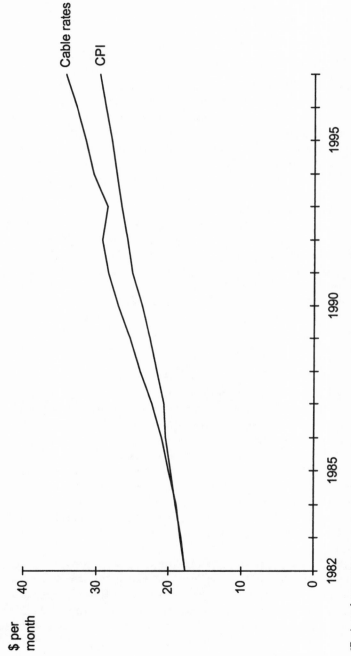

Exhibit 14
Cable Television Monthly Rates*

$ per month

Cable rates

CPI

40

30

20

10

0

1982   1985   1990   1995

*Basic and pay rates.
Source: National Cable Television Association, *Cable Television Developments* (Washington, D.C.: NCTA, 1997). Reproduced with permission.

new entrants, or at least to put them on notice not to expect existing price levels to remain stable. Another way to deter entry was to deny crucial programming, widely acknowledged as a key ingredient for the success of a multichannel distributor.[36] While it is impossible to determine the extent of foreclosure behavior through the denial of access to programming for competitive multichannel distributors, there is a record of activity that the FCC has declared to be "anticompetitive."[37]

The fact that there have been very few overbuilds, even in municipalities that have invited overbuilders in the franchising process,[38] supports this argument that cable operators have been protected by entry barriers and may have taken actions that have deterred entry.

While these tactics have worked against overbuilders and pose a threat to SMATV, MMDS, and telephone companies, any entry-deterring behavior has had less impact on DBS operators. Cable operators were denied the chance to use their strongest competitive weapon. They were not successful in preventing Congress from giving DBS access to programming owned by cable operators in the 1992 Cable Act. Nor can cable operators deter DBS operators with selective price reductions in isolated geographic areas, as DBS has national coverage.

With the distribution bottleneck and its associated tactics persisting into the Cable Era, it should come as no surprise that distribution, both on the broadcast side and on the cable side, was very profitable. While viewers have not increased their viewing time, they have opened their wallets and are willing to spend ever-increasing amounts to receive subscription multichannel television. Given the presence of the distribution bottleneck, cable system operators have been able to take advantage of this spending. They have enjoyed rising prices without competition to improve some parts of their service. This is a formula for profitability. And, sure enough, the data prove this formula correct.

The performance measurement that economists use to measure monopoly profitability is long-run social marginal costs versus prices. Monopolists face downward-sloping demand curves and set price greater than marginal costs, thus restricting output, increasing profit above the risk-adjusted cost of capital, and wasting social resources. In the absence of data on long-run social marginal costs, economists use proxies and other tests. Our case is no different. Let us first examine accounting returns and then consider other tests.

The persistently high accounting profits found in the distribution segment, especially in combination with high entry barriers, are an indication that there is a gap between marginal costs and price and, hence, monopoly returns. Accounting profits to distribution, as well as the entire television industry, are above the average for other American firms. Returns to distribution, both to the local stations and the cable operators, are higher than returns to other segments, especially if cash flow is considered (see Exhibit 21 later in this chapter).[39] The exception is videocassette retailers, whose returns are lower than all other segments. The reason is that the structure of the videocassette retailer segment—significant market fragmentation, low entry barriers, commodity products—ensures that conduct is highly competitive.

Hazlett conducted two other analyses, which we can apply to the persistently high accounting profits of cable operators, that indicate that they earned returns in excess of their cost of capital: Q-ratios and competitive system sales price differentials.[40] The Q-ratio is defined as the market value of an asset divided by the cost of replacing that asset from scratch. The logic of the Q-ratio is that in a competitive market, it should not cost much more to build an asset than it does to buy it; in other words, the Q-ratio should approach 1. If it were significantly higher, the difference should be due in some part to market power. In analyzing Q-ratios for cable systems, he found a ratio of Q = 3.51, an extraordinarily high figure that cannot be explained by entrepreneurial foresight, high riskiness, built-up goodwill, or returns to monopsony power, the reasons often given for high Q-ratios.[41] His study of competitive system sales price differentials showed that "sales prices for systems in competitive markets were 17–20% less, on a per subscriber basis, than contemporaneous sales of cable systems in monopoly markets."[42]

Another interesting way to look at who earns what in the industry is to examine the total dollar amount of profit that each part of the supply chain earns. As in the Broadcast Era, more operating profit continues to stop at the level of distribution than anywhere else (Exhibit 15). In fact, distribution now accounts for about three-quarters of all of the operating profit in the supply chain, with production and networking splitting the remainder almost evenly. The cable side of the supply chain has grown to rival the broadcast side at the level of distribution and to surpass the broadcast side at the level of networking.

The Phenomenon of Cable Networks

The distribution bottleneck may not have been broken, but changes did occur that would soon have a profound impact. In their effort to attract subscribers, cable operators encouraged, and even financed, networks that would be available only to their subscribers. These networks would soon become almost as recognizable as the broadcast networks.

During the course of the Cable Era, cable networks would:

- fragment the television audience
- separate the packaging function from the distribution function
- introduce a new paradigm for profitability in packaging
- create new demand for programming

Exhibit 15
Flows of Operating Profit through the Supply Chain: Cable Era, circa 1996

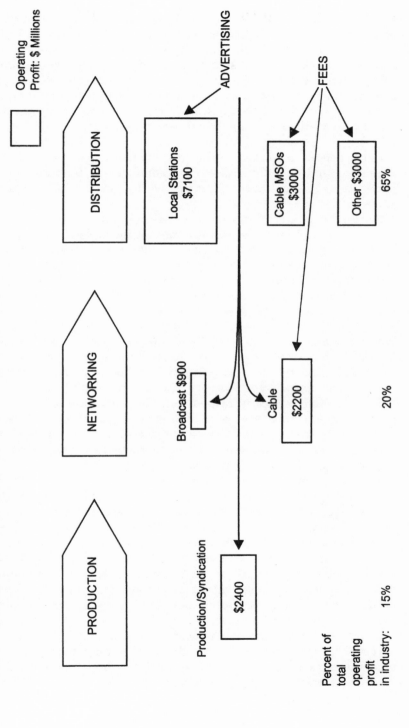

How were cable networks born, and why did they bring about this epochal change? Recall that cable operators were able to continually raise price throughout the Cable Era. The lack of price competition is understandable, as cable operators had no major rivals capable of charging a subscription fee. But pricing is only one element of competitive conduct. In other important ways, cable operators had to compete: they had to make sure that their product was sufficiently better than that of their "freely" available rivals, the broadcasters, to justify the cable price premium.

Cable operators worked to improve their product in two areas: programming and everything else. Programming had the most important implications for the industry, but it is worthwhile to review other areas as well.

Since cable operators did not have serious competition in the market for multichannel video in the beginning of the Cable Era, they did not have to worry too much about making their service better than anyone else's. Operators simply had to get consumers a good enough signal to justify their subscription fee. Non-programming product benefits, such as signal reliability and good service, were not very important in the early years of cable. In recent years, however, these non-programming benefits have been increased and improved. In 1990, in part to deflect the need for re-regulation, the cable industry adopted a set of service standards that included guidelines for rapid response to customer service inquiries, standards for installation times and response times for service calls, and formats and rules for billing and refund procedures.[43]

These initiatives clearly helped cable operators improve their value proposition to consumers vis-à-vis their broadcast rivals. But, more important, they served to anticipate and respond to regulators and to deter entry by signaling commitment to the market and raising the stakes for alternative providers using new technologies.

The most important area of competition was in programming. Since most subscribers were able to get acceptable reception of terrestrial signals without cable, good, fresh programming was the reason for viewers to subscribe to cable.[44] Early in the Cable Era, the pioneering operators realized that they needed more than just good reception to build a national business. HBO was launched in the early 1970s with $150,000 in seed money from Time Inc., an owner of the cable system in Manhattan, because a pioneering cable entrepreneur named Chuck Dolan was looking for programming that would make Time Inc.'s investment in a cable system in New York profitable.[45]

Other services that are now household names, like CNN and The Discovery Channel, were financed with cable operator money, and many others were actively encouraged by the operators. They are known as cable "networks," although "packager" may be a better word for them because they buy or make programming, package it into schedules of programming, distribute them to cable systems, and sell time on their schedules to advertisers. Since they do not maintain a network of affiliates, calling them cable networks is more an historical artifact of the Broadcast Era than an accurate description of their activities.

Cable system operators have continued to support cable networks by spending increasing sums on programming: from $1.7 billion in 1984 to over $4 billion in 1994. There are 164 cable networks in existence today with hundreds more planned (Exhibit 16). They have made significant inroads against the viewership of the broadcast networks. The 100 percent of the audience held by terrestrial television during the Broadcast Era has dwindled to 70 percent during the Cable Era in a process known as audience fragmentation. While no one knows whether this pattern will stabilize or continue, it has left the cable networks splitting 30 percent of viewing share (Exhibit 17). While many of the cable networks, occupy tiny niches, several larger packagers have emerged, CNN, Nickelodeon, HBO, and the largest of which in terms of revenue, ESPN. In terms of viewing share, the top eight networks garner 59 percent of the total share of viewing and over 60 percent of the total share of advertising devoted to cable networks, with the remainder split into tiny fractions by the smaller niche packagers (Exhibit 18).

Cable networks have achieved this feat with programming. They have attacked the broadcast networks with two concepts: niche programming and general entertainment. Niche programming means filling an entire schedule with programming about a narrow area of interest. The Weather Channel and the various music and sports channels are examples of this strategy. The strategy is effective because with national distribution enough interested viewers can be aggregated to provide a revenue base. General entertainment networks present a variety of programs that appeal to viewers of all stripes. Often these networks rely on unique content: TBS, the Atlanta superstation, has exclusive rights for some Atlanta sports teams, and TNT has access to the MGM film library. In addition, the general entertainment cable networks, like the independent broadcast networks, counter-program against the broadcast networks. Counter-programming consists of scheduling programs that address audiences not being addressed by other networks. For example, while the broadcast networks air the national news, cable networks can air off-network situation comedies.

These programming strategies were easier to execute because the number of cable networks was kept artificially low. Throughout the Cable Era, cable networks were protected by barriers to entry. The most important barrier in the cable environment has been the limited channel capacity of systems.

As cable began competing for subscribers, operators decided not only

Exhibit 16
Growth in Number of Cable Networks: 1977–1997

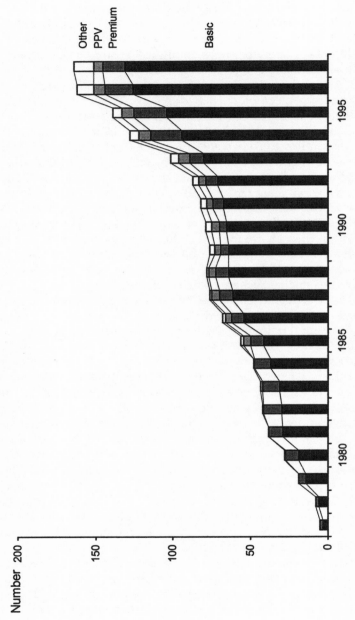

Source: National Cable Television Association, *Cable Television Developments* (Washington, D.C.: NCTA, 1997). Reproduced with permission.

Exhibit 17
Television Viewing Shares*: 1983–1993

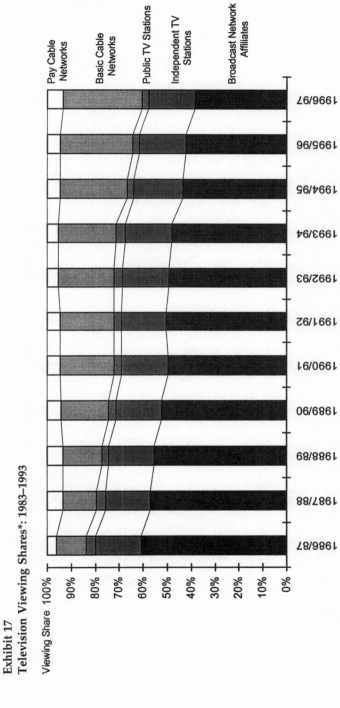

*Data for all TV households and all television viewing during a broadcast year. Independent shares include Fox.
Source: National Cable Television Association, *Cable Television Developments* (Washington, D.C.: NCTA, 1997). Reproduced with permission.

Exhibit 18
Dominance of Top Cable Networks

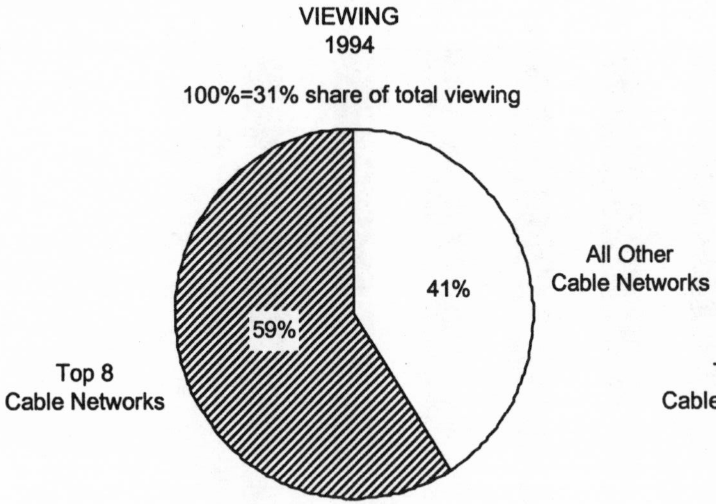

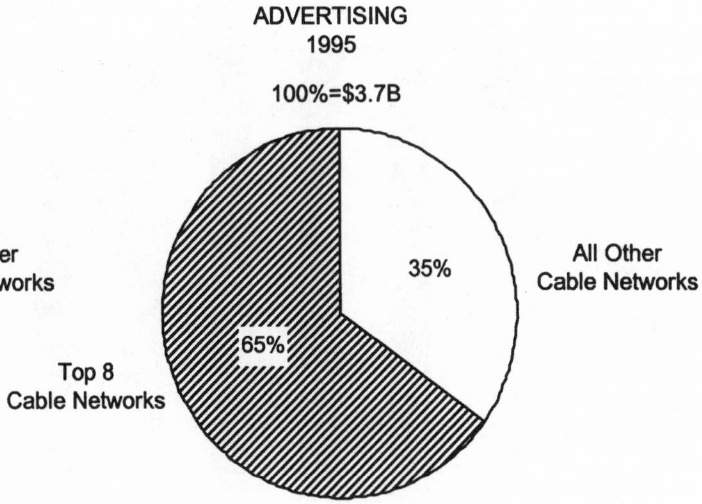

VIEWING
1994

100% = 31% share of total viewing

All Other
Cable Networks

41%

59%

Top 8
Cable Networks

ADVERTISING
1995

100% = $3.7B

All Other
Cable Networks

35%

65%

Top 8
Cable Networks

Sources: For viewing: Nielsen Cable Activity Report for the second, third, and fourth quarters of 1994 (New York: Nielsen Media Research, 1994). For advertising: Mary Meeker, *The Internet Advertising Report* (New York: HarperCollins, 1997).

that they needed new programming, but that they needed lots of it. Unfortunately, this required significant investment. Early systems had no more than a dozen or so channel slots. Towards the close of the Cable Era, systems were rebuilt with the capability of offering vastly more channels. The percentage of systems with channel capacity of 30 to 53 increased from 35.9 percent of all systems in 1985 to 59 percent in 1993, the percentage of systems with channel capacity of 54 or more increased from 5.8 percent of all systems to 17 percent, and the percentage of subscribers on these large systems increased from 9.8 percent to 57 percent over the same time period.[46]

While this additional channel capacity obviously was an improvement, it was not enough to satisfy all of the entrepreneurs who wanted to launch new cable networks. Given their limited channel capacity, operators typically limited the number of networks in any one programming niche so that they could transmit a bouquet of complimentary channels. In this way, they could provide a variety of program choices to attract as many subscribers as possible.[47]

From the mid-1980s on, new cable networks had to go hat in hand to cable operators to try to secure distribution. Without distribution, it was impossible for new cable networks to achieve profitability. In fact, in the mid-1990s, it took about 30 million subscribers just to break even (Exhibit 19).

The only new packagers able to secure a position on cable systems in this period of strained capacity were those owned by broadcasting entities, Fox's fx, for example, or those owned by cable MSOs, like Outdoor Life. As part of the 1992 Cable Act,[48] broadcast networks took slots for new channels from cable systems in return for retransmission of their broadcast signals. In many cases, cable systems have had to drop established packagers to make room for them. C-Span I and II have been particularly hurt as cable systems try to find some capacity for the broadcast-owned cable networks.[49]

Protected by this barrier to entry, the established cable networks had a considerably easier job implementing their strategies. But their phenomenal success has not changed the fundamental fact that the distribution bottleneck reigned in the Cable Era. While strong, the cable networks were no match for the operators that distributed them.

Internecine Rivalry: Cable Networks Versus Distributors

During the Cable Era, the operators enjoyed control of the bottleneck that separated packagers and viewers. This was part of the reason that cable operators could retain so much of the revenues from subscriber fees to themselves.

As there were always more packagers than openings on cable systems,

Exhibit 19

Cable Network Subscribers versus Cash Flow: 1994

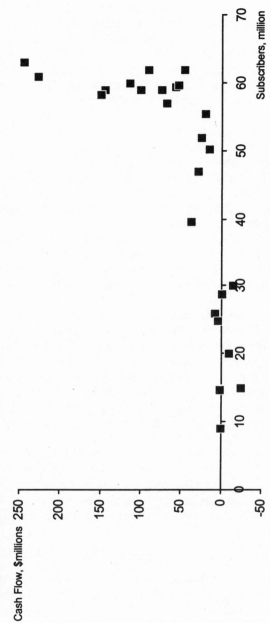

Sources: Paul Kagan Associates, *Cable TV Programming* (Carmel, Calif.: Paul Kagan Associates, 23 May 1994), p. 1; National Cable Television Association, *Cable Television Developments* (Washington, D.C.: NCTA, 1994).

packagers had to make the pilgrimage to the headquarters of the cable operators to get access to their subscribers. Without access to subscribers, it did not matter how good the programming was. Making this trip more difficult was the fact that many cable systems and therefore many cable subscribers were often in the hands of a single entity, a Multiple Systems Operator (MSO). Clearly, the larger the MSO, the greater the power it will have over packagers trying to get distribution on their systems. Rising since the mid-1970s, concentration levels are now so great that the top four MSOs control over 75 percent of all cable subscribers in the United States.

Cable operators used their control of the distribution bottleneck to improve their leverage relative to packagers that were selected for carriage on their systems. They did this by differentiating among the products sold on their delivery system. By influencing viewers' decisions on which channels they would subscribe to and watch, cable operators put themselves in an advantageous position with regard to the packagers.[50] The packager that wanted to build a base of viewers would need favorable treatment from operators.

Of course, packagers can differentiate their product and advertise it so that viewers do not need the cable operator to make their purchase. However, advertising may not be as important in influencing the buying decision as the tools available to the cable operator. One indicator of this is that advertising is not effective in achieving differentiation.[51] There is no correlation between advertising levels and cable network profitability (Exhibit 20). This means that packagers have had a hard time using advertising to differentiate their products.

During the Cable Era, operators influenced consumer purchasing decisions in five ways:

- acquisition of programming
- tiering
- sales assistance
- direct marketing
- channel positioning

This influence has been much stronger for weaker and newer services than over established services.

The first way that cable operators have exerted power over packagers has been by selecting and acquiring the programming to be transmitted over their systems. This was not important at the dawn of cable television, when operators were desperate for original cable programming. Later, there was more programming than channels on which to transmit it. Therefore, cable operators served as the gatekeepers selecting which

Exhibit 20
Cable Network Media Spending versus Cash Flow: 1993

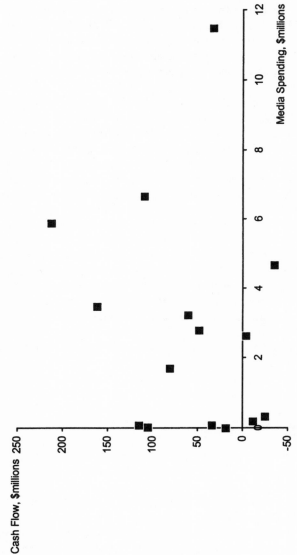

Note: Includes BET (ex. PPV), CNN, Headline News, TBS, TNT, Comedy Channel, Discovery, ESPN (ex. ESPN2), Lifetime, Family Channel, TLC, Nickelodeon, Sci-Fi Channel, Travel Channel, TWC, USA.
Sources: Paul Kagan Associates, *Cable TV Programming* (Carmel, Calif.: Paul Kagan Associates, 15 April 1994); Cabletelevision Advertising Bureau, *1994 Cable Facts* (New York: Cabletelevision Advertising Bureau, 1994).

channels would be transmitted. As we noted, this served as a barrier to entry to protect established cable networks from upstart competitors. Established networks were able to check the power of the operator; the operator needed to select popular programming that would attract subscribers. Programming like that of HBO, ESPN, or CNN has been considered "must-have" for any system, and these networks have been able to counter operator power. Less attractive networks and new networks, eager to stay on or get onto systems, have been in a weaker position. The vigorous defense of the "must-carry" rules, requiring cable operators to carry a number of broadcasters in their system areas, by independent VHF and UHF stations is recent evidence of the strength of cable operators. Without these rules, many stations believed that they would be dropped.

In the establishment of tiers of service, as in the "basic" tier or the "expanded basic" tier, cable operators have sought to maximize viewing and profits by price discrimination among viewers.[52] Cable operators sell cable television in tiers, or bundles of channels. Lower-priced tiers have advertising-supported fare, while higher-priced tiers have subscription-based channels. Networks have been dependent on operator decisions as to in which tier and at what price they would be placed. Again, this has been more important for newer and weaker services than it has been for established services that could draw subscribers to a tier on their own. Less attractive networks had to rely on cable operators for placement in tiers that have been attractive to subscribers, priced well, and available without any additional required purchase. Channels that were left out of inexpensive tiers, popular tiers, or possibly any tier altogether have had a hard time surviving, especially if they were new or marginal. In the 1992 Cable Act, cable operators were limited to an extent in their tiering policy, but these rules are still in flux and the latest promulgations give the cable operator discretion on tiering decisions beyond the basic tier. The only way that networks could counter this power is by stipulating different prices in their contracts for different penetration levels that their networks achieve. For example, USA Network's contracts stipulated that if distribution fell below 85 percent, the operator and the network must negotiate how the situation would be rectified.[53]

Sales assistance has been another way that cable operator could influence the purchasing decision of subscribers. Cable operators' sales helped influence decisions by explaining to subscribers the nature of different tiers and channels. When a new subscriber is trying to decide between HBO and Showtime, for example, sales assistance could swing the decision with a description of the type and number of movies, exclusives, length of breaks between movies, and special events.

Cable operators also had another marketing tool at their discretion that could influence purchasing decisions: direct marketing. Cable operators market directly with mail to residents of a cabled area and to previous subscribers. In their mail packages, they can promote certain channels and tiers in a variety of ways, including free trial months and other discounts. The networks cannot afford this kind of marketing since the marginal cost for them is significantly higher[54] and since they do not have the databases for the target market. Networks have to expend more resources to be included in various marketing activities if they wish to promote their service.

A final tool that the cable operator had to influence the ultimate viewing decision has been channel positioning. This is important since channels depend on viewing for ad revenue and, ultimately, for their share of the subscriber revenues. If a channel has low ratings, the cable operator can threaten to drop the channel and argue for lower payments to the network. Cable operators can directly influence a channel's ratings by channel positioning. The lower the channel number, the higher are the channel's ratings. Network affiliates are usually carried on low channel numbers, between 2 and 13, and still attract the largest viewing share. Since most viewers select programming passively either by watching adjacent programs on the same channel or by switching between adjacent channels, networks can achieve higher ratings if they are positioned at lower channel numbers. ESPN and MTV were among the first to offer cable operators monetary incentives in return for placement on low-number channels;[55] and channel placement is still important to them today. Today, this practice is more widespread: In 1994, the Family Channel, for example, would refund a cable operator 15 percent of its license fees if it was positioned on any channel between 2 and 20.[56] Channel positioning is also important for broadcasters. In 1994, Fox purchased twelve VHF stations to replace UHF affiliates. Fox claimed that these VHF stations with lower channel numbers would increase ratings by 40 percent, while CBS countered that the ratings boost would be *only* 25 percent. Even UHF broadcasters with relatively high terrestrial channel numbers have an interest in channel positioning since "being located uniformly 'on-channel'[57] greatly simplifies the marketing task of UHF independent stations and reduces audience confusion with respect to program promotion."[58]

How was this bargaining power manifest in the actual transactions between cable network and operator? A look at the prices that packagers charged operators for their services provides the answer. Operators pay packagers a per-subscriber rate for their programming. It is difficult to assess prices since contract terms are generally not known. Published rate cards do circulate, but they are only a starting point for negotiations that take place in private. Of course, the fact that price negotiations do occur is a signal that packagers do compete to the benefit of operators.

There are several publicly available examples showing that price competition between basic cable networks actually does occur. CNN cut its price in response to the launch of Satellite News Channel (SNC), a competing general cable news channel, in 1982 and again in 1985, when TCI was encouraging competition to CNN.[59] New services price aggressively in order to overcome entry barriers. New shopping services were offering operators $5 per household "launch support payments."[60] Viacom planned to offer cable operators three minutes of commercial time every hour to sell for themselves as well as to lift any per-subscriber charges for transmitting their new channel, TV Land.[61] Price competition was evident when the 1992 Cable Act was passed, allowing broadcasters to elect to charge a fee for carriage. At the outset of the negotiations, the expectation was that some fee would be required of the cable operators for network carriage. However, during the negotiations, the broadcasters, one by one, agreed to waive any fee and instead take a position on the cable system for a new channel.

Finally, although the exact terms of contracts are unknown, MSOs are known to get large discounts on programming. In 1988, TCI apparently formed Satellite Services, Inc., "which had the stated purpose of negotiating on behalf of TCI's consolidated and unconsolidated holdings with program suppliers in wholesale rate negotiations."[62] The National Telecommunications Information Agency also cites reports of discounts that large MSOs receive from cable networks, although it points out that these could, in theory, be due to transactions efficiencies.[63] These discounts are so attractive that smaller cable operators formed the National Cable Television Cooperative in order to combine their programming purchases. In addition to these discounts, operators can get discounts for long-term contracts and multinetwork packages. These discounts taken together can reduce operators' costs by anywhere from 20 percent to 50 percent.[64]

Clearly, although there is price competition between services, it is not as intense as one might think. While examples of entry-deterring and entry-seeking price cutting can be found, there are fewer examples of price cutting in the course of normal business. Any price competition that does exist is likely to be greater for the larger systems and between packagers that are less differentiated and have less appeal to viewers. A highly differentiated and popular service, like ESPN or MTV, is unlikely to cut price for a small operator; a less differentiated and less popular service, like an independent station, is likely to cut price for a large operator. The data bear out these predictions. Average rate card fees have steadily increased over the last decade, averaging between a 10 percent and a 20 percent increase per year, and show no signs of abatement. Actual rates, which include discounts given to operators, have also steadily increased, although at a slower 5 to 15 percent annual average.

A New Paradigm for Network Profitability

Although they would have been even more profitable but for the enormous power of the operators, cable networks became one of the most powerful and profitable links in the supply chain. The cable network prosperity formula was achieved by changing the broadcast network paradigm for both costs and revenues.

On the cost side, the breakthrough that cable networks made was to realize that they did not have to spend vast sums on programming, like the broadcast networks, to satisfy a small audience. All they needed to do was to spend enough to attract their small audiences and retain carriage on cable systems.

There are three different categories of programming that cable networks transmit: programming produced internally, original programming purchased from program producers, and non-network programming, first run or rerun, purchased from syndicators. Networks make choices among these options depending on their particular value proposition: Some general entertainment cable networks rely on non-network programming and other cable networks, like CNN and ESPN, produce their own programming. By avoiding costly original productions, cable networks drastically reduce programming expenses. The Cartoon Network is an example of a cable network with extremely low programming costs. At its launch in the early 1990s, it spent about $6 million per year, 33 percent of its total costs, or about the cost of a couple of episodes of a top-rated situation comedy.[65]

Cable network revenues have increased at the phenomenal compound annual rate of 13 percent for the last ten years and now total about 70 percent of broadcast network revenues, or $7.5 billion. This growth is so strong because of cable networks have gotten access to a new source of revenue: subscriber fees. Actually, by relying on advertising alone, broadcast television and radio parted from the successful formula used in the print media world. Cable networks have returned television to the print model and now earn revenue from both subscription fees and advertising.

Low costs and high revenues usually result in strong profits. Cable networks were no exception. Cable networks quickly became one of the most profitable parts of the entire industry (Exhibit 21). They are the most profitable segment on asset-based performance measures, because of their relatively small asset base, and almost as profitable as distributors on sales-based measures. Recognized by the investment community, the stock prices of these companies have increased more rapidly than have the prices for companies at other points in the supply chain (Exhibit 22).

With their investment in cable packaging and programming, cable op-

Exhibit 21
Comparative Performance Data

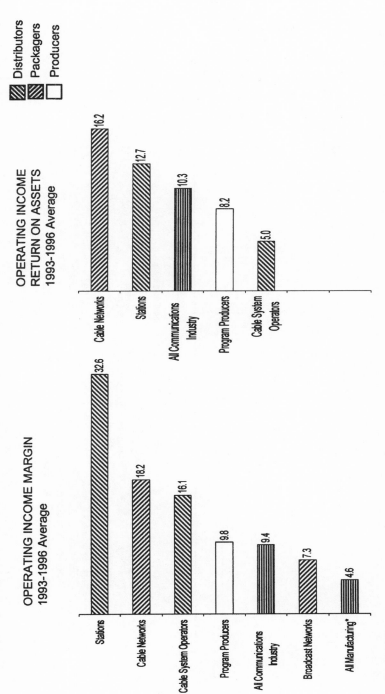

OPERATING INCOME MARGIN
1993-1996 Average

Stations	32.6
Cable Networks	18.2
Cable System Operators	16.1
Program Producers	9.8
All Communications Industry	9.4
Broadcast Networks	7.3
All Manufacturing*	4.6

OPERATING INCOME
RETURN ON ASSETS
1993-1996 Average

Cable Networks	16.2
Stations	12.7
All Communications Industry	10.3
Program Producers	8.2
Cable System Operators	5.0

Distributors
Packagers
Producers

*1993 to 1995.
Sources: Veronis, Suhler, and Associates, *Communications Industry Report* (New York: Veronis, Suhler, and Associates, Inc., 1998); A. C. Jacobs, *Handbook of US Labor Statistics* (Lanham, Md.: Bernan Press, 1997); Steve McClellan, "ABC Takes Top Network Profit Honors," *Broadcasting and Cable,* 3 April 1995; Geoffrey Foisie, "ABC, CBS Tie for TV Network 1993 Revenue Honors," *Broadcasting and Cable,* 16 May 1994; Geoffrey Foisie, "CBS Edges Out NBC in TV Network Revenue," *Broadcasting and Cable,* 10 May 1993.

Exhibit 22
Stock Market Performance through the Supply Chain: Annualized Return, 29 March 1996 to 31 March 1998

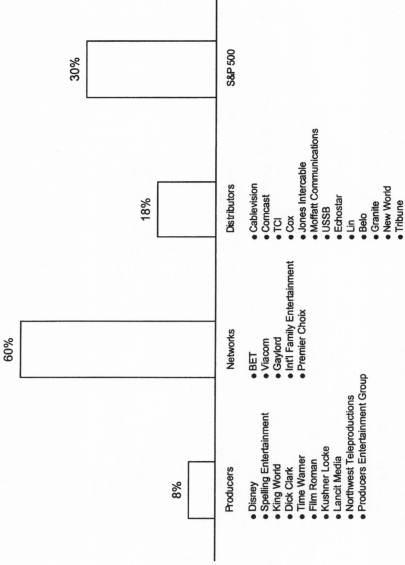

8%	60%	18%	30%
Producers	Networks	Distributors	S&P 500

Producers
- Disney
- Spelling Entertainment
- King World
- Dick Clark
- Time Warner
- Film Roman
- Kushner Locke
- Lancit Media
- Northwest Teleproductions
- Producers Entertainment Group

Networks
- BET
- Viacom
- Gaylord
- Int'l Family Entertainment
- Premier Choix

Distributors
- Cablevision
- Comcast
- TCI
- Cox
- Jones Intercable
- Moffatt Communications
- USSB
- Echostar
- Lin
- Belo
- Granite
- New World
- Tribune

Source: Bloomberg Financial and Commodity Market data.

erators may have created a monster: The cable networks they have financed and nurtured may have become more powerful than their forebears, the operators. This is a story that will unfold as we move to the Digital Era later in the book. Its roots can be seen in the Cable Era. Although cable networks were often owned by cable operators, they began to emerge as independent entities. While the broadcast networks exist to feed programming to their station groups, cable networks—once they had fulfilled their early role and attracted subscribers to cable operators—existed to make a profit. They were not limited to distribution on any particular cable MSO or, for that matter, to distribution via cable technology generally. Cable networks were sold to any distributor that would pay for them—other MSOs and even rival distributors.

The creation of cable networks is the first stage in a massive migration of profits from the conduit to content. This Great Value Shift was made possible by cable networks that separated content from the conduit. No longer were networks simply vehicles to supply programming to distributors; they were on their way to becoming independent, branded, and profit-oriented entities. Entities that ultimately could give distributors more trouble than they had bargained for.

Broadcasters in the Cable Era

Broadcasters survived the cable challenge, but woke up to a newly competitive era. In the Cable Era, the harbingers of the coming Great Value Shift, the migration of profits from distribution to content, could be seen. The pressure on broadcasters would come from two major forces:

- New entrants in distribution
- New networks and audience fragmentation

Together, these forces would change the landscape of the broadcast industry; ultimately, they would end the status of the local stations as the only means of distribution of television signals, end the cozy triopoly in network broadcasting, and usher in the Great Value Shift.

However, at the same time these changes were occurring, the FCC was deregulating the broadcast industry. With competition from the cable industry growing, the FCC loosened many of the regulations that had constrained broadcasters. These changes were welcomed and would benefit the industry. They would mask the fundamental forces of the Great Value Shift. But they would be short-lived.

The cabling of the country did not undermine the privileged position of broadcast stations as the sole vehicle for ubiquitous distribution throughout the country. Since one-third of the country still had not subscribed to cable at the close of the Cable Era, broadcast networks did not yet consider cable to be an alternative to their local stations for distribution. We will see later that the changing structure of distribution, of which cable is a part, would soon have an effect on the broadcasters.

Not only did the local stations prosper during the cabling of America, they actually became even more valuable. This was the result of the lifting of the regulation that had been imposed on the industry during the Broadcast Era. Now the 12-12-12 Rule was changed to allow groups to acquire and amass ever larger numbers of stations. Prices shot up as stations became the target of bids by competing station groups. As, the networks increased their number of O&O's, their performance improved, owing more to the stronger economics of their stations than to their broadcast networks. As formerly independent stations became part of groups, their economics changed. They earned some of the benefits that their rival stations, the O&O's and the network affiliates, had enjoyed. Specifically, they gained buying power and scale to produce and purchase better programming. They used this programming effectively against the networks by counterprogramming local fare against the national programming distributed by the networks.

While these dynamics have increased station margins and values, other structural changes were occurring that would make life more difficult for the broadcast industry in the long run. These changes would have an immediate and serious effect on the broadcast networks. Later, during the Digital Era, they would even be poised to strike the distributors.

After decades of a "golden age," the broadcast triopoly broke down. Not only did the big three networks have to face new cable networks, but they also had to compete with new broadcast networks. How could new networks be viable during the Cable Era when they had not been viable during the Broadcast Era?

Several changes made it possible for new networks to emerge. Recall that the number of networks during the Broadcast Era was constrained by the number of available stations in markets across the country: without an available station of acceptable power in most every market in the country, new terrestrial networks did not have enough distribution to be viable. In the Cable Era, two developments occurred that eased this constraint.

The first development was that the FCC licensed more stations. In the beginning of the Cable Era, from 1979 to 1986, just over 300 new UHF station and 20 new VHF stations went on the air. The number of stations licensed was impressive, as was their geographic distribution throughout the country. Since 85 percent of U.S. television households could be reached with affiliates in the top 100 markets, it was critical for there to be stations available in these markets. Most of these new stations were located in top and middle population markets.

Combined with this new FCC spectrum was the effect of the cable distribution. Carriage on cable systems equalized UHF and VHF reception because, on cable, viewers could not tell the difference. Cable allowed a broadcast network to use UHF stations for coverage without suffering all of the technical handicaps that had been associated with UHF in the past. Moreover, if a station did not reach an adjacent market, the cable system in that market would often import signals from nearby markets.

With regulation and technology eroding some of the barriers to entry, the Fox Network was able to launch at the end of 1986. With 99 affiliated stations covering 80 percent of the country, Fox entered the broadcast network fray as a much smaller entity than its rivals. It used its own production studio, low costs, and a streamlined and counterprogrammed schedule to work its way into the mainstream.

Today, Fox is an equal of the original three networks; in fact, it is the highest-ranked network in some of the ratings categories. Fox paved the way for two more recent efforts to form broadcast networks, Warner Brothers and Paramount. In these efforts, the limitations of available spectrum are apparent. Warner and Paramount are pushing up against the limit of available stations. This can be seen by the fact that these networks have had to sign up smaller stations—and even cable operators—for distribution in markets where larger and more powerful stations were simply unavailable. Even with these smaller stations, coverage remains less than ubiquitous for these new broadcast networks: in 1994, when the Warner and Paramount networks were about to begin, they had achieved only 40 to 50 percent coverage with terrestrial signals and between 70 and 80 percent coverage when cable was included.[66]

Recall that the networks enjoyed a period of calm and prosperity in the Broadcast Era. They were able to agree on conventions and practices—pricing, quantity of advertising per hour, amounts of original programming—thus limiting some of the most damaging aspects of competition. During the Cable Era, the entry of Fox and the cable networks began to break these rules down.

The environment for advertising sales began to change during the Cable Era. Advertising pricing became more competitive than it had been during the Broadcast Era. In the Cable Era, new players entered the market eager to muscle their way into a lucrative advertising market. Buyers of time, advertisers and their agencies, became larger and more savvy. The effects could be seen in many ways: in price discounts to large buyers,[67] in decreasing prices as airtime approached, and in the intense negotiations between buyers and sellers during which sellers often adjusted various aspects of their prices.

However, the market did not become as competitive as a commodity market.[68] During the Cable Era, broadcast networks could still maintain high prices despite loss of audience share because they maintained an oligopoly that could provide mass audiences. There is statistical evidence for this.[69] One can also observe industry practices that enabled sellers to keep prices higher than they might have been in a more competitive market: networks still tried to sell most of their inventory in the up-front market minimizing the risk of selling a perishable product too close to the time at which it becomes useless; the traditional pricing formula[70] was still widely used with "the industry leader initiating changes in the price level"[71]; and overall price levels tended to steadily increase at a rate roughly two times greater than the Consumer Price Index, pausing only during times of serious recession, if at all.[72]

It is, of course, impossible to know just how collusive the advertising market really was during the Cable Era. As advertising prices resume their increase after the recession of the early 1990s—up-front sales for network time in the 1995–1996 season totals an estimated $5.6 billion, a 27.3 percent increase over the previous season[73]—and total revenues to all sellers of advertising grow (Exhibit 23), it is unclear the extent to which they are due to collusion or simply to robust demand growth by advertisers in the face of more slowly increasing supply. What is certain is that whatever the conditions were during the Broadcast Era they were more competitive in the Cable Era.

Even if the networks could limit price competition for advertiser spending, it would be very difficult to curtail programming competition. Programming is simply too critical a part of the packagers' product and too difficult an attribute to control in cartel arrangements.

Networks have fewer product attributes than did distributors. Without a distribution system or picture and sound quality to tinker with, programming is just about the only attribute left on which a network can differentiate itself. Not only can programming attract viewers, it can also draw distributors: A cable network with better product will be more valuable to a cable operator since it will be able to attract more subscribers, and a broadcast network with better product will be more valuable to a station since it will increase the value of its advertising time.

Broadcast networks spend enormous sums on programming. As they are dependent solely on advertising revenue and as advertisers want large audiences, broadcast networks must maintain large viewing share to remain financially viable. The only way to do this is through investment in attractive programming. In 1990, the three networks devoted about 85 percent of total expenditures to programming. This meant that they spent roughly $6 billion on programming in a year, with most of it

Exhibit 23
Growth in National Advertising: 1980–1997

$Billion

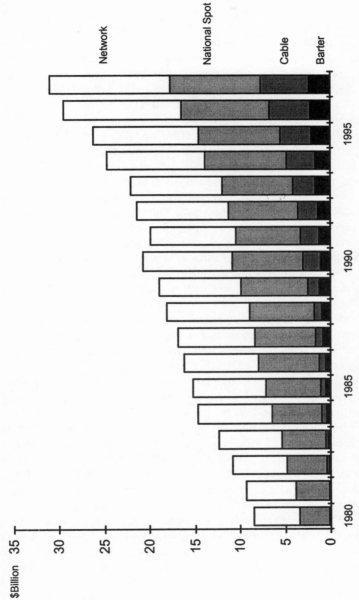

Note: Up to 1989 Fox is included in Barter; thereafter it is included in Network.
Source: Robert J. Coen and McCann-Erickson, *Annual U.S. Advertising Expenditures* (New York: Advertising Age, 1997). Reproduced with permission.

going to lavishly filmed mini-series, made-for-television movies, dramas, and situation comedies purchased from production companies. In addition, $300 million is left over for each network to spend on national and international news departments, with the remainder going to sports departments covering all of the major national sports, late night schedules, and daytime fare as well.[74]

While most cable networks do not spend anywhere near the sums that broadcasters spend for programming, it is still their largest single cost. From 1992 to 1994, programming expenses for basic cable networks averaged 68 percent of total expenses,[75] although this number will vary depending on the type of network.

Not only is programming important to packagers, it is also a notoriously difficult area to control. In fact, program quality cannot even be measured ex ante: It is only possible to create a quantitative measure of program quality after the audience is known—and even then, it is problematic. Even if there were a measure, such as program budgets, it would be difficult to identify cheaters and enforce the rules of any collusive arrangement since budgets are opaque.[76]

However, there were ways to at least partially control competition. The first way it could be limited was by controlling the quantity and timing of programming produced and aired. Since repeat programming has no marginal cost, one way of limiting competition would be for the networks to agree to limit the amount of original programming made and aired. This would be relatively easy to measure and enforce. There is evidence that agreement of this kind was achieved in the Broadcast Era: Original "seasons" were limited and declined in length while reruns were programmed at the end of these seasons.[77]

While the vestiges of this agreement remain, the proliferation of networks has made collusion in this area more difficult. In 1989, Fox stunned the industry by starting its 1989–1990 season in early July to get a jump on its competitors who started theirs in late August or early September. Moreover, since many of the new cable networks do not follow the same format of the traditional broadcast networks, agreement in detail would be difficult: ESPN, CNN, and Court TV, for instance, cannot show any substantial amount of reruns without jeopardizing the vitality of their concept. The premium services have entirely different scheduling parameters; since they only show feature films, their reruns cannot be coordinated with the traditional networks at all. Those cable networks that do use more traditional entertainment programming are increasingly airing original programming in the summer in an effort to steal viewers from the broadcasters who are showing reruns.[78]

Competition could also be limited to the extent that different networks can decide to serve different demographic groups. Advertising-supported markets exist so that advertisers can buy access to viewers.

Advertisers prefer viewers who are in their target market: Companies selling beer, for example, seek 21- to 35-year-old male viewers. Networks talk to advertisers to determine which types of audiences are in demand so that they can buy or make programming to attract these audiences. In making their programming choices, networks are in a position to differentiate their product to advertisers on the basis of audience size, demographics, geography, and day of the week. Broadcasters could, for example, serve 18- to 49-year-olds while cable served children and seniors. The problem is in tacitly reaching a differentiation scheme that is equitable and can be enforced over time.

A final dimension on which collusion could occur is the total hours of programming. Collusion on this dimension, quantity of supply, is similar to collusion on the number of commercial minutes per hour. It is visible and relatively easily enforced. There is evidence that three networks successfully colluded on this front during the 1960s and 1970s. They cut back from supplying programming to local stations during the marginal slots before prime time, the 7:00 p.m. to 7:30 p.m. slot at first, and then they responded to new FCC regulations by cutting back the 7:30 p.m. to 8:00 p.m. slot later.[79] But, since the dawn of the Cable Era, collusion along this dimension has become more difficult. The proliferation of channels has brought a vast increase in the number of hours programmed. These channels have changed the meaning of prime time: CNN's value proposition can be expressed as "the latest news, all the time," while MTV's is music at all hours, Court TV provides trials all of the time, the Weather Channel provides weather reports all of the time, and so on. Even the traditional networks have expanded programming into new dayparts in response, primarily late night and early morning.

Collusive conduct, if it ever existed, had disappeared by the Cable Era. The broadcast networks could only counter the cable threat by spending more money on programming to retain viewers, even at the expense of lowering profit margins:

The television networks experienced an average annual compound increase in advertising revenues of 13.7 percent from 1978 to 1980, while program expenses increased at an average compound rate of 17 percent over this same period. This finding is in sharp contrast to the "pre-audience decline" in the average annual compound growth rates of revenue and program costs experienced by the television networks from 1973 to 1977 (15.1 percent and 15.0 percent respectively).[80]

Since then, broadcast networks and local stations have continued to vastly increase the quality of programming in response to cable television and new stations: broadcasters have increased spending "at an estimated rate of 8% annually between 1980 and 1990."[81]

This pattern has been apparent in the case of news. In the case of local news, a positive correlation between intensity of competition and size of newsroom budgets was established by Lacy, Atwater, and Qin[82] and between the intensity of competition and the hours of news per day.[83] Total affiliate spending on local news increased 250 percent between 1987 and 1991 as competition with cable networks intensified. At the national level, the linkage has not been established statistically. However, since 1980, when the Turner Broadcasting System launched CNN, the dynamics of product competition in the national news business have been readily observable. CNN's offering of 24-hour news caused the broadcast networks to add more news of their own:

In response to SNC and CNN, CBS, NBC, and ABC expanded their own news into the late night and early morning time periods. They added a total of 33 weekly hours of news in response to CNN's entry. . . . In particular, the networks sharply increased the quantity and quality of news material available to their affiliates for insertion in local news broadcasts. . . . NBC implemented a major expansion and improved the quality of its news feed; ABC increased the quantity of news material in its feed by 35 to 40 percent.[84]

Such massive spending has forced cable to respond by increasing its own programming expenditures threefold in ten years, from about $1.5 billion in the mid-1980s to $4.5 billion by the mid-1990s. This has set into motion a spiral of increased spending on programming by all parties. The dynamic can even be seen in intra-cable competition. In niches like premium services in which there are numerous providers, the product competition is plainly evident. HBO and Showtime have continually increased the overall programming that they schedule, the number of costly original programs that they produce, and the number of block-buster films that they schedule. More recently, premium services have begun to launch additional services in an effort to compete: Encore launched several mini-pay channels that were quickly followed by Showtime; HBO took the route of multiplexing, offering HBO movies starting at different times.

So far in the 1990s, broadcast networks have not been as profitable as they were in the 1960s and 1970s nor as profitable as cable networks and distributors are today (see Exhibit 21). The reason for this is that broadcast networks were trapped in the paradigm of the Broadcast Era. They did not earn a share of subscription revenue like the cable networks. In fact, they had to pay the stations to distribute their signals. Dependent on advertising for all revenues, broadcast network profitability was particularly hurt by the soft advertising market caused by the recession of the early 1990s. In the mid-1990s, profitability has been improving, but without structural changes, it will never reach that of the cable networks.

Local stations went relatively unscathed while the networks were in this crunch, but their enviable position will not last forever. As we will see, the Digital Era will make life more difficult for them too.

This cycle of spending has forever changed the television industry. It made life more difficult for networks and distributors during the Cable Era than ever before. However, the money was not poured down a drain: there was a recipient of all of that spending. That recipient was the programming business itself.

Programming in the Cable Era

While the Cable Era saw seismic shifts in the distribution and packaging functions, what happened further upstream to the programming function? Remarkably little. As spending on programming increased, the revenues of the programming companies followed. But, profits were another matter. The lives of production companies remained competitive, risky, and short.

Demand for programming exploded during the Cable Era. The broadcasters went through the traditional sources for their programming. On the cable side, some programming was produced in-house—CNN's news and features, MTV's video shows, and ESPN's beach volleyball tournaments. But much of the programming used by cable networks was programming that was originally produced for broadcast television. Old situation comedies found a new outlet on Nick-at-Nite and TV Land, classic films were bought by Turner Classic Movies and American Movie Classics, one-hour dramas were placed on general entertainment networks like TNT and the USA Network, and children's programming became the staple of the Cartoon Channel and Nickelodeon.

Unfortunately for producers, this added demand did not spill over into the bottom line. No less than Steven Spielberg, Jeffrey Katzenberg, and David Geffen, the gifted trio that founded the Dreamworks studio, learned how difficult the television production business is. Despite all of their talent and $100 million in backing from partner ABC, they were considered a disappointment with only one show in prime time and one show getting readied for syndication in 1997. They were not the only ones who were disappointed: investors who held stocks of production companies earned returns far lower than the stock market average and among the lowest in the industry (see Exhibit 22).

The reason is that the structure of the production business remained as competitive as ever: it was still characterized by fragmented supply (Exhibit 24), inability to predict demand, and low entry barriers. As in the Broadcast Era, the fortunes of the production companies that supply the broadcast networks with prime-time programming continued to fluctuate with each year's hits and flops (Exhibit 25). Analysis of the syndication market showed that that market was also characterized by

Exhibit 24
Market Shares of Prime-Time Series Sales in the Cable Era, 1984–1988

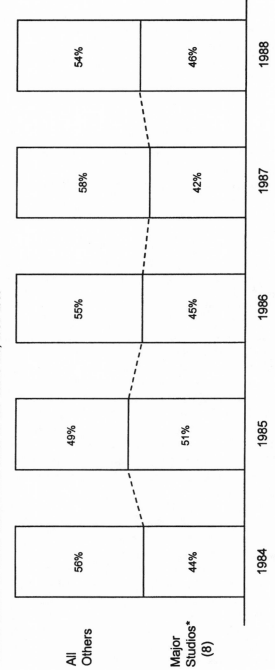

*Warner Bros., Disney, Columbia, 20th Century Fox, Paramount, Universal, MGM/UA, Lorimar.
Source: Bruce M. Owen and Steven S. Wildman, *Video Economics* (Cambridge, Mass.: Harvard University Press, 1992). Reproduced with permission.

Exhibit 25
Market Shares of Top Five Sellers of Prime-Time Series, 1984–1988, in Percentages

1984		1985		1986	
Producer	Share (%)	Producer	Share (%)	Producer	Share (%)
1. Universal	12	1. Universal	17	1. Universal	11
2. Columbia	10	2. Columbia	11	2. Lorimar	8
3. Spelling	7	3. Lorimar	6	3. Warner	6
4. Warner	6	4. Paramount	5	4. Columbia	6
5. Stephen J. Cannell	6	5. MTM	5	5. 20th Century Fox	5

1987		1988	
Producer	Share (%)	Producer	Share (%)
1. Universal	11	1. Lorimar	10
2. Lorimar	10	2. Universal	8
3. Warner	6	3. Columbia	7
4. Columbia	6	4. Paramount	6
5. Stephen J. Cannell	5	5. MGM/UA	5

Source: Bruce M. Owen and Steven S. Wildman, *Video Economics* (Cambridge, Mass.: Harvard University Press, 1992). Reproduced with permission.

fragmentation and share instability during the Cable Era.[85] This volatility in market share is often found in industries in which profits are scarce.

In addition to these structural characteristics, program producers had another problem: content creators had strong bargaining power. As revenues to program producers went up, so did compensation to talent. In fact, in one study, Woodbury, Besen, and Fournier show that talent compensation levels are a precise function of revenues to the program suppliers. The authors persuasively argue that program producers serve as vehicles for transferring profits from networks to content creators: that for every marginal dollar generated by higher prices from the networks, a marginal dollar gets spent for talent.[86]

How were content creators able to extract these marginal dollars from the producers? In the Cable Era, demand for all labor associated with television programming expanded as a result of product competition in the network and distribution segment. All labor does not present program producers with a "hold-up" problem: only content creators are capable of this. There were two typical situations in which content creators could negotiate extremely large levels of compensation.

The first was demand for that small pool of content creators that program producers believe has the ability to differentiate programs and consistently attract large audiences. Often, however, "star power," at least in television, has proven elusive. The success of particular content creators is due to skillful marketing and the particular combinations of creators that are assembled.[87] This can be seen most spectacularly when individual "stars" fail to attract audiences in new programs—Ted Danson in *Ink*—while entirely unknown talent leads other programs to success—Drew Carey in the *The Drew Carey Show*. Nevertheless, the task of the program producer is daunting. Facing pressure to make hits, it is often easiest to take the least risky path and sign up a star. After all, in the event of failure, there is an obvious scapegoat. Demand for proven content creators has thus always been large relative to the small and, at least in the short term, fixed supply.[88] This small pool of talent—Bill Cosby and Oprah Winfrey were two of the most prominent examples during the Cable Era—was compensated extremely well as a result.

The second situation in which compensation levels get bid up in the television business is for talent that begins in a program as a relatively unknown entity but, during the course of a successful program's exhibition, becomes associated with that program's success. In this way, labor relatively easily replaced prior to the scheduling of a program becomes more difficult to replace after becoming closely associated with the program after it has achieved success, for example, the stars of *Dallas* in the 1980s or Heather Locklear of *Melrose Place*. This pool of talent, obviously vital to the successful continuation of the program series, is in a strong position relative to the producers. Compensation can become extremely high and, since the late-1980s, is increasingly linked with the total expected revenue of a program. However, if demands become too high, producers do have the option, and have often exercised it, of rejecting compensation demands, altering a story line, and replacing lost personnel; this was done early in the Cable Era in the case of Suzanne Somers in *Three's Company* and more recently with David Caruso in *NYPD Blue*.

Compensation for actors and directors who are difficult to replace and perceived to attract audiences has reached dazzling heights and continues to grow. For example, the average compensation for a film or television star who made the Forbes "Top 40" list, actors and one director, went from $13.5 million in 1986 to $28 million in 1993, an average annual increase of 11 percent while inflation was only 4 percent. Certain writers can also be in high demand if they have the ability to write programming that can consistently attract audiences. Average compensation for writers increased by about 9 percent from 1982 to 1994, but the average is lower than that of the Forbes "Top 40" list since it includes many writers that have not been able to identify themselves with hit programming and are not irreplaceable. Compensation for top writers, truly unique inputs, is extremely high and increasing rapidly. This has been especially true for comedy writers in recent years as the number of situation comedies produced has multiplied. According to Jamie McDermott, the senior vice president in charge of prime-time series for NBC, "all over town, bidding wars are breaking out even for second- and third-level writers on successful comedies."[89]

Using the measure of profits, we could compare the returns of firms in industry segments to national averages to measure how well the television industry performs relative to the economy as a whole. A similar comparison for compensation is more difficult. However, there is no reason to believe that content creators were not being fairly compensated for their service. Increases in compensation levels were well in excess of consumer price inflation, and absolute compensation levels were much higher than levels for their closest alternative use on the theatrical stage.[90]

Compensation for top stars is so high that it begs the opposite question: How can it be justified? Small differences in actual talent get magnified into large differences in earnings. Lesser talent cannot substitute for greater talent in a symmetrical fashion: seeing ten episodes of a mediocre drama does not equal one episode of a great drama. Just as a surgeon with a success rate that is 10 percent higher than that of another surgeon will earn more than a 10 percent premium over his rival, so will a star earn a large premium over other talented actors.

There have been frequent reports in the press about labor not getting compensated "fairly" for work in the production of motion pictures. For example, Winston Groom was promised a share of net profits from the film *Forrest Gump*, which was based on his novel. Since the film had yet to earn a net profit, Mr. Groom had not received his compensation as late as one year after the film was released.[91] The issue raised is not a question of "fairness," but a question of the bargaining power of Mr. Groom. Actor Tom Hanks and director Robert Zemeckis received $31 million in the same time period because their bargaining power was large enough for them to have negotiated for a share of gross profits. If talent is critical enough to the production process, it receives a significant portion of the profits, if it is not, it must be content with wages that are set at a level at which the rest of the labor market clears.

We are now moving into the television industry's third era: the Digital Era. This era cannot be characterized by a single revolutionizing technology like those of the previous eras, but by many. While the cable operators were hyping their visions of the 500-channel universe, a plethora of new platforms have emerged that are capable of competing with cable to provide subscribers with television service.

These platforms range from satellites to the copper line. Breakthroughs are being made based on the fundamental fact that data can be transmitted in a digital format. By converting video, voice, or data to a stream of 1s and 0s, large amounts of information can be scrambled, compressed, and delivered with high quality and little delay to users. Today, these technologies are being deployed; digitalization is breaking the distribution bottleneck.

NOTES

1. The available frequencies for television.

2. Inferior signal strength, higher transmission costs, and channel tuning and receiver problems.

3. Mark J. Fratrik and Theresa J. Ottina, *1994 Television Financial Report* (Washington, D.C.: National Association of Broadcasters, 1994).

4. Bruce M. Owen and Steven S. Wildman, *Video Economics* (Cambridge, Mass.: Harvard University Press, 1992); Stanley M. Besen et al., *Misregulating Television: Network Dominance and the F.C.C.* (Chicago: University of Chicago Press, 1984).

5. Network programming that goes on sale after it has completed a run on the affiliated stations.

6. Independently produced programming sold to the highest bidder in any given market.

7. W. Brian Arthur, "Competing Technologies, Increasing Returns, and Lock-in by Historical Events," *Economic Journal* 99, no. 394 (March 1989): 116–131; Paul David, *Path-Dependence: Putting the Past into the Future of Economics*, I.M.S.S.S. Tech Report No. 553 (Palo Alto, Calif.: Stanford University, 1988).

8. B. M. Owen, J. H. Beebe, and W. G. Manning, Jr., *Television Economics* (Lexington, Mass.: Lexington Books, D. C. Heath, 1974), p. 101.

9. Owen, Beebe, and Manning, *Television Economics*; Barry R. Litman, *The Vertical Structure of the Television Broadcasting Industry: The Coalescence of Power* (East Lansing, Mich.: MSU Business Studies, 1979).

10. In this environment, we can predict that while cooperative equilibrium might be easy to maintain in markets in which the number of local stations matches the number of networks, it is harder to maintain in other markets or in times of changing economic conditions for the negotiating parties. In fact, during the years of three network dominance, there was not much competition in this area. An exception was ABC's use of higher compensation payments in the 1960s to lure affiliates in one- and two-station markets as it was establishing itself as an equal to NBC and CBS. More recent evidence of the difficulty in achieving cooperative equilibrium without a symmetrical structure comes from West Palm Beach in 1988: With the situation reversed, as there were more local stations than networks, competition reversed the flow of compensation from a network to a station for the first time. See Besen et al., *Misregulating Television*.

11. Prices were broken down into cost per thousand (CPM) times audience size. This convention makes it easier to converge on a consensus CPM and limit competition to attracting audiences.

12. There were, and still are, "seasons" during which original programming is aired. Repeats were aired in the summer.

13. Litman, *The Vertical Structure of the Television Broadcasting Industry*, p. 26.

14. Owen, Beebe, and Manning, *Television Economics*, p. 31.

15. This is discussed in the the chapter on programming.

16. Owen and Wildman, *Video Economics*, pp. 58–59.

17. Harold L. Vogel, *Entertainment Industry Economics*, 3rd ed. (Cambridge: Cambridge University Press, 1994), p. 117.

18. Oliver E. Williamson, *Markets and Hierarchies, Analysis and Antitrust Implications: A Study in the Economics of Internal Organisation* (New York: Free Press, 1975).

19. William J. Baumol, *Performing Arts, the Economic Dilemma: A Study of Problems Common to Theatre, Opera, Music and Dance* (New York: 20th Century Fund, 1966).

20. Programming that is made to be premiered outside of a network schedule.

21. Vogel, *Entertainment Industry Economics*, p. 121.

22. Owen and Wildman, *Video Economics*; Vogel, *Entertainment Industry Economics*.

23. Vogel, *Entertainment Industry Economics*, p. 117.

24. See Beebe, Owen, and Manning, *Television Economics*.

25. Ibid., p. 40.

26. Eva E. Jacobs, ed., *Handbook of U.S. Labor Statistics* (Lanham, Md.: Bernan Press, 1997).

27. R. Smith, *The Wired Nation* (New York: Harper and Row, 1972), p. 3.

28. Paul Kagan Associates, *Marketing New Media*, 20 June 1994, p. 4; Paul Kagan Associates, *Marketing New Media*, 15 August 1994; Paul Kagan Associates, *Cable & Pay TV Census*, 22 August 1994.

29. Other regulatory barriers might have existed if Congress had not given competitors to cable the right to buy cable system–owned programming, like CNN, considered to be critical for success.

30. Thomas W. Hazlett, "Duopolistic Competition in Cable Television: Implications for Public Policy," *Yale Journal on Regulation* 65 (1990): 7–34.

31. Leland L. Johnson, *Toward Competition in Cable Television* (Cambridge, Mass.: MIT Press, 1994), p. 22.

32. Bruce L. Egan, *Information Superhighways Revisited* (Boston: Artech House, 1997).

33. This makes our situation a good example of a "noncontestable" market. See William J. Baumol, John C. Panzar, and Robert D. Willig, *Contestable Markets and the Theory of Industry Structure*, rev. ed. (New York: Harcourt Brace Jovanovich, 1988).

34. Thomas W. Hazlett and Matthew L. Spitzer, "Public Policy toward Cable Television. Volume 1: The Economics of Rate Controls," working paper for the Program on Telecommunications Policy, Institute of Governmental Affairs, University of California, Davis, 1996.

35. Ibid.

36. David H. Waterman and Andrew A. Weiss, "Vertical Integration in Cable Television," paper prepared for the American Enterprise Institute for Public Policy Research, Washington, D.C., 17 September 1993, p. 74.

37. Ibid.

38. Eli M. Noam, "Economies of Scale in Cable Television: A Multiproduct Analysis," in *Video Media Competition: Regulation, Economics, and Technology*, edited by Eli M. Noam (New York: Columbia University Press, 1985); Hazlett, "Duopolistic Competition in Cable Television," pp. 7–34.

39. Performance is measured using returns to sales and returns to assets. Both measures use pre-tax profit numbers in their numerator, but a second asset measurement is added that uses cash flow in its numerator. These two indices of profit are employed because certain types of firms with high depreciation, notably cable operators, will have low earnings, but high cash flows. Examining returns based only on earnings will not tell the entire story. In the denominator of the performance measures, both sales and assets are used. Typically, sales-based numbers are not as valuable as asset-based numbers because sales can vary depending on strategy choices while assets represent capital employed in the business. Consider, for example, a company that successfully lowers its prices to increase volume. This company would have a low ratio of operating income to sales. However, this strategy may make sense if the company can generate the extra volume with a low level of assets. Nevertheless, returns on sales are included because returns on assets were not available for all of the industry segments under study.

40. Hazlett and Spitzer, "Public Policy toward Cable Television."

41. Ibid., pp. 33–38.

42. Ibid., p. 44.

43. National Cable Television Association (NCTA), *How to Apply For or Renew Your NCTA Seal of Good Customer Service* (Washington, D.C.: NCTA, 1991).

44. David H. Waterman and Andrew A. Weiss, "Vertical Integration in Cable Television," paper prepared for the American Enterprise Institute for Public Policy Research, Washington, D.C., 17 September 1993.

45. George Mair, *Inside HBO: The Billion Dollar War between HBO, Hollywood, and the Home Video Revolution* (New York: Macmillan, 1988), p. 5.

46. NCTA, *Cable Television Developments* (Washington, D.C.: NCTA, 1997).

47. Economic models show that a monopolist has greater incentive, other things being equal, to offer more differentiated radio or television programming than do firms engaged in competitive markets. See Peter O. Steiner, "Program Patterns and Preferences and the Workability of Competition in Radio Broadcasting," *Quarterly Journal of Economics* 66 (1952): 194.

48. The act allowed broadcasters to negotiate agreements with cable operators for carriage of their signal.

49. Paul Kagan Associates, *Cable TV Programming*, 23 June 1994, p. 1.

50. For a discussion of how retailers can exert power over wholesalers, see Michael E. Porter, *Interbrand Choice, Strategy, and Bilateral Market Power* (Cambridge, Mass.: Harvard University Press, 1976), p. 22.

51. Porter, *Interbrand Choice, Strategy, and Bilateral Market Power.*

52. There are two ways in which they can achieve this: taking advantage of scale economies and extracting additional buyer surplus. Owen and Greenlaugh in their 1986 work showed that a cable operator can offer a multichannel cable bundle at a lower price than an individual channel. Wildman and Owen in their 1992 book, building on earlier work of Stigler and others, show how bundling allows operators to increase the revenue they get from subscribers.

53. Kim Mitchell and Rod Granger, "Operators Call New Contracts Obscene," *Multichannel News*, 29 March 1993, p. 1.

54. The cable operators have the advantage of marketing their complete transmission service as well as individual channels.

55. Michael O. Wirth, "Cable's Economic Impact on Over-the-Air Broadcasting," *Journal of Media Economics* (Fall 1990).

56. Interview with Frank Hughes, National Cable Television Cooperative, 5 October 1994.

57. On-channel refers to having the same channel number in a cable system as in the terrestrial environment.

58. Wirth, "Cable's Economic Impact on Over-the-Air Broadcasting," p. 49.

59. Waterman and Weiss, "Vertical Integration," p. 18.

60. Paul Kagan Associates, *Cable TV Programming*, 31 March 1994, p. 1.

61. Bill Carter, "Nostalgia Gets a 2d Chance, Via Cable," *New York Times*, 30 October 1995, Business section.

62. Waterman, "A New Look at Media Chains and Groups: 1977–1989," 8–12.

63. National Telecommunications Information Administration, *Video Program Distribution and Cable Television: Current Policy Issues and Recommendations*, NTIA Report No. 83–233 (Washington, D.C.: NTIA, 1988).

64. Kim Mitchell, and Rod Granger, "Operators Call New Contracts Obscene," *Multichannel News*, 29 March 1993, p. 1.

65. Ibid.

66. Steve Coe, "Warner Brothers Fifth Network," *Broadcasting and Cable*, 4 April 1994, p. 6. This situation, too, could change as compression techniques become available. Clearly, regulators would also have to make the decision to give newly available spectrum to new entrants and not incumbents.

67. Gary M. Fournier and D. L. Martin, "Does Government Restricted Entry Produce Market Power? New Evidence from the Market for Television Advertising," *Bell Journal of Economics* 14 (1983): 44–56; Gary M. Fournier, "The Determination of Economic Rents in Television Broadcasting," *Antitrust Bulletin* 31 (1986): 1045–1066; W. J. Kelley, "How Television Stations Price Their Service," *Journal of Broadcasting* 11 (1967): 313–323; S. M. Besen, "The Value of Television Time," *Southern Economic Journal* 42 (1976): 435–441; Benjamin J. Bates, "Determining Television Advertising Rates," in *Communications Yearbook 7*, edited by Robert Bostrom (Beverly Hills, Calif.: Sage Publications, 1983); and W. A. French and J. T. McBrayer, "Arriving at Television Advertising Rates," *Journal of Advertising* 8 (1979): 15–18.

68. Litman, *The Vertical Structure of the Television Broadcasting Industry*; Michael O. Wirth and Harry Bloch, "The Broadcasters: The Future Role of Local Stations and the Three Networks," in *Video Media Competition: Regulation, Economics, and Technology*, edited by Eli M. Noam (New York: Columbia University Press, 1985).

69. Michael O. Wirth and James A. Wollert, "The Effects of Market Structure on Television News Pricing," *Journal of Broadcasting* 28 (Spring 1984): 215–224; Bates, "Determining Television Advertising Rates."

70. Cost per thousand multipied by thousands of viewers.

71. Litman, *Vertical Structure of the Television Broadcasting Industry*, p. 117.

72. Benjamin J. Bates, "Determining Television Advertising Rates," in *Communications Yearbook 7*, edited by Robert Bostrom (Beverly Hills, Calif.: Sage Publications, 1983).

73. Stuart Elliot, "Advertising," *New York Times*, 9 June 1995, Business section.

74. Vogel, *Entertainment Industry Economics*, pp. 165, 167, and 171.

75. Paul Kagan Associates, *Cable TV Programming*, 23 May 1994, p. 2.

76. Owen, Beebe, and Manning, *Television Economics*; Litman, *The Vertical Structure of the Television Broadcasting Industry*.

77. Ibid.

78. Bill Carter, "Cable Plans to Pounce in Networks' Off-Season," *New York Times*, 26 June 1995, Business section.

79. Litman, *The Vertical Structure of the Television Broadcasting Industry*.

80. Wirth and Bloch, "The Broadcasters," p. 134.

81. Vogel, *Entertainment Industry Economics*, p. 171.

82. Stephen Lacy, Tony Atwater, and Xinmin Qin, "Competition and the Allocation of Resources for Local Television News," *Journal of Media Economics* 2 (Spring 1989): 3–13.

83. Angela Powers, "Competition, Conduct, and Ratings in Local Television News: Applying the Industrial Organization Model," *Journal of Media Economics* (Summer 1993): 39–44.

84. Owen and Wildman, *Video Economics*, pp. 175–177.

85. Sylvia M. Chan-Olmsted, "A Structural Analysis of Market Competition in the U.S. TV Syndication Industry, 1981–1990," *Journal of Media Economics* (Fall 1991): 9–27.

86. John R. Woodbury, Stanley M. Besen, and Gary M. Fournier, "The Determinants of Network Television Program Prices: Implicit Contracts, Regulation, and Bargaining Power," *Bell Journal of Economics* 14 (1983): 351–365.

87. Owen, Beebe, and Manning, *Television Economics*.

88. Supply does tend to expand in the long term. Consider, for example, the case of syndicated talk show hosts. At the beginning of the most recent television talk show phenomenon, Phil Donahue reigned supreme, virtually inventing a new kind of television talk show. Today, there are so many hosts available that Donahue has actually left television.

89. Bill Carter, "Not a Laugh Riot: Comedy Writers in Short Supply," *New York Times*, 17 July 1995, Business section.

90. Wages in New York for the Actor's Equity union are only $1,000 per week. Lead actors can earn a small multiple of this and a small share of earnings, in the range of 5 percent (see Vogel, *Entertainment Industry Economics*, p. 267). But, since most plays do not earn profits, this does not usually add up to a substantial sum.

91. Bernard Weinraub, " 'Gump,' a Huge Hit, Still Isn't Raking in the Profits? Hmm." *New York Times*, 25 May 1995, Leisure section.

Chapter 2

The Digital Era: How Technology
Broke the Distribution Bottleneck

In classical microeconomics, technology is considered to be one of many basic conditions, like the availability of raw materials, that set industry structure. As such, technology helps determine basic structural features like the nature of costs and the level of concentration, of entry barriers, and of product differentiation. Technology's importance so far in our story cannot be denied. The industry owes its very birth to a technological innovation. At the end of the Cable Era, technology continues to play a major role in the television industry, thrusting it into the Digital Era.

Today's technological change is most profoundly affecting distribution. While the processes of producing a television program and aggregating programs into networks are similar to what they were when television was first introduced, the distribution of television signals changed in the Cable Era and will continue to change in the next era.

Classical economics refers to technology being exogenously determined: proceeding at a pace determined by "other" factors that are usually left untouched. A quick look at the pace of technology development in the real world reveals that technological breakthroughs do not always appear magically out of nowhere. Often there lurks a more pedestrian cause. In the television industry, the pace of technology change has often been dictated by regulation. Since media has to use a public right-of-way to get to its audience, regulators have never been very far away. As we tell the story of how technology broke the distribution bottleneck and led television into the Digital Era, regulatory change will play a key role in unleashing technological innovation.

BITS AND BANDWIDTH: AN INTRODUCTION TO THE DIGITAL ERA

Not much has changed to improve productivity in the content business in the last 50 years. It still takes a few dozen players several hours to complete a baseball game; four people must spend the better part of an hour to play a Beethoven String Quartet; an author, even with a word processor, still has to spend months or years writing a book; and it continues to require a battalion-size group several weeks to finish a one-half-hour comedy and an army a year to make a feature film.

Once this content has been made, its distribution is another story entirely. This segment of the supply chain is undergoing a revolution. In the Broadcast and Cable Eras, media was transmitted in analog formats. Analog formats can be thought of as continuous and fully representational of each particular producer's content. In the analog eras, text and graphics were printed on paper, and audio and video were transmitted through the electromagnetic spectrum using waves.

Analog delivery had profound effects that we have come to take for granted. With printed material, it meant that newspapers and magazines had to be delivered by the postal system or by legions of paperboys, that old papers piled up and were thrown away, that retrieving archived issues or getting timely updates was difficult. With television, it meant that the transmission of relatively few stations used a large amount of spectrum or that viewers had to buy videocassette recorders and trudge out to rent—and return—videocassettes.

At the heart of the digital revolution lies the bit. Whereas analog signals are continuous, a *bit* simply indicates to the recipient a binary response (a 1 or a 0, positive or negative). Bits were first used in computing to represent numbers. Now they can be employed to represent all kinds of information, including audio and video. An image, for example, can be digitized by first dividing it into small squares. The color in each square can be coded into bits using a range of values representing the colors of the rainbow. The bits can be transmitted and rearranged at the other end using a computer program. If you examined the picture under a microscope, you would be able to identify the squares and see the abrupt changes in coloration, but, these distortions would not be noticeable by the naked eye.

Once media is transmitted digitally, a world of new possibilities emerges. Digital media can be transmitted with a clarity that even today's relatively static-free media provide. By including information that corrects errors like static and television snow and by sending it with the content itself, digital media can deliver studio-quality audio or video.

As attractive as this might sound, it is only the beginning of what the Digital Era will bring. Since all media can be reduced to the same level of bits, the distinctions that we have historically made between media begin to blur. Text, graphics, audio, and video used to be with in the purview of separate industries: print, radio, and television respectively. Once digitized, as one observer described it, bits can commingle effortlessly.[1] Content can travel down the same distribution path and can be used interchangeably. Newspapers can add video to their mix of information, and television can provide depth using text and graphics.

The technology of this new information age also provides a means to sort through all of this new media. All content providers can add information to their bit streams that describes their content. This information is called headers. Think of headers as containing keywords or other information that describes content. In much the same way as researchers look through massive quantities of literature by searching for keywords in abstracts, viewers searching through headers will be able to find the content that they are interested in.

As revolutionary as bits are, they are only one-half of the story. No discussion of the Digital Era would be complete without telling the story of bandwidth. *Bandwidth* refers to the capacity to distribute content. In the previous eras, when television was distributed through spectrum or on coaxial cable using analog transmission techniques, bandwidth constraints created the distribution bottleneck.

In the Digital Era, the bottleneck in distribution will finally disappear. Two technological forces now at work will loosen and then eliminate the bottleneck. The digital environment is both bringing new ways of packing more information on existing distribution paths and creating entirely new paths.

Digitized information can be made to take up much less space than analog signals. In a process known as compression, unnecessary information can be removed from video signals. For example, because only parts of a television picture change from frame to frame, it is possible to save bandwidth by transmitting only the portion of the picture that is changing. If, say, the background remains constant, one compression technique is not to re-transmit this unchanging background.

The digital environment also enables networks to be designed to transport more information. In previous eras, wireline networks like the telephone network were engineered so that when two people exchanged information a circuit was dedicated to them. With bits, it is possible to make much more efficient use of the network. The technique, the packetizing of bandwidth, involves converting information into bits and sending them through the network. What makes it so thrifty in its use of bandwidth is that other bits from other messages can be sent at intervals *between* the original bits. This technique forms the basis of information flow on the Internet.

While new ways are found to send more information down television's existing distribution channels, the electromagnetic spectrum and coaxial cable, the Digital Era is also bringing new distribution channels altogether. Powerful new satellites, the copper plant of the telephone network, the electricity plant, and a brand-new fiber backbone are part of the digital revolution's end to the distribution bottleneck.[2]

There is no reason to debate the relative merits of these technologies. As we will learn in this chapter, each distribution channel has its strengths and weaknesses. The important point for our story is that they all exist and compete with each other for subscribers. Let us learn more about the basic technological forces of the Digital Era and how they are turning television's familiar distribution channels into the new distributors.

CABLE AND ITS EARLY COMPETITORS

The technology of cable is based on its origins as a community antenna. CATV was a simple system whose sole purpose was to transmit television signals from a single source to individual households without too noticeable a decline in signal quality. It consisted of a well-placed television antenna connected to users with copper wire. The early systems were capable of transmitting a handful of channels, which was more capacity than was necessary since there were only three networks and perhaps another independent or two in most markets. Picture quality was fine when the mostly aerial plant was not damaged.

Throughout the 40 years since their inception, cable systems have improved but have not fundamentally changed. Today they remain a "tree and branch" architecture with programming sent from a headend to subscribing households. Of course, advances have occurred: Satellite reception equipment resides at the headend to import distant signals; backbones are now fiber and the rest of the system is coaxial cable in order to increase the capacity of the system, improve quality, and ease maintenance; much wiring has gone underground to decrease vulnerability to damage; and amplifiers have been added to increase the geographic scope of the system.

Since cable technology has been around since the 1950s and has experienced only marginal improvement, the long incubation period before its rapid diffusion in the 1980s can only be explained by regulatory changes. At a very early stage, broadcasters and programmers perceived cable to be a threat. Local broadcasters felt threatened by the importation of distant signals, and programmers demanded compensation from the reuse of their copyrighted material. The FCC responded with a series of decisions throughout the 1960s, culminating in the 1972 Cable Television Rules, protecting broadcasters from the importation of distant signals onto cable systems and giving municipalities the authority to regulate basic cable rates. However, FCC authority to regulate distant signals and pay programming distributed by cable was challenged in the courts in a series of decisions, *FCC v. Midwest Video Corp.* (440 U.S. 689, 1979) and *Home Box Office v. FCC* (434 U.S. 829, 1977), and the 1972 Rules were rolled back. Congress passed the Cable Communications Policy Act of 1984, organizing the remaining patchwork of federal cable regulations under one law and freeing cable operators from rate regulation by municipalities. Together, the decisions in the courts and in Congress set the stage for cable's growth.

Buoyed by dramatic growth in the 1980s and attracted by the potential to develop new sources of revenue, cable operators have begun a process of upgrading their systems toward a goal of providing broadband interactivity. To do this, operators will have to escape from the prison of cable's original one-way architecture. Operators will drive fiber deeper into their systems, upgrade nodes with reliable two-way optoelectronic equipment, and provide digital modems. The cable infrastructure in the United States represents a special asset that many other countries do not possess. It offers more bandwidth into—and out of—the home than many of the other alternatives combined. Without it, the revolution in television would not have begun.

Several related technologies also can deliver multichannel television signals into the home. Satellite Master Antenna Television (SMATV) can be thought of as a cable system in miniature whose development parallels the development of cable. A SMATV system consists of reception equipment that is shared between units in a multi-unit dwelling, such as an apartment building, through the use of a coaxial cable distribution system. Typically these systems have had fewer channels than cable systems. They emerged to fill gaps left in cable systems coverage.

Wireless cable is another technology that has been commercialized during the Cable Era as a means of distributing television signals to those unserved by cable operators. Wireless cable systems are microwave systems[3] that use a fixed omnidirectional transmitter with a range of less than 50 miles. Subscribers need microwave antennas to receive transmission and often a decoder, since operators often scramble signals to keep pirates from intercepting signals. MMDS has technical handicaps such as its limited channel capacity (up to 33 channels), its requirement for a direct line of sight from the transmitting tower to the receiver, and its generally lower-grade picture than that of cable systems.

Microwave distribution was used before 1970 as a means of transmitting data to business users and of transmitting voice. As with other technological developments, its diffusion as a means of television distribution was triggered by regulatory change: FCC policies in the 1970s and 1980s reassigned more spectrum to wireless services in an attempt to make them more competitive with cable. Technological hand-

icaps have limited the deployment of wireless to areas that are too poor
or too rural to attract cable operators. However, these handicaps are
being overcome with the development of digital wireless systems that
could increase the transmission capacity to 250 channels.[4] Recently these
systems have attracted the attention of telephone companies, who are
using them as a means to enter the business of video programming.
These are seen as interim technologies that provide quick entry at relatively low cost.[5]

VIDEOCASSETTES

The development of cable was not the only radical change in the distribution of television upsetting the industry during the Cable Era. If
cable was a second channel of distribution for programming into the
home, the development and diffusion of home video equipment allowed
the creation of a third. The technology dates back to the 1950s, but it
was advanced in the 1970s to create a mass consumer product priced
well below $500. Essentially, videotape represents the same type of tech-
nology used in audio recording. Electric current is used to align mole-
cules of a magnetic coating storing video and audio on a strip of plastic.
Owners of a video recorder can both play and record tapes. In the early
1980s the industry, with the help of consumers who began buying video
recorders, settled on the VHS standard out of what were as many as five
different and incompatible technologies.

Viewers could go to a store, buy or rent a videocassette of a film,
television program, or program specifically made for video, and return
home and watch it at their convenience. In the early days, pornography,
low cost to make and high priced to buy, drove diffusion. It was not
until the Sony-Betamax case was decided in the Supreme Court in 1984
that diffusion accelerated. The case cleared the way for consumers to
legally view rented movies and recorded television programming without infringing on the rights of copyright holders. Hollywood abandoned
any effort to stop the VCR and began to release titles to the home video
market at lower prices. As the VHS standard achieved mass penetration,
it also elbowed away another technology, the videodisc. One of the main
reasons was that videotapes, unlike videodisks, also gave viewers the
opportunity to record programming from television for viewing at a later
time.

During the Digital Era, this technology will jolt the television industry
for a second time. Already the first digital VCRs are being made available
to the public through two firms: Replay Networks Inc. and Tivo, Inc.

Digital VCRs offer users enhanced features for recording, storing, and
replaying programming. Unlike their analog predecessors, digital VCRs
can record programming that is already in progress, that fits predeter-

mined criterion (like programming starring a viewer's favorite actor or featuring a particular sports team). It can be done without having to follow difficult instructions in manuals and while skipping commercials. These advances are possible because the digital revolution allows the new VCRs to scan databases and download digital bits onto a home storage drive.

Digital VCRs are not a new pipeline into the home. However, they can fundamentally alter an existing pipeline. By making it easier to record, alter, store, and retrieve programming, they have the potential to impact the advertising paradigm under which traditional television operates. Digital VCRs force us to ask such core questions about our industry as: how will traditional methods of measuring audiences be sustained in an environment in which many more viewers are watching programs from their hard drives? Will the new technology allow—or even require—networks to push programming directly to viewers without advertising?

Together, these two developments moved the industry from the Broadcast Era to the Cable Era. No longer was television three networks and an independent or two, but rather thirty to fifty networks and a selection of thousands of titles in a video store. There was still more to come.

No sooner had cable been made available to 90 percent of U.S. households and subscribed to by 50 percent and VCRs reached saturation, than technology struck again. Several new technologies have been evolving during the 1970s, 1980s, and 1990s that are capable of delivering traditional television programming, as well as new products, into the home. As these technologies get commercialized, they move us into a new era. What are these new technologies, and why are they so important?

SATELLITES

The first development is the advance of satellite technology. Despite the recent surge in interest in satellite television, satellite delivery of television and telephones has been around since the early 1960s. Leveraging advances from the space program, satellite technology was applied to communications as way of achieving long-distance transmission of signals without the interference, cost, and other problems of wireline transmission. The initial systems sent out weak signals, were capable of carrying only limited traffic, and required huge reception equipment. Given the state of this early technology, the heavy-handed regulatory scheme outlined in the Communications Satellite Act of 1962, which gave the newly created Communications Satellite Corporation (COMSAT) a regulated monopoly, was probably appropriate.

Throughout the next decade advances in satellite technology occurred rendering this initial regulatory approach inadequate. Satellites transmitted more powerful signals with more information and remained in geosynchronous orbit.[6] These improvements coincided with the phenomenal journey of cable and the VCR into the American household and combined to transform space into a tool for television.

Satellites became part of the Cable Era revolution with two developments. First, satellites in the mid-1970s became a means through which cable networks could deliver their signals to operators. HBO, after the success of the satellite delivery of the 1975 Muhammad Ali–George Foreman "Thrilla in Manila," realized that they could build subscribership faster and more cost effectively if they delivered their service via satellite. Just following this move, Turner understood that there might just be an audience for TBS, his Atlanta-based broadcast station, around the country and acted on his hunch by delivering it to program-hungry cable operators by satellite.

Second, satellite entrepreneurs began to dream of transforming their technology from an intermediate relaying device to a means of delivering television directly to consumers. In the early 1980s, after policy makers responded to the advances in satellite technology by relaxing regulatory constraints, four direct broadcast satellite (DBS) ventures were launched with the idea of supplying television programming directly to viewers, who would receive signals with their own purchased, on-premises, and relatively small reception antennae. The most significant of these ventures was COMSAT, which ended in 1984 after four years and $145 million in write-downs against revenues.[7] COMSAT and the other ventures all failed because they had relatively little programming to offer and the reception equipment that they required subscribers to purchase was large and expensive. COMSAT's plans, for example, were for only three satellites, each with a capacity of three channels.[8]

Despite the failure of these initial efforts, there remained an attractiveness about the idea of beaming television directly to consumers. It was like a massive "overbuild" of all the cable systems throughout the country—without laying a single wire. Plans for DBS ventures were discussed throughout the 1980s; in the meantime, consumers in areas not cabled went out and bought their own reception equipment for higher-power satellite services. This equipment, called "home satellite dishes" (HSDs) and "television receive only" (TVRO) terminals, was extremely bulky, over six feet in diameter, and costly, over $3,000. But, the programming was abundant and free since all of the programming that went to cable headends was literally up for grabs. Sales grew rapidly in the early 1980s until signal scrambling was introduced by HBO in 1986. Other pay services and some of the more popular basic services followed and required HSD owners to buy a decoder and pay for their services.

Of course, this was too late for the early DBS ventures, which had lost an important segment of their market to the HSD market.

About ten years after the first DBS ventures, a second set of ventures were launched that have proven far more successful and are finally breaking the distribution bottleneck. These ventures owe their success in part to advances in technology, but in part to the actions of regulators. The story continues with the success of cable and HSD demonstrating to DBS entrepreneurs that a market existed; it continues with the efforts of these entrepreneurs to overcome the weaknesses of the early ventures, notably the reception equipment problem and the quantity of programming problem.

The reception equipment problem was fundamentally a regulatory problem since the International Telecommunications Union (ITU) controls the international allocation of orbital slots and the FCC controls the allocation of frequencies. This control is important because the size of the antennae is driven by the distance separating satellites sharing the same frequency and the power of the satellite, itself a function of the distance separating satellites. In other words, the further apart the satellites, the easier it is to distinguish between adjacent signals, the higher the power that can be used by the satellite, and the smaller the reception equipment needed. In the early 1980s, the FCC allocated additional spectrum within a portion of the Ku-band. In the orbital positions operating within this band, the spacing between satellites was large enough to minimize disturbances on the ground between adjacent signals and permit high-power transmission. This meant that the antennae diameter of the required reception equipment could shrink to eighteen inches.

Since the DBS systems of today are digital, the other problem of programming could be addressed with digital compression. At $100 million earth stations, digital signals are compressed before being up-linked to a satellite using a standard such as Moving Picture Experts Group 2 (MPEG-2). A decoder at the television set decompresses the signals and converts them back to analog for presentation on the viewer's television set. Using today's compression techniques, which can acheive compression rates of 4 to 1 and even 6 to 1, high-power DBS operators can deliver about 150 channels to subscribers. The technology continues to advance in this area: TCI, using Imedia's statistical multiplexing equipment, has demonstrated 24-to-1 multiplexing.

With these two issues settled, the path was cleared in the early 1990s for the second set of DBS launches. The first satellite was launched in 1990 by K Prime Partners, now known as PrimeStar Partners, and has only served as a prelude. Since PrimeStar is owned by cable systems operators, it was treated as a supplemental means of distribution and marketed to unwired areas within the operator's franchise area. Furthermore, since it is a medium power DBS system, subscribing households had to purchase reception equipment with an antennae diameter of three feet.

The real breakthrough came with much fanfare in 1994 with the launch of the high-power DBS-1 satellite by Hughes (DirecTV) and United States Satellite Broadcasting (USSB). The satellite has 32 transponders, or satellite-based transmitters, of which one-half are used regularly and the others serve as backups. Both DirecTV and USSB use a common receiver system called DSS, or Digital Satellite System. Subscribers to either service would need a DSS eighteen-inch dish and a set-top box to descramble the signal and convert the digital DBS signals to analog so that they can be displayed on conventional TV sets. With the system's smaller requirement for reception equipment, 150 channels, and aggressive marketing, it is currently being marketed around the country. Other providers like EchoStar, AlphaStar and ASkyB followed DirecTV and USSB into the satellite business.

Despite the initial success of high-power DBS, cable operators are quick to point out the limitations of the technology. Although the picture quality of the service is generally higher than that of cable, it is subject to deterioration in signal quality during heavy rain. Even more daunting for DBS operators is the fact that, unlike cable operators, satellite operators cannot send signals from local stations to interested households.[9] Finally, DBS systems can never be fully interactive as switched wireline because individual households would need an enormous power source and transmitter to send transmissions back to satellites.

Given the impressive march of technology in satellite communications thus far, it should not be surprising that these limitations are being overcome as these words are written. New satellite systems like the Intelsat 7 series are built with steerable spot-beam transponders that can be configured on orbit. This means that operators will be able to use narrower spot beams with a footprint of only several hundred miles in diameter to target metropolitan areas. By establishing regional up-link facilities to compress and up-link local terrestrial signals, satellite operators claim to be able to deliver local signals to subscribers in about three-quarters of the country. With compression techniques advancing, these subscribers will not even have to sacrifice the hundreds of channels of national programming. Even existing players like DirecTV and USSB say they can overcome the problem using a hybrid receiver dish and conventional antenna that can pick up both satellite transmission and local broadcasts. In the long term, satellites will be developed that use the Ka band, an even higher frequency range than the Ku-band, to increase channel capacity and to target small areas.

The issues of signal interference and interactivity are also being addressed. New electronics in the satellite decoders can clean up shadows and other picture problems. Of course, if used in conjunction with a telephone system, DBS systems provide interactivity today. But, satellite communications systems are being developed in conjunction with video systems that will provide users with full interactivity.

It is interesting that the dance of technology with regulation in this area is not over. Issues like cross-ownership of DBS and local stations, retransmission rules, and the restrictions against one company controlling more than one of the full-CONUS slots[10] have to be resolved before the most ambitious DBS plans can be unveiled.

TELEPHONE COMPANIES

The second technology revolutionizing the distribution of video into the home is fiber-optic transmission technology. The commercialization of fiber optics—with its virtually unlimited transmission capacity—creates the potential for the telephone companies to distribute broadband services, including video, into the home.

The telephone companies have what engineers consider to be an ideal architecture for the delivery of interactive broadband services. The telephone companies use a "star" architecture that was designed for two-way voice traffic. Without the upstream bottlenecks that the cable systems have, the telephone companies can more easily construct interactive systems.

Many telephone companies are already aggressively deploying fiber for the purposes of improving telephone service only. These local exchange carriers (LECs) are installing fiber in their networks to connect central offices to remote distribution units. These units are the points at which copper is used to transmit signals the rest of the way to subscribers' homes. This application for fiber, the digital loop carrier, can be justified by the savings it brings from aggregating voice traffic into the central office. At the same time, of course, it serves to break one of the telephone companies' bandwidth constraints.

While the telephone companies have an architectural advantage over the cable companies, they also have an important technical disadvantage. The basic problem is that copper local loop is not ideal for the delivery of video since it lacks the necessary bandwidth. The copper wires that connect each household to the network have the capacity of 64,000 bits per second (bps) each, while video requires 1.5 million bps (Mbps) at a minimum. Live-action scenes and fast-action scenes require 3 Mbps and 6 Mbps respectively.

This problem could be solved by simply extending optical fiber and coaxial cable to the neighborhood or even to the home, but such fiber optic transmission systems can only be constructed at great expense. Cost estimates range from $1,500 to $5,000 per subscriber access line.[11] These costs can be compared to the $300 to $500 per household passed that a conventional coaxial cable system would cost. The high costs of fiber optic systems are due to the optoelectronic components required to allow existing customer premises equipment (CPE) to use the network.[12] The day may come when this solution looks attractive, but for now the telephone companies are exploring other avenues.

One can bet that with billions of dollars in installed copper wire, the telephone companies would put some resources into determining ways to use it. Sure enough, technology, funded generously by the telephone companies, is advancing to present ways of using copper to get video into the home.

An option that is quickly evolving is called digital subscriber line (DSL) technology. At $500 to $600 per subscriber,[13] this solution looks economically attractive. It uses digital signal compression to support the downstream transmission of video over the existing copper wire. A video channel would come from the central office of the telephone company and be converted to a digital signal. Each television set, as always, would need a decoder that decompresses the digital signal and converts it back to analog. The first asymetrical digital subscriber line (ADSL) systems were limited to only 1.5 Mbps, thus limiting the potential video applications: Live sports programming, for example, would not be available for transmission, and there would be a noticeable delay as the viewer changed from one channel to another. Second-generation systems will provide from 4 Mbps to 10 Mbps of downstream bandwidth, which will allow high-quality digital video service using the standardized MPEG-2 compression technique.[14] Moreover, this is not the maximum speed that telephone lines can carry. If the lines are short enough, very-high-bit-rate digital subscriber lines (VDSL) can operate at high speeds. If a subscriber's access line is 500 feet long, (the national average is 10,000 feet), VDSL can operate at 52 Mbps; a LAN service, copper distributed data interface (CDDI), exists that hits 100 Mbps.[15]

LECs are not limited to DSL in their quest to distribute video to the home. In marked contrast to the grand announcements that were made only a few years ago, the LECs are slowly beginning their entrance into the video marketplace with a variety of options. Some LECs are using conventional cable systems out of their territory, others are trying DSL, others are bridging the time gap with wireless cable, and still others are exploring fiber/coax hybrids.[16]

The question of whether LECs could enter the video market was hotly debated throughout the Cable Era. With the appearance of technological solutions and the ten- to 15-year announced time frames for deployment of many telephone companies,[17] the debate has shifted to whether the LECs can cost-effectively compete with cable companies.

THE INTERNET

Another wireline distribution channel that has emerged as an alternative for video is the Internet. Unlike the other closed proprietary systems, the Internet is an open system that anyone with a telephone line and a computer can access. Perhaps more important, anyone with a video camera can easily and cheaply distribute the product to Internet users: a school, church, or entrepreneur could become a broadcaster with a microphone, a camcorder, a PC, and a telephone line.

The Internet is a global communications network linking computer terminals that was initially funded by the U.S. federal government in the 1960s as a means for academics and government researchers to communicate more efficiently. Today, of course, its role has expanded dramatically to facilitate communications among a multitude of users around the world. Not only has the Internet's infrastructure—things like host computers and bandwidth in the backbone—grown at a dramatic rate, but so has actual usage. According to a recent IDC/Link study, there were 18 million American households connected to the Internet in 1997. This number is expected to grow at a compound annual growth rate of 30 percent over 5 years and reach 51.5 million, or 50 percent of all households, by 2001.

One part of the Internet that has particular importance for the transmission of video is the World Wide Web. The World Wide Web is a multimedia, hypertext-based,[18] electronic publishing system within the Internet that allows users to navigate easily through thousands of international data bases stored on archival computers, called file servers, and to transfer desired data to their own computer. These data bases consist of text, diagrams, color photographs, sound, and video. It was created in 1989 at the European Laboratory for Particle Physics, or CERN, in Geneva for the academic and scientific community to exchange complex documents. Early in 1994, however, scientists were joined on the Web by increasing numbers of private individuals and commercial users. With the adoption of browser software—Mosaic and then Netscape's Navigator and Microsoft's Explorer—the complexity of navigating the Web was eliminated. Today, businesses use the Web to publish detailed product information and catalogues, to offer 24-hour technical support, and to gather instantaneous customer feedback; individuals use it to access information; publishers create and distribute information and entertainment; governments distribute information on the political process and public resources, like libraries and museums.

Much of what is available on the Web consists of new information formats combining text, graphics, and sound. Video, too, is already making its way onto the Internet in snippets. Recorded digital videos with larger pictures and steadier pictures are also available in an MPEG-2 format. While very little full-length television programming is currently available in this digital format, there are hints of the Web's capability. For instance, television networks and distributors have sites that describe and even disseminate their content, and advertisers are using the Web as a vehicle to reach their target markets. Already, there are 620 Web sites devoted to commercial television programming.[19] Most of these sights simply promote conventional broadcasters, using text, graphics, and photos and perhaps making video clips available for downloading. Once downloaded, the clips' sound is of low quality and the video is small, jerky, and fuzzy.

The problem blocking the dissemination of full-motion video is the limited bandwidth of the copper telephone lines that are most often used deliver the Internet to consumers. Most users get video trickling through their 28.8 Kbps modems at a rate of two frames per second (fps), users with older modems receive only one fps, and films are delivered to television audiences at a rate of 30 fps. A specialized Internet service called multicast backbone (MBONE) was launched in 1992 to allow video applications like real-time videoconferencing. Even with its dedicated routers, MBONE offers only 500 Kbps speeds, still way short of the 6 Mbps required for television.

Internet technology, though, has no shortage of entrepreneur interest. Several new ventures have been launched to solve this problem. Microsoft, with its purchase of Vxtreme and its investment in VDOnet, has moved aggressively into video. The market leader at this early juncture is a tiny firm called RealVideo. RealVideo offers a streaming technology that compresses live video for transmission over standard telephone lines and improves the picture when a faster connection is used. The technology also uses a new communications protocol that "can adjust the quality and speed of its video transmissions depending on the amount of communications capacity available at any given moment."[20] The technology will only allow fifteen frames per second to be sent, one-half the number of frames of the broadcasters. This could improve to broadcast-quality when transmitted over the larger bandwidth of integrated services digital network (ISDN) lines that are being installed in the telephone network.[21]

The ultimate solution to this problem awaits the deployment of cable modems and ADSL modems for telephone lines. Cable firms can use the enormous bandwidth of their coaxial cable to send Internet data to users at peak speeds of 10 Mbps, and telephone companies with their advances in ADSL are not far behind.

A second issue delaying Internet development is that the Internet itself has fundamentally different properties than telephone or cable networks. It is a network of networks with a variety of different kinds of routers and transmission links. Moreover, instead of dedicated lines operating without interruption being set up between users, packets of data are sent over this network without any method of prioritization. This means that without a pricing mechanism or some sort of routing hierarchy, video sent over the Internet can be subject to unknown delays. A community of Internet users, scholars, and would-be regulators are at work on this issue, which must be solved if users are ever to rely on the Internet for video.

Of course, video via the Internet has an even more expensive customer premises unit (CPU) problem than does DBS. Not only must viewers have a computer, currently available in only about one-third of all households in the United States, and a modem, available in only one-half of the computer households in the United States, but to take full advantage of the video capabilities of the Internet, an early 1990s unit will not do. Computers are slowly being transmogrified into television sets as displays are becoming larger, graphics chips are increasing in speed and memory with the addition of graphics-accelerator cards, MPEG cards are being added to configurations to allow computers access to digital programming, and modems are now standard parts of PC packages that consumers buy.

Since so few Americans have computers, perhaps the answer lies in making television sets into Internet reception devices. This process, too, is under way as the communications industry realizes the value of the massive deployment of television sets across America. There are many different approaches to this issue. The industry is offering high-end television sets for several thousands of dollars that have built-in computing capacity to support Internet access, as well as stripped-down PCs for several hundreds of dollars that use existing TV monitors as display devices for Web browsing.

ELECTRIC UTILITIES

Yet a third wire into the home could eventually become a conduit for video transmission: the power line owned by the electric utilities. As of 1992, 39 of the 62 cable systems that were municipally owned were associated with a municipally owned electric power system.[22] The idea behind utility involvement in television is that they can pay for the cost of such a system with savings that they can earn from electricity load management. With a wireline connection to the home, utilities can monitor patterns of electricity consumption in order to better manage load usage. The cost savings from this could pay for any infrastructure investment in television.

Although some may disagree with the conclusion, even the threat of a utility-owned wireline television service could be enough to change the behavior of cable operators.[23]

BROADCAST TELEVISION

Finally, no discussion of technological change in our industry would be complete without mention of what is happening with conventional broadcast television. The Digital Era is also revolutionizing this technology.

Conventional broadcast television follows the technical standards, National Television System Committee (NTSC) standards, that were adopted for black-and-white television in the 1940s and color television in the 1950s. The clearer and more powerful VHF bands were licensed first, and the inferior UHF bands—weaker signal strength, higher transmission costs, channel tuning and receiver problems—were licensed later as the FCC sought to satisfy demand for television broadcasting. Since mid-century, the technology of broadcasting has advanced; today, it is possible to deliver larger and better quality television pictures and CD quality sound. With digital signals and the video compression techniques that were described earlier, it is possible to accomplish this using no more than the 6 Mhz bandwidth used for today's NTSC broadcasting. In fact, broadcasters can even offer viewers these better pictures on multiple channels. To do so, they would need a new national standard for television broadcasting.

The search for a new standard, referred to as High Definition Television (HDTV) or Advanced Television (ATV), was launched in the United States by the FCC in 1987 in response to earlier efforts to develop a standard in Japan and Western Europe. The progress of this quest has often been slow and tortured as political concerns and business rivalries have interfered frequently with technology questions. The FCC went back and forth as competing consortia argued and merged and split again in their efforts to persuade the regulators of the merits of their technologies.

Finally in 1997, the FCC had had enough and decided to delegate the decision to the marketplace. The FCC allowed the broadcasters to select from any one of eighteen possible formats in which to broadcast in their new spectrum. The formats have different technical specifications that affect the degree of resolution of the picture, the shape of the display screen, and the method that is used to "paint" the picture on the screen (Exhibit 26). This last point has become very important because computer screens use one method, progressive scanning, and television uses another, interlaced scanning. Computer makers have been pushing hard for a standard that mandates progressive scanning so that television programming can be seen on computers.

Exhibit 26
Possible Formats for Digital Television (DTV)

	Scanning Lines (Vertical)	Pixels (Horizontal)	Aspect Ratio (Screen Dimensions)	Frame Rates Per Second	
High Definition	1,125	1,920	16 x 9	60	Interlaced
				30 } 24	Progressive
High Definition	750	1,280	16 x 9	60 } 30 } 24	Progressive
Standard Definition	525	704	16 x 9 or 4 x 3	60	Interlaced
				60 } 30 } 24	Progressive
Standard Definition	525	640	4 x 3	60	Interlaced
				60 } 30 } 24	Progressive

Identical to today's NTSC STANDARD

Source: Courtesy of Sony Electronics Inc.

With this decision, it will be possible that the broadcasters could use their spectrum to transmit data, multiple video channels, a high-definition channel, or a little bit of each. As Negroponte puts it, each broadcaster could become its own FCC, dictating just what to do with its valuable real estate.

Given the choice, many broadcasters will no doubt choose to use video compression techniques to deliver multiple channels of traditional television instead of using them to deliver a single high-definition channel. The logic behind such a decision is understandable: If all a new standard has to offer viewers is prettier pictures and better sound, not many people would actually go out and buy the required new television set. Those who would are probably the same viewers who subscribe to cable and satellite services already.

There is another consequence of the FCC decision. Whatever the broadcasters do, they will have to transmit digital signals. When they do, the long-suffering UHF signals will have finally come to parity with VHF signals. The quality differences between the two are due to artifacts of analog technology long gone in the Digital Era; digital streams of 1s and 0s are no different whether broadcast from UHF or VHF transmitters.

Far from being left out by the revolution in video technology, the conventional over-the-air broadcasters may land right in the middle of it. In fact, with all of their bandwidth, they alone could break the distribution bottleneck themselves.

With a little help from the regulators, technology is breaking the distribution bottleneck and ushering in the Digital Era. Many of these technologies already exist, and others are so close to existing that they figure into the strategic plans of the current players. However, their mere existence does not guarantee that there will be dozens of distribution channels into the home. Several visions for the "end game" of our information infrastructure have been advanced. One vision assumes that each new distribution technology survives with part of the market for communications services. Another assumes that the wireline technologies merge into a single, perhaps regulated, integrated broadband network to save the duplicative costs of multiple networks. Yet a third vision is that households will choose among several wireline and wireless options to connect to an Internet-like national information infrastructure. Regulatory models, political clout of players, level of required investment and relative cost structures, consumer demand, and historical sequencing will all play key roles in determining the outcome.

This book does not attempt to predict an outcome. From the perspective of relative profitability of content and conduit, it hardly matters. Rather, the book sets out to predict the common impact of all of these outcomes. This is possible because all of the outcomes share a set of implications for industry players. In all of the outcomes, the distribution bottleneck is broken. Regardless of what replaces it, the world will be a far less friendly place for distributors.

NOTES

1. Nicholas Negroponte, *Being Digital* (New York: Vintage Books, 1995).

2. For a full discussion, see Negroponte, *Being Digital*.

3. Wireless refers to services transmitting television in the 2 GHz band. The spectrum that operators use consists of 33 analog channels of which 16 channels use IFS frequencies, two channels use MDS frequencies, and eight use the Multipoint Multichannel Distribution Services (MMDS) band.

4. Patty Wetli, "Getting There with Wireless Cable," *America's Network*, 15 July 1995.

5. Mark Landler, "In a Video Rush, Phone Groups Aren't Waiting for Fiber Optics," *New York Times*, 18 April 1995, Business section; Wetli, "Getting There," p. 38.

6. The basic idea of geosynchronous orbit is that a satellite placed 22,300 miles above the equator circles the earth at the same speed at which the earth rotates on its axis, thus making the satellite appear stationary above any particular part of the earth. This means that with a single beam from a properly positioned satellite, a television distributor can cover all of the United States. In the early days, satellites were used to provide video signals from remote locations to local broadcasters and cable systems that then transmitted the signals to their local viewers and subscribers.

7. Communications Satellite Corporation, *1984 See Form 10-K*, 1985, p. 4.

8. Leland L. Johnson, *Toward Competition in Cable Television* (Cambridge, Mass.: MIT Press, 1994).

9. In order to do so, satellite operators have to send local stations on spot beams to local regions or, alternatively, have enough capacity to send all of the local stations to the entire country.

10. Orbital slots that cover the entire continental United States.

11. Bruce L. Egan, *Information Superhighways Revisited* (Boston: Artech House, 1997), p. 68.

12. Ibid., p. 69.

13. Ibid., p. 65.

14. MPEG-2 would require the use of a video decoder box, which will cost about $400, although the price is expected to fall to $200 within two years.

15. Egan, *Information Superhighways Revisited*, p. 37.

16. See an article by Reshma Kapadia entitled "Carriers Wade Slowly into Video Waters" in *Telephony*, 27 November 1995, for a carrier-by-carrier update.

17. Johnson, *Toward Competition in Cable Television*, pp. 48–49.

18. Hypertext allows users to jump from one source of information to another at the click of a mouse despite the physical location of the data base.

19. "Video on the Internet: Webbed," *The Economist*, 20 January 1996, pp. 82–83.

20. Ibid.

21. Peter Coy, "Get Ready for the TV Station on Your Desk," *Business Week*, 6 November 1995, p. 149.

22. Ibid., p. 22.

23. Leland Johnson asks, if this logic is correct, why don't today's cable operators take advantage of this revenue stream and provide the service to utilities? His answer is that there is currently no low-cost interface between the electric meter and the set-top box of the cable operator. Once this interface is provided, there is no reason that utilities have to own a network. Cable operators will likely provide this service at a cost lower than what a utility would pay to replicate the network. See Ibid.

Part II

The Great Value Shift

Introduction:
The Digital Dilemma

Technology is ushering in the third era of television: the Digital Era. It will erode the distribution bottleneck and throw owners of the conduit into a new period of competition. It will bring on a Great Value Shift in which the bottle will be turned upside down: profits will migrate from distribution to content.

As television passes from its second to its third era, firms in the television business will face two major questions: (1) where in the digital supply chain should they be? and (2) how should they compete against other media?

In answer to these seminal questions, many companies seem obsessed with two strategies that lead in the wrong direction. Some firms believe that they can replicate the distribution bottleneck by controlling the set-top box; other firms maintain that they can dominate the media supply chain through the creation of massive content/conduit combines. Both strategies will fail, because they do not recognize that technological change has irreversibly changed the nature of distribution.

There will be two winners in the Digital Era, and both will be in the content business. Content creators will be in increasing demand as firms down the supply chain seek to differentiate their commodity-like products. A handful of digital brands will emerge as the principal means to organize content for the information-weary consumer. The firms that have an opportunity to create the best digital brands are television networks.

Television firms face two major questions in the Digital Era: the vertical question and the horizontal question. Part two of the book will address these questions and in so doing separate the winners from the losers of the Digital Era.

THE VERTICAL QUESTION

We have seen that the television business is a multistage process. The first question, the vertical question, is at which stage in this process are the profits likely to be largest? Will profits be higher upstream than downstream? Complicating the question is the fact that in the Digital Era the definitions of upstream and downstream will be different from what they were in the previous eras of the business. What are these new definitions?

The Internet, with its broadband backbone, packet-switching technology, and computer terminal as display device, is evolving to be the best model for understanding the New Information Age. The supply chain of the World Wide Web with its multimedia content therefore serves as a good model for the television supply chain of the future.

The World Wide Web's supply chain is more complex than the supply chain in the traditional television business (Exhibit 27). As the traditional television business, it starts with content creators, the actual people or software that generate content. Content creators are music stars, sports leagues, writers, cartoonists, actors, and directors who create and make video, software, printed material, or anything else that can be transmitted digitally over the Internet to users. Content creators often have their own sites on the Web; for example, the National Football League, the White House, the Metropolitan Opera, and even advertisers all have sites that visitors can visit. Just as often, they do not have their own sites. The *New York Times* columnist Maureen Dowd is a creator whose work appears at the *New York Times* site, not at her own personal site.

In the traditional television business, the next stage in the supply chain was program producers, the firms that employed the creators and completed the production process. These firms still exist in the Digital Era supply chain as the producers of television programs and of any new kind of content that will require them. They may even have their own Web sites. In contrast to the traditional television business in which content creators were dependent on producers, content creators can often make do without producers on the Web. If creators merely want a presence on the Web, all they have to do is to hire designers and programmers in order to build their own sites.

At the next stage in the supply chain are digital brands. These are entities that package the work of content creators together and create sites on the Web. Digital brands are Pathfinder, the site that contains the Time Warner stable of media products; Boston.com, the site of the *Boston*

Exhibit 27
The World Wide Web Supply Chain

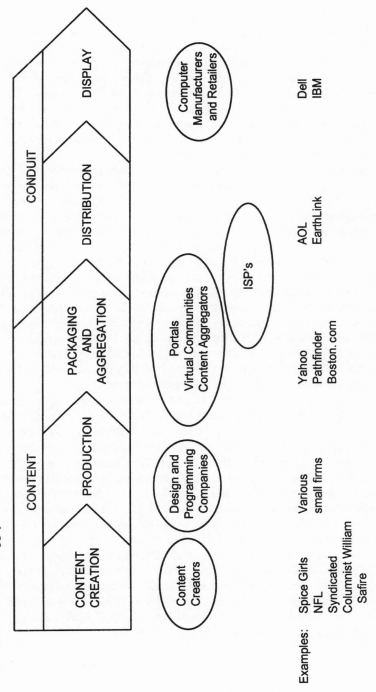

Globe and related material; and CNN Interactive, the Web site for the cable network CNN.

This is point in the traditional television industry supply chain at which content ends and distribution begins: the packagers, the television industry equivalent of media brands, simply pass their products on to the cable operators, DBS companies, and local broadcast stations that distribute them on to viewers. In the Internet world, there is could yet be another level of aggregation at which content is organized. This level is still wide open. Some of the contenders are on-line services, portals, virtual community organizers, and agents.

The task at this level is to access and order the content of the media brands and the creators themselves. On-line services, like America Online, are services that provide subscribers access to the Internet via their computer and modem. With their Internet connection, subscribers get access to a Web site that includes proprietary and non-proprietary content, electronic mail facilities, chat spaces, and other services. Virtual communities are evolving as places on the Web that aggregate content, commerce, and users focused on particular areas of interest, like travel or finance. Portals are sites that are built around search capabilities that allow users to find information on the Web. Yahoo, Lycos, and Microsoft's Start.com are examples of gateways to the Web that give users the opportunity to easily identify and package their own content from all that is available on the Web. Agents are a more sophisticated version of search engines; they can be thought of as personalized and programmable software that customizes content for users.

The roles and relationships of these products and stages in the supply chain have been changing since the dawn of the Digital Era and are still in flux. Proprietary on-line services and interactive television were the first efforts to build digital brands. They both failed as users embraced the more open model of the Internet. The latest rage is for the portals that serve as entry points for Web users: NBC, Disney, Microsoft, AT&T, and Netscape have all made plays for portals that make use of search engines and indexing technology. Will portals be the next casualty or the enduring organizing principle of the Digital Era? Will they be able to retain the attention of users who are simply employing them to find customized content? Will they be displaced by intelligent agents?

While it is not clear whether portals will be sucessful, their existence raises a question that did not exist in the traditional television business: Which organizing and packaging entity will have the potential of creating the most value for shareholders of firms? Will the media brands or the organizing and packaging software win?

THE HORIZONTAL QUESTION

The other major issue that the television industry faces is competition from the print media, radio, and new media formats. Up until now, television was separated from print and radio in the sense that each offered a product with different features and different reception equipment. While all three media formats presented the evening news, newspapers did it with text and pictures, radio with audio, and television with video.

Obviously, there is still competition among the media. They compete both for users and for advertisers. As individual users, we have only so much time in a day, and so much money, to devote to getting the news. We rarely consume news in all three major formats; we usually choose among them. Furthermore, advertisers can choose among the media formats to reach viewers.

Therefore, because of the basic constraints of time and money, media formats with entirely different functionality actually do compete. Up until today and the dawn of the Digital Era, the media formats had settled into a pattern of reasonable coexistence, but not before television took its toll on radio and then the print media. In well-documented fights for the attention of viewers and the dollars of advertisers, television first displaced radio for the position of evening entertainment provider into the home and then displaced the evening newspapers for the position of nightly news source.

In today's world, television assumes the dominant place as provider of news and entertainment throughout the day and particularly in the morning and evening. It is also the best vehicle for national advertising campaigns. Morning newspapers still are a major source of news and provide advertisers a large, but unsegmented, local audience. Magazines reach national and often highly targeted niche audiences. Radio is the best medium for automobile drivers and people who want to work while they consume media. In addition to providing advertisers with different kinds of audience demographics, the media formats also offer advertisers the opportunity to take advantage of their different functionality: Print, for example, gives an opportunity to present detailed information, while television can show a product "in action."

This relatively pleasant equilibrium is about to be disrupted. In the Digital Era, traditionally separate media formats will be able to compete. Digitalization is the great equalizer. Newspapers, magazines, radio stations, and television all have sites on the Web and compete for users. No longer limited to text and pictures or audio, print and radio can compete using any format for their content that they choose. Moreover, entrepreneurs have an unprecedented opportunity to enter the fray and create new media formats based on some combination of audio, video, text, and graphics. The first efforts at these new formats have already been created on the World Wide Web and are drawing larger audiences in cyberspace than the traditional media players.

The horizontal question is: What happens when television loses its monopoly on video? How will the struggle between content providers shake out on a digital battlefield? What should media companies do in the face of this challenge?

Chapter 3

The Commoditization
of the Conduit

A Great Value Shift is under way in which value is migrating from distributors to content providers. The distribution bottleneck strategy is being eroded. Technology is eliminating the monopoly that distributors once enjoyed. A new era of choice is coming for both consumers and content providers. With several distributors competing, consumers will be able to choose television suppliers and content providers will be able to sell their products to different pipelines. Distribution profits will ebb and content providers' profits will flow in this Great Value Shift.

This chapter will show how the Great Value Shift will commoditize distribution. It will examine the transformation as local stations and cable operators evolve from being the bottleneck to the consumer to being one of many possible "pipes" into the home for the scarce resource of programming.

Prior to the Digital Era, distributing television signals was an immensely profitable business; there should be no great mystery as to why. Distribution was the bottleneck through which programming had to pass. There was only one cable operator in each locality and a handful of local terrestrial stations. These lucky distributors were in a powerful position vis-à-vis both consumers and upstream suppliers. They could increase prices regularly and limit product competition. This meant that margins were hefty and profits strong.

The technology revolution is ushering in a new era—and this era will not be so kind to the distributors. The new technologies, coupled with regulatory change, are breaking down the barriers to entry that once protected distribution. New competitors are emerging with distribution channels that can offer the same features as established channels.

As competition intensifies and differentiation between distribution channels becomes more difficult, prices to subscribers will fall and costs will increase as distributors compete harder for subscription revenue. Packagers will drive better and better deals as capacity increases in distribution and as they gain leverage over distributors in negotiations. For cable operators, DBS, and MMDS, this will mean higher prices for programming; for local stations, this will mean reduced compensation and maybe even less advertising time from the packagers for their own advertising.

This increased level of competition will eventually have an impact on the bottom line. The massive profits of the distribution bottleneck era will disappear. Ultimately, distribution could become a commodity. Instead of their exalted status in the prior eras, they could resemble the video store business where stores have trouble differentiating themselves and battle it out against each other, destroying their margins in the process. As distribution loses, the profits will migrate upstream in the supply chain (Exhibit 28).

The seeds of the Great Value Shift were planted with the rapid technological developments of the 1980s and 1990s. Once the technology of distribution advanced such that it could end the bottleneck held by the broadcasters and the cable operators, the stage was set for more competition between distributors and lower profits.

The revolution in technology is introducing a basic change in the structure of television distribution: It is lowering concentration levels without increasing the potential for differentiation. This fundamental change in structure will have profound implications on the performance of the industry. But, before getting ahead of ourselves, let us understand the new structure.

THE LOSS OF THE BOTTLENECK

During the Cable Era, both cable operators and local stations operated in markets that were highly concentrated: In most municipalities there was only one cable system and a handful of terrestrial stations. This situation was due to a combination of technology, economics, and policy. But now, technology is changing rapidly and economics and policy are following. New technologies of distribution are emerging that are eliminating the bottleneck. As the bottleneck is eliminated, the consequences are felt both downstream and upstream: (1) more distributors are selling programming to consumers, and (2) more distributors are buying programming from networks for transmission to viewers.

The process is neither smooth nor predictable. The technologies outlined in the preceding sections are all at different stages of development

Exhibit 28
Flows of Operating Profit through the Supply Chain: Digital Era, circa 2005

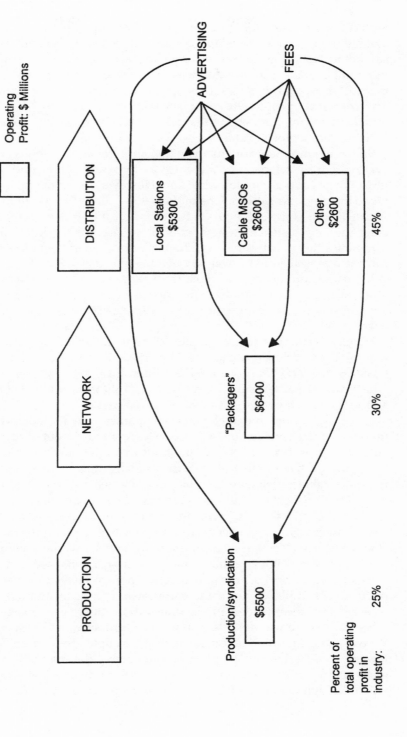

with different timetables for deployment. For example, it was once fashionable to argue that the telephone companies would become the major competitor to cable. Telephone companies announced trials for their technology and major investments in television programming. Now many of these trials have been discontinued and investments abandoned. The very same people who were speaking of the coming of two wires into the home are now saying that telephone companies will never prove a viable competitor to cable.

Still, announcements of advances in compression techniques are made every week by telephone companies as they attempt to find ways to utilize their copper wire for television. However, the initial rush into the video business has slowed. One of the results of the Telecommunications Act of 1996 was to set the groundwork for local telephone companies to enter the long-distance business and vice versa. For the local telephone companies this new business is a higher priority than the video business since it represents more revenue potential at a lower cost. For now, development continues on the video front as telephone companies look for a breakthrough that minimizes the capital costs required for video; full-scale telephone company entry into video has become a medium-term event.

Wireless cable is being championed by some of the telephone companies eager to find a cheap and immediate way to get into the video business. In 1995, PacTel paid $175 million for Cross Country Wireless, which owned a 42,000 subscriber system in California, while Bell Atlantic and NYNEX invested $100 million in CAI Wireless.

Having given up on the telephone companies, industry observers took up the next fad: satellite. Indeed, the fastest alternative out of the starting block has proven to be DBS. With about five million subscribers, up to two-thirds of whom are within cable municipalities,[1] DBS is already offering a viable alternative to cable. The aborted merger of Murdoch's ASkyB with Echostar would have created the strongest DBS competitor to enter the field thus far. With the delivery of local signals, advanced compression techniques used to deliver 500 channels, and the marketing clout of Murdoch's News Corporation, the service would have been an important competitor to cable. When this merger collapsed and sales of DBS subscriptions did not immediately jump to levels that were competitive with cable, some of the enthusiasm cooled on the technology. Nevertheless, the relentless pace of innovation and investment continues; other players are willing to step in where Murdoch and Echostar left off.

Today, the Internet juggernaut is what occupies the attention of followers of the industry. The phenomenal pace of the Internet's development continues as attention is turned to the problem of sending more video through the network's bottlenecks. With nothing to lose, entrepreneurs have turned from graphics to audio and now to video to find ways to attack the giant media and communications firms.

The important point here is not the viability or timing of any single competitor to conventional television. We have shown that not one, but several alternative distribution paths to conventional television are on the horizon. Any one of them, not to mention the development of digital terrestrial television, if viable will change the nature of the distribution business.

HOW DO YOU DIFFERENTIATE A PIPE?

The easy days for the broadcasters and the cable operators are over. No longer can they simply build their systems and have a differentiated product. No longer will they be able to influence viewer decisions by virtue of their control over a distribution bottleneck. Life will become much more difficult during the Digital Era.

Not only will there be new competitors in the distribution business, but these new competitors will look increasingly alike. The distribution of television signals may not get to the level of the salt business, in which differentiation is well-nigh impossible. But, it may start to look more like, say, the transportation business, a business in which providers are virtually identical and compete on price while turning small advantages in productivity into gains on the bottom line.

In theory, there will still be many attributes of traditional multichannel video services on which distributors could base differentiation in the Digital Era. For example, distributors can attempt to differentiate their products by offering different billing options, better reliability, service, sound, and picture quality or by changing the tiering of packages, requiring different reception equipment, and bundling with other telecommunications services. They can go further and improve their systems to offer expanded channel capacity and interactive products. Unfortunately, though, for the distributor of video, none of these options are as easy as providing a clear picture was for their cable predecessor. Furthermore, most of the new distributors can or soon will be able to copy any promising innovation. Obviously each technology has its strengths and weaknesses: DBS cannot offer on-line interactivity, telephone companies using ADSL currently cannot provide rapid channel surfing or live programming, and the mostly aerial cable plant has problems with reliability, but these differences are relatively small and will be disappearing as technology advances.

Not only will differentiation vis-à-vis their competitors become onerous, but distributors will also lose the control they had over their suppliers upstream, the packagers and programmers. Distributors will find it harder to influence the viewing and buying decisions of consumers as technology evolves and distributors lose the sources of leverage they once had. The power of a cable operator or any other distributor, so evident in the Cable Era, to control which programming gets transmitted will diminish as the cable operator itself increases its bandwidth and as the number of distributors multiply. TCI, for example, will not control the fate of a new programming service when it has huge amounts of additional capacity to fill, when other distributors may be prepared to distribute the programming on their services, or when it is available to anyone with access to the Web.

Tiering, another toll used by cable operators to exert control over networks, could also come under pressure in tomorrow's video marketplace. Tiering may be limited as new distributors compete by offering viewers choices of individual channels, without having to pay for those channels that they do not watch, or even individual programs.

Finally, the importance of channel positioning may diminish in importance as new menu-driven on-screen guides emerge. These descendants of today's directory channels will eliminate the last vestiges of the concept of the "dial" and allow viewers to select programs without the need to surf through all of the channels, a process that often stops viewers at a particular low-number channel before that viewer has previewed the higher-number channels.

This is all pretty serious stuff for an industry that used to consider a congressional hearing on the fate of children's television a problem. What does it all mean?

THE END OF THE INFLATING SUBSCRIBER FEE

The Great Value Shift will be precipitated by a consumer price war. As entry barriers fall and new distributors emerge, competition will intensify. Where companies lack meaningful ways to differentiate their products, the quickest way to take market share from the incumbent cable operators and each other will be to cut price.

This is not a daring prediction when one considers the record of price competition thus far in the industry. The industry is known for steadily advancing prices, but this pattern was established in communities where cable operators provided the only multichannel service. Whenever a second competitor is present, the record is different. In fact, the presence of a second competitor is always accompanied by price competition.

Measuring prices for cable television services is not as easy as measuring prices for a commodity like gold. For example, each operator offers a variety of different program tiers with different types of programming in different time periods. But, study after study has shown, as can be seen in Exhibit 29, that in the handful of municipalities around the country in which two cable systems have competed for subscribers, these

Exhibit 29
Studies and Surveys of Competitive Pricing Differential in Municipalities with "Overbuilds," by Study and Data Year

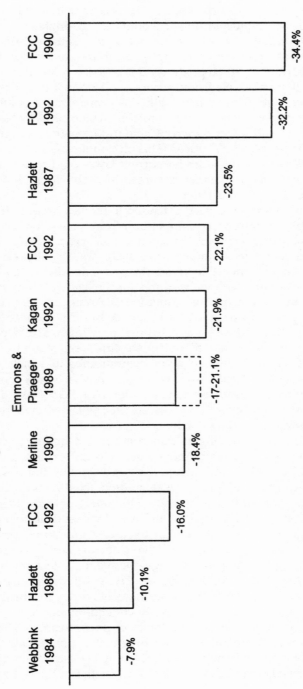

Source: Thomas W. Hazlett and Matthew L. Spitzer, "Public Policy toward Cable Television, Volume 1: The Economics of Rate Controls," working paper for the Program on Telecommunications Policy, Institute of Governmental Affairs, University of California, Davis, 1996. Reproduced with permission.

systems cut prices to win subscribers. The result is that prices in municipalities with overbuilds are lower than prices in single-system areas.

Some have argued that overbuilds are a rare fratricidal phenomenon
that easily leads to overanalysis. However, it does not take a cable overbuild for distributors to compete on the basis of price. Any other provider of multichannel television services will do just fine. For example,
in areas where subscription television was available, prices for cable television were 9 percent lower.[2] In areas in which SMATV is available,
retail prices are still lower: Liberty Cable in Manhattan charged only 55
percent of Time Warner's price.[3] This discount was not answered by
Time Warner since to do so under current law would mean offering the
same discount to all in their service area, those able to get SMATV services and also those who are not.

This pricing pattern has been extended to the few areas in the country
in which cable operators face competition from a telephone company. In
the Midwest, Ameritech has launched a new video service in several
communities as a direct competitor to such large MSOs as TCI, Continental, and Time Warner. Despite its rhetoric claim that it had been competing with nascent telephone ventures for the last ten years, it was only
two weeks after the arrival of Ameritech's Americast service that TCI
reduced the price of expanded basic service by 15 percent to $23.95 per
month and included the Disney Channel, previously $10.45 per month,
in that tier at no extra cost. Similar price cuts were made by TCI, Continental, and Time Warner in other communities in which Ameritech
launched its service. Cablevision went even further when it offered potential Ameritech subscribers the Evander Holyfield–Mike Tyson title
fight, a pay-per-view event that was sold for $49.95 elsewhere and gen-
erated important cash flow, for free.[4]

These situations, as telling as they are, are not frequent occurrences.
However, to them we can add the pricing behavior exhibited by the new
distributors. Take DBS, for example. With a satellite build and launch
costing between $150 million and $300 million, fixed costs are huge. Once
this initial investment has been made, DBS operators turn to signing up
subscribers. So eager are they for the marginal revenue that each subscriber brings, that as in other high fixed-cost industries, price cutting
can become an attractive option. We have already seen this option used.
DBS has one big pricing disadvantage relative to cable companies: users
need a satellite dish to receive the service. At the dawn of the satellite
age, users were expected to pay large sums of money for the equipment.
In the pre–high-powered DBS era, such equipment sold for several
thousands of dollars. DBS brought the price down to about $700 by 1995.
The dynamics of competition have brought that down even further. A
price war began in the summer of 1996, led by Echostar, then the smallest
of the satellite players. Echostar first shocked the industry by dropping

its dish price down to $199[5] at a time when DBS rivals were selling their reception equipment for $400. Once DirecTV and USSB matched the offer, Echostar said that it would slash prices even further. The price wars continued into 1997, as rumors were that Sky might be willing to give the equipment away entirely while trying to recoup its investment in a small monthly fee.

This price war illustrates the lengths to which satellite operators are willing to go to sign up subscribers. There is no reason that they will not extend this activity to the programming service itself. In fact, they already have. While it is difficult to compare prices of packages of programming, prices for individual movies can be compared: in early 1997, DirecTV offered pay-per-view movies for $2.99 each, about $1.00 less than the price on most cable systems. Not to be outdone, Charlie Ergen of Echostar has said, "Whatever they do, I'll be cheaper."[6]

Despite its history, the distribution business is not immune to the price-cutting disease. The days of the uniform increases in multichannel video prices are over. Even in markets served by a single cable operator, the recent liberation from the 1992 Cable Act's price controls does not offer the potential that it was once thought to have. When TCI pushed through a 7.5 percent rate hike at the end of 1997 to cover some of the programming price increases that it was getting hit with, it saw an alarming number of cancellations.[7] As competition evolves, things will get worse. Retail price competition will be unavoidable in the Digital Era.

THE SPECTACLE OF PRODUCTION

The intense product competition of the Cable Era is not likely to end in the Digital Era. Rather, it will continue and will accompany price competition. Product competition can take many forms. Distributors can compete on programming quality or quantity, video quality, sound quality, service levels, billing, and other features of their service.

Will there continue to be programming competition between distributors in the future? Since distribution companies will find it difficult to differentiate their pipeline from their competitor's, they will turn to programming to get a leg up. Should they be able to carry exclusive programming—according to current law, vertically integrated MSOs cannot—it would be the most important attribute by which services are differentiated. Consumers are likely to care much more about programming than slight differences in the technology of delivery.

The pattern of competing with more and better programming has already emerged. The race is on, using compression and digital technology. In 1997, DBS entrant DirecTV offered subscribers 150 channels, and the Time Warner system in Queens offered subscribers 150 channels. In fact, the ability to deliver large numbers of channels to subscribers is already an important competitive weapon that DirecTV uses in its advertising: a direct-mail piece features a section entitled "TOTAL CHOICE," in which highlights of the 150 channels available on DirecTV are listed. The service includes all of the most popular programming on cable systems and other new services like the entire schedule of the National Football League.

According to Frost and Sullivan, by 1999 cable companies will spend $2.36 billion per year to upgrade their systems, up about $.5 billion from 1995. Much of this will go to upgrades that offer subscribers more programming. For example, cable systems will gradually use digital technology to offer more channel capacity and other features.

These numbers are really only the beginning. High bandwidth connections from individual households to a fiber optic network make any notion of limited channel capacity an anachronism. Viewers will have access to literally thousands of channels and even more programs on video servers around the world. Wireless technology, too, will experience significant increases in capacity through compression.

Of course, it can be taken for granted that distributors will continue to improve the technical quality of their service, especially if distributors must offer their programming to their competitors. Product competition will intensify in other areas like picture and sound quality, service, reliability, and new products. DBS is already investing in digital compression and spot beaming local stations, MMDS is going digital, and the telephone companies are looking for ways to improve the performance of their copper plant for high-bandwidth tasks. This will continue in the never-ending game of technical follow-the-leader.

POWERFUL SUPPLIERS

Distribution was the bottleneck between upstream suppliers and downstream consumers. Until now, we have discussed the effect of the disappearance of the bottleneck on competition for consumers, the buyers of television. Let us turn now to its effect on the suppliers of television

In addition to their power in retail pricing, bottleneck distributors were also in a very desirable position vis-à-vis their suppliers. With supplier access to viewers limited to only one wireline distributor and a handful of local broadcast stations, those distributors had a strong bargaining position. During the Cable Era, we saw that they were the gatekeepers to the viewing public, deciding which programming would be transmitted and which would not. Many cable packagers, launched with great fanfare, never became economically viable simply because they were not carried by enough cable systems. During the Cable Era, distributors used this power to extract reasonable terms and conditions from established content providers and to dictate unfavorable terms and conditions to marginal providers that were desperate to gain access to viewers. Even today, content providers still complain that distributors hold the balance of power.

In the coming Digital Era, however, the struggle between content providers and distributors will tilt in favor of content providers—not necessarily the small entities that launch a niche network, but clearly the large media firms that own popular programming. Distributors will evolve from privileged gatekeepers to desperate competitors.

The logic is straightforward. As distribution technology advances, new distributors will emerge to exploit these technologies. With these distributors competing vigorously for business, the number of households subscribing to some form of subscription television will grow; but as the market is split, the number of households subscribing to any particular service will fall. This will weaken the existing distributors, cable MSOs and local stations, and benefit content providers.

Instead of having to convince the cable MSOs to buy and transmit their programming, content providers will be able to take their product to two, three, or even four distributors. Content providers will win increased bargaining power. They will be able to play one distributor against another. Eventually, they will have a credible threat to withhold programming; they can tell a distributor that does not meet their terms that they will simply rely on the other distributors. New content providers will no longer have to beg from the gatekeeper cable MSOs; they will have several other distributors who may select their services in an effort to find a competitive advantage.

Experience from other industries supports this commonsensical prediction. Lustgarten found evidence across the national economy that decreased buyer concentration tended to increase supplier bargaining power.[8] And, back to our industry, the facts are already coming in to prove this prediction correct.

The advent of DBS has fundamentally changed the nature of distributor-packager negotiations. "Competition is changing the dynamic between programmers and operators," according to Classic Sports Network, a packager that is now carried on both cable and satellite systems.[9] Packagers can now pressure distributors for carriage in ways never dreamed of before. The Golf Channel reminds cable operators with advertisements in the trade press that viewers are willing to buy satellite dishes to get certain channels. To get reinstated on some cable systems, MTV organizes "MTV Shelters" in local record stores where viewers can see the channel via satellite. It is easy to see the impact that the threat of satellite distribution has had by looking at the prices that cable operators pay for programming. In the last two years since the advent of satellite distribution, some of the more popular cable networks have raised their rates by close to 50 percent per year.

To be sure, there will still be checks on the bargaining power of content: the threat to withhold programming is checked by the content providers' interest in being available to as many households as possible; attracted by the new opportunities for distribution, new content entrepreneurs will emerge to give the distributors alternatives to recalcitrant negotiators; and content providers will still be delighted to gain carriage on the large distributors in order to gain access to millions of viewers in one deal. Nevertheless, the bottleneck will be broken. The specter of having to go before TCI President John Malone in a desperate, all-or-nothing bid for carriage will become a memory.

The local stations are in a better position than the other distributors with regard to their bargaining power vis-à-vis their suppliers, the broadcast networks. The reason is that the local stations are the only distributor that provides ubiquitous coverage: virtually every household in America can receive the local stations for free with "rabbit ears" hooked up to their television set. This is what the FCC's policy of localism was all about. It meant that during the Cable Era, broadcast networks had a choice of distribution via local stations for 100 percent coverage or via cable for coverage of only about two-thirds of the country.

Although the balance of power swings back and forth between networks and local stations continually, it is heresy in network-affiliate circles to even suggest that the networks will someday be in the position to use alternate distributors to displace stations. In 1990, when TCI asked NBC for permission to build channels around NBC programming in areas where no NBC affiliate even existed, affiliate stations blew up. An NBC affiliate said that the proposal was " 'an extreme threat' to the network-affiliate partnership system that has served the country well. I can see no circumstance where such an agreement would be attractive or acceptable to any NBC affiliate."[10]

So far this kind of reaction—as well as the emergence of the Warner Brothers and United-Paramount mini-networks and the increased viability of the strategy of independence—has kept the networks in line. To be sure, the networks have asserted some power. In the 1980s, as the networks suffered from a deteriorating market position, they began reducing compensation.[11] Between 1987 and 1992, the three networks cut compensation by 18 percent, from $425 million to $350 million, before it started to trend back up in the mid-1990s.[12] As the local stations have begun to suffer from reduced profitability in the more competitive environment, they too have become more assertive over price, successfully resisting even further cuts through the threat of pre-emption. But, the fact is that while there is always noise between the networks and affiliates, the basic terms of relationship, the compensation payments and the transfer of about one and-one-half minutes of advertising time every hour from the networks to the stations, is unchanged.

However, the day is not far away when local stations will begin to feel the effects of the Great Value Shift. Recall that the local stations are still enjoying the fruits of their historical position as the government-sanctioned bottleneck. As we saw for the broadcast networks, distribution through local stations does not come cheap. Not only do the local stations get free programming, but they also take hundreds of millions of dollars in compensation payments and a valuable minute or two per hour in advertising time. Even then, they reserve the right to pre-empt network programming when they find something local that they believe will draw higher ratings. During the Broadcast Era, affiliates cleared over 95 percent of network programming.[13] Since then, clearances dropped to about 90 percent in the 1980s as network ratings decreased.[14]

Eventually this artifact of the Broadcast Era will disappear. In fact, major cracks in the bargaining position of the stations are just appearing. For the first time, networks are succeeding in getting affiliates to share costs of program acquisition. First Fox and now CBS, in the enormous expenditure to acquire the rights to NFL football, share the cost of acquisition with their affiliates. Although the affiliate contribution amount to less than 10 percent of the total acquitision costs, it is critically important important assistance to network economics.

The networks will gain even more leverage when digital technology virtually eliminates the difference in picture quality between UHF and VHF stations. As we learned earlier, the terms of the affiliate contract are favorable to the affiliates because there have only been a handful of the powerful VHF stations in any given market. UHF signals, inferior in signal strength and quality, are perceived as less attractive since, all other things equal, they generate lower audience numbers. Clearly, in situations in which there are more networks than VHF stations, bargaining power shifts to the stations.

Technology is eliminating the difference between the "Vs" and the "Us." In doing so, technology will increase the supply of stations for networks to choose from. Cities will go from having two or three prized VHF stations and four or eight weaker UHF stations to having six to ten digital stations. At that point the bargaining terms cannot help but shift away from the stations in favor of the networks.

In the longer term a more ominous threat lies on the horizon for stations that make their living as distributors. That threat comes from the new distributors. Soon new distributors will be able to offer the broadcast networks a better deal than they currently get through the local stations. New distributors, growing their subscribership, will soon be able to offer near-ubiquity without asking for compensation or advertising minutes. At some point, this will be more attractive than total ubiquity with the terms that local stations offer (Exhibit 30).

Consider this. An hour of programming distributed by conventional terrestrial stations delivers a network $1.76 million in revenue—fifteen

Exhibit 30
Network Revenue: Traditional Terrestrial Distribution versus Alternative Distribution

Revenue
$M

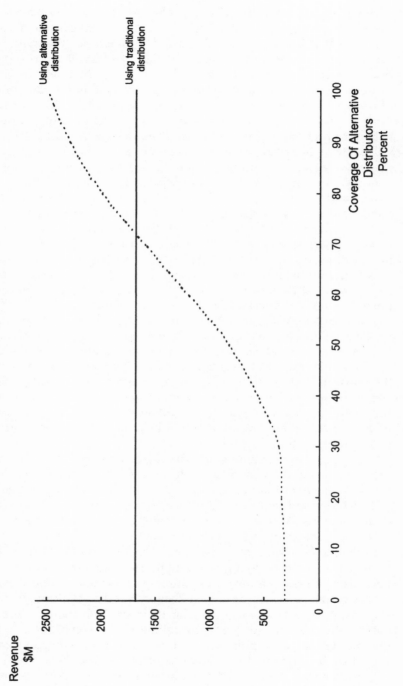

30-second slots at an average of $125,000 per slot minus compensation payments and non-clearances. If alternative distributors were able to provide coverage of 75 percent of the country and forsake compensation payments, they would deliver the same network $1.80 million—20 slots at an average of $90,000 per slot in areas not covered by network O&O's and the same for areas covered by O&O's.

This is not to suggest that broadcast stations will abandon their affiliates. By offering advertisers near 100 percent coverage they maintain a premium price. They also have a political necessity to provide free television to all in return for their free use of the electromagnetic spectrum. By keeping their end of the deal, they have maneuvered into position to get a bargain on the spectrum that the government is making available for advanced television.

Nevertheless, the numbers presented are compelling. New entrants without the baggage of history are already challenging the network-affiliate paradigm. Fox began its existence without the baggage of affiliate compensation and recently told its affiliates that it would keep for itself 20 percent of the commercial time that the affiliates had been selling to advertisers. Barry Diller is cobbling together a national network using a combination of cable networks, USA and Sci-Fi, and local terrestrial stations. By combining cable and terrestrial distribution, he will be able to achieve near-ubiquity without the drag on profits of the affiliate relationship. Even ABC is challenging the network-affiliate paradigm. The network just announced that it would launch a cable network that would replay ABC's soap operas on the same day that they are shown on the network's affiliates.

At a certain point, when the alternative distributors achieve around 75 percent penetration, a very serious conversation will take place between affiliates and the broadcast networks. And it would not be surprising to find out that the outcome of that conversation is worse terms for the distributor.

OTHER OUTCOMES?

Some might argue that this scenario of increasing competition for distributors is unnecessarily pessimistic. They might point out that the field of microeconomics is more art than science, that the business of predicting the future should not be taken lightly, that the new Digital Era might be kinder to distributors than we have suggested.

We cannot ignore this warning. No less than Rupert Murdoch himself was humbled when Time Warner denied carriage of his startup Fox News Channel in New York City. In the new era there will only be a handful of new distributors, hardly the "perfect competition" of the agricultural commodity markets in which thousands of producers toil and

Exhibit 31
Structural Features Increasing Likelihood of Competition

Structural Feature	Impact on Conduct
• Decreasing concentration	• More difficult to collude
• Substantial fixed costs	• Greater incentives to gain share to cover fixed costs
• Some new distributors may have a cost advantage over others	• New distributors can use their cost advantage to compete and maintain profits
• High exit barriers	• Incentive to compete, even if desperately, instead of exiting
• Large profits	• Potential to have price competition and still maintain some level of profitability
• Undifferentiated products	• Makes product competition problematic and encourages price competition

sell without the slightest knowledge of their competitors' actions. Can we be sure of robust price and product competition in the television market? No. In these conditions, economic theory is not well developed: the textbooks tell us that anything from a tightly colluding cartel to a vicious rivalry could emerge.

However, the evidence that we have points to a higher likelihood of competition than collusion. The business of television distribution has many structural features that point toward the emergence of a more competitive environment. According to industrial organization theory, the structural elements shown in Exhibit 31—all found in distribution of television services—are associated with more competitive conduct. These structural features coupled with the experience of competition thus far make a strong case for increased price competition in the future.

PERFORMANCE: POOR

What does the future hold for returns to the owners of the conduit? Can the money machine of the golden age of television and the Cable Era be sustained into the Digital Era? By now, it should be clear that many obstacles lie in the way of strong distributor performance in the Digital Era. Gone is the distribution bottleneck that gave the conduit among the strongest profits in the economy. New distributors bring price competition, product competition, and supplier power, which will devastate distributor profit margins.

The situation of cable operators and their new competitors will start to move in the direction of videocassette retailers, a highly competitive business with low profitability. Recall from the introduction that barriers to entry in retailing are low and that retailers are fragmented. As a consequence, price competition is fierce, product competition—in the form of maintaining a vast inventory of titles and multiple copies—is strong, and payments to suppliers are high. This mode of conduct has resulted in relatively low operating margins in the range of 7 to 8 percent. The distribution of television may never become this fractious, but it is clearly the direction that the business is headed in.

A Modeling Exercise

One way to show the effect of increased competition on profits is with a modeling exercise. With such an exercise, we can demonstrate the catastrophic effects of competition on distributor profits in the new era. In the modeling exercise, we will create a profit-and-loss statement for sample distributors before and after the arrival of competition. To complete the model with competition, we will make a series of assumptions on market share, retail prices, and costs. To simplify the exercise, we will model a situation in which new distributors emerge but resemble a cable operator in their product offerings and costs.

The situation before competition is similar to the situation facing distributors during the Cable Era. But, based on the previous discussion, the situation after the arrival of new distributors will be one in which market share is split, retail prices are reduced, and programming and capital costs are higher.

A typical cable operator had the following financial vital statistics in the Cable Era (refer to Exhibit 32 for a summary of distributor performance under various scenarios discussed).

On the revenue side:

• Subscriber penetration: 60 percent of all homes passed
• Average monthly bill: about $30.00 per subscriber
• Total annual revenue in a municipality of 25,600 homes: $5.5 million

On the cost side:

• Capital costs: $740 per subscriber
• Operating costs: $204 per subscriber
• Total annual costs: $300 per subscriber

Given these numbers, the operators financial performance would be:

• Annual operating profits of $60 per subscriber and an operating profit margin of about 16 percent

Exhibit 32
Distributor Performance under Competitive Pressure, by Cash Flow to Revenue Margin

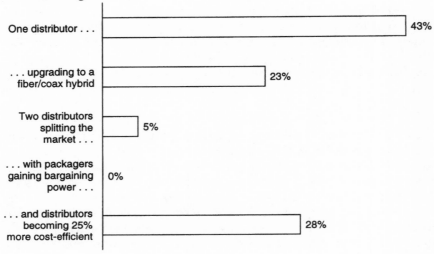

- Cash flow of $155 and a cash flow to revenue margin of 43 percent and a cash flow to asset margin of 13 percent

If a second competitor enters the market, we can make the following assumptions:

On the revenue side:

- Penetration expands by 20 percent, consistent with experience in competitive cable markets,[15] from 60 percent of all households passed to 72 percent.
- Average monthly bill falls by 20 percent, roughly in the middle of the range of data from overbuild situations, from $30 to $24.
- Total revenue in the modeled municipality will fall by 4 percent to $2.6 million.
- The two distributors split this new market evenly, so that total revenue for each distributor is $1.3 million.

On the cost side:

- No new capital investment
- No increase in supplier prices
- Scale elasticity of production: 2.5
- With fewer subscribers to serve, capital costs increase to $1,119 per subscriber and operating costs increase to $274 per subscriber. This brings total annual costs per subscriber to $419.

Given this set of assumptions, operating profits would be wiped out completely. In addition,

- Annual operating profit would fall to −$132 per subscriber.
- Cash flow would drop to $13, the cash flow to revenue margin to 5 percent, and the cash flow to assets margin to 1 percent.

This dramatic decrease in performance would be worse if an increase network bargaining power were added to this set of assumptions. If networks were able to increase their prices by 20 percent, cash flow would disappear entirely (Exhibit 32).

Clearly, this scenario is a financial nightmare for distributors of video. We have not even introduced a third competitor, which could fragment the market even further. If the market were split into thirds, penetration of video services would have to go from 72 percent to 100 percent just to maintain the dismal margins just presented—and this holds only in the unlikely event that another round of price cutting could be avoided.

Is the situation really this bad? Is there anything that distributors can do to stave off disaster? We have already explained why collusion is unlikely and differentiation difficult. But, optimists will suggest that there are three possible ways out for distributors:

- Penetration for subscription video could dramatically rise.
- Competitive pressure could force companies to reduce costs.
- Newer or better products could be developed.

While possible, these three rescues are not probable and certainly should not be counted on by managers or investors. Here is why.

After two decades of mature existence, cable operators have penetrated about two-thirds of the market. Despite extensive marketing efforts like repeated mailings and door-to-door sales visits, offers of free installation and free packages of premium programming, giveaways, and tie-ins with local retailers, about one-third of the population has said "no, thanks" to cable. This segment of the population is either too poor to be able to afford multichannel television, too busy with other activities to watch much television, or in one of those handful of rural communities that are not reached by cable.

With the exception of rural America, these groups will pose problems for distributors. While DBS represents an attractive alternative to cable, it is unlikely to be either cheap enough or unusual enough to attract the terrestrial-only crowd. Moreover, it is difficult to imagine that cable can attract these segments with measures that it has not already tried.

Clearly, the market will grow if prices drop, but growth in the market for multichannel video without price discounts is unlikely.

Successful efforts to reduce costs driven by competitive pressure are not unheard of. In our case, distributors could compensate for the reduction in revenue by increasing operating efficiencies. These reductions are known in economic terms as X-efficiencies. X-efficiencies of as much as 25 percent are documented.[16] Of course, no one knows if distributors could achieve such X-efficiencies: On the one hand, cable operators have never felt the competitive pressure of new entrants against which they could benchmark their performance; but, on the other hand, cable operators have had to manage costs carefully due to the high levels of debt that they have incurred to build their infrastructure.

If distributors achieved efficiencies of about 25 percent in all operating costs except programming,[17] distributors' cash flow to revenue margin would still fall, but to 28 percent instead of 0, while the cash flow to assets margin would fall to 7 percent instead of 0 (Exhibit 32). While an improvement over the nightmare scenario, it still represents a near halving of existing performance.

What about the potential for newer or better products? The great hope is that some new product will come along and rescue the distributors, justifying costly upgrades, and sustaining multiple providers. The answer, though, is doubtful. To provide a new product, a distributor would have to increase capital costs and operating costs while seeing all its competitors do the same. Unless the new product were priced high enough to cover the upgrades, profits would suffer. This result should not be surprising, since an upgrade of this sort is basically a type of product competition that a monopolist bottleneck provider would be able to avoid.

Variations of this scenario are being played out in the real world: Cable operators are upgrading their plant to offer newer and better products than their competitors will be able to offer. TCI, in fact, has committed to spending $1.9 billion by 2000 for upgrades to digital video. The move that most cable operators are now making or contemplating is the upgrade to fiber/coax (coaxial cable) hybrids. With such an infrastructure, cable systems would have increased capacity for more channels of programming, the ability to offer limited interactive products such as near video on demand (NVOD), and Internet access. Let us return to our modeling exercise to determine what the magnitude of price increases or market growth would have to be to cover the investment in an upgrade. With a fiber/coax hybrid, costs could be:

- Annualized capital costs of $44 per subscriber. Installation of fiber in the backbone at the cost of $250[18] and discount rate of 17 percent with 20-year depreciation schedule[19]

- Programming costs to double from $73 per subscriber to $146 per subscriber as channel capacity triples from 50 to 150 channels[20]

In order to make up for this total annual cost increase per subscriber of $117, the average revenue per subscriber would have to increase by $9.75 per month, a 40 percent increase. If revenue remained constant, operating profit would be −$58 and cash flow would be $82, thus decreasing the cash flow to revenue margin to 23 percent and the cash flow to assets margin to 7 percent. All this would happen even if no other competing distributor emerged (Exhibit 32).

The difficulty for distributors in this scenario is that no ideas for new products are being considered. The revenue is thought to come from stealing share of existing products. But, to get an idea of just how difficult this would be, consider the existing markets for some products that the operator of a fiber/coax network could sell. One product that is often mentioned is movies-on-demand. Since total home video spending in 1995 was only $6.59 per person per month[21] and distributors have to pay Hollywood about 50 percent of retail prices, each distributor would have to draw three-quarters of the average four-person family's spending on home video just to cover the cost increase. Making this virtually impossible is the fact that distributors would only be able to show about ten titles in an evening[22] combined with the fact that the top ten titles account for only about 10 percent of all rentals.[23] This means that a distributor multiplexing with as many as one hundred channels would still only be able to compete for 10 percent of a consumer's video rental spending.

Another product that is often discussed as having the potential to provide needed new revenue is video games. It is difficult to imagine the revenues from this product rescuing the distribution business. For example, total home video game revenues per person per year on average were only $16.86 in 1995.[24] Even if 100 percent of these revenues went to a single distributor, it would still cover less than 40 percent of the annualized investment costs.

An idea that has recently picked up momentum is the offer of high-speed Internet access. As was discussed in the technology chapter, cable has big advantage over its competition in delivering Internet access: It can offer much speedier connections. At 800 to 3,000 Kbps, coaxial cable is 700 times faster than a copper wire telephone line, 80 times faster than an ISDN telephone line, and two to ten times faster than DSL technology.

Will this advantage translate into the needed revenue? Probably not. First of all, it is unclear whether or when Internet access will become a mass market. Spending on on-line services and Internet access is still relatively small: Despite having quadrupled between 1991 and 1995, at $16.24 it is still less than spending on home video games. Furthermore, to use cable for Internet access, viewers would need a cable modem. As its price is unlikely to fall much below $150 in the near future, this requirement will either slow down diffusion if the modem must be purchased by the viewer or increase capital requirements if it is to be provided by the distributor.

Finally, Internet access is fast becoming a competitive business. The conventional copper-line business shows the direction of things to come. Prices have been pushed down below $20 per month for unlimited Internet access, and some long-distance companies like AT&T have decided to give Internet access and support free with long-distance service. Competition is also heating up for high-speed access and, with it, the prospects for high prices and margins are fading. The satellite alternative is DirectPC with connection speeds of 200 to 400 Kbps. Unlike its wireline competitors, this service is available throughout the United States and starts at only $20 per month. With the market rapidly growing, the telephone companies have finally gotten serious; they are now preparing to offer "DSL lite," a version of DSL that is cheaper to install and only slightly slower than standard DSL. It can be bought for only $40 per month and can also serve as a second telephone line. DSL offers a major advantage over cable competitors in that it allows users to send data at high speeds. Since most cable systems were designed as one-way systems, data must be sent back over the telephone line at the glacial pace of 33.6 Kbps.

Internet access, even high-speed Internet access, is likely to be a commodity service and not the boon that distribution companies are hoping for. For example, even if users paid for the modems themselves and monthly prices for Internet connection stayed in the $35 per month range, cable operators would need almost 30 percent of all their subscribers to sign up to make up the necessary revenue. This does not even begin to address the revenue loss that a second competitor would cause to the operator's core video business.

So far our modeling exercise has used the costs of a wireline competitor assumed to resemble a cable operator. Is the situation for a satellite operator any better? Since huge fixed startup costs are involved in providing satellite television, the answer clearly depends on the number of subscribers that the service would get. Obviously, DBS pioneers believe that they can make significant inroads into cable's subscriber base. What would it take to make an above-average return on their money?

Some preliminary numbers have emerged on the investment that Sky is making in the market. The magnitude of these numbers is not for the timid investor. Sky paid $682.5 million at auction for the last prime orbital slot covering the United States and reckons that total capital costs will be about $2.8 billion to get launched. If operating costs resemble those of cable system operators and the capital is charged over five years, the system will need about 3.5 million subscribers paying an average of $30 per month in fees to break even. This excludes any additional cost in subsidizing the purchase of satellite dishes (Exhibit 33).

If the satellite distributors were to take 15 million subscribers from the cable operators—a devastating loss for cable in the absence of new replacement revenues—and split these subscribers among three providers, it could be a sustainable business with operating profit margins in the range of 20 percent. These numbers are not the numbers of the distribution business in its heyday, nor are they available without making a great marketing effort. The investor after this segment has to be willing to tolerate massive up-front investment and operating losses before reaching stability.

The preceding analysis applies for subscription-based distributors, but the performance of local stations is also easy to model. Local stations do not depend on subscriptions, but on advertising revenue. Therefore, they can be thought of as packagers of programming playing the ratings game and will be discussed in the next chapter. While removed from some of the new competitive pressures in distribution, like retail pricing, they could become the victims of increased supplier bargaining power.

Currently about one-third of television households do not subscribe to cable television. As long as such a significant part of the population is served by local stations, they will retain a critical distribution role without which broadcast networks would not be able to offer ubiquitous coverage. In the short term, then, networks will not play off new distributors against the local stations in order to extract more favorable conditions.

But in the long term, local stations will not remain untouched by this turmoil. As digital technology eliminates the difference between UHF and VHF stations and as new distribution channels approach ubiquitous coverage, networks will begin to toughen their bargaining stance toward local stations. Local stations will no longer be able to assume that they are a necessary conduit to audiences for networks. In these conditions, affiliation payments, which averaged 3.8 percent of local network affiliate compensation in 1993,[25] will be reduced, eliminated, or possibly reversed. Should they be eliminated, the average affiliate's operating margin would drop from 31 percent to 28 percent. Moreover, as we saw above, the advertising minutes that affiliates get from the networks and the level of affiliate preemptions could also be reduced. The potential impact for a typical affiliate could be more severe, since it means the loss of, say, four minutes per evening over the course of the year. At an average price of $1,000 per 30-second slot, that could amount to lost revenue of close to $3 million annually. This would reduce the sky-high operating margin down to 12 percent.

Exhibit 33
Economics of a Satellite Distributor, in $ Millions

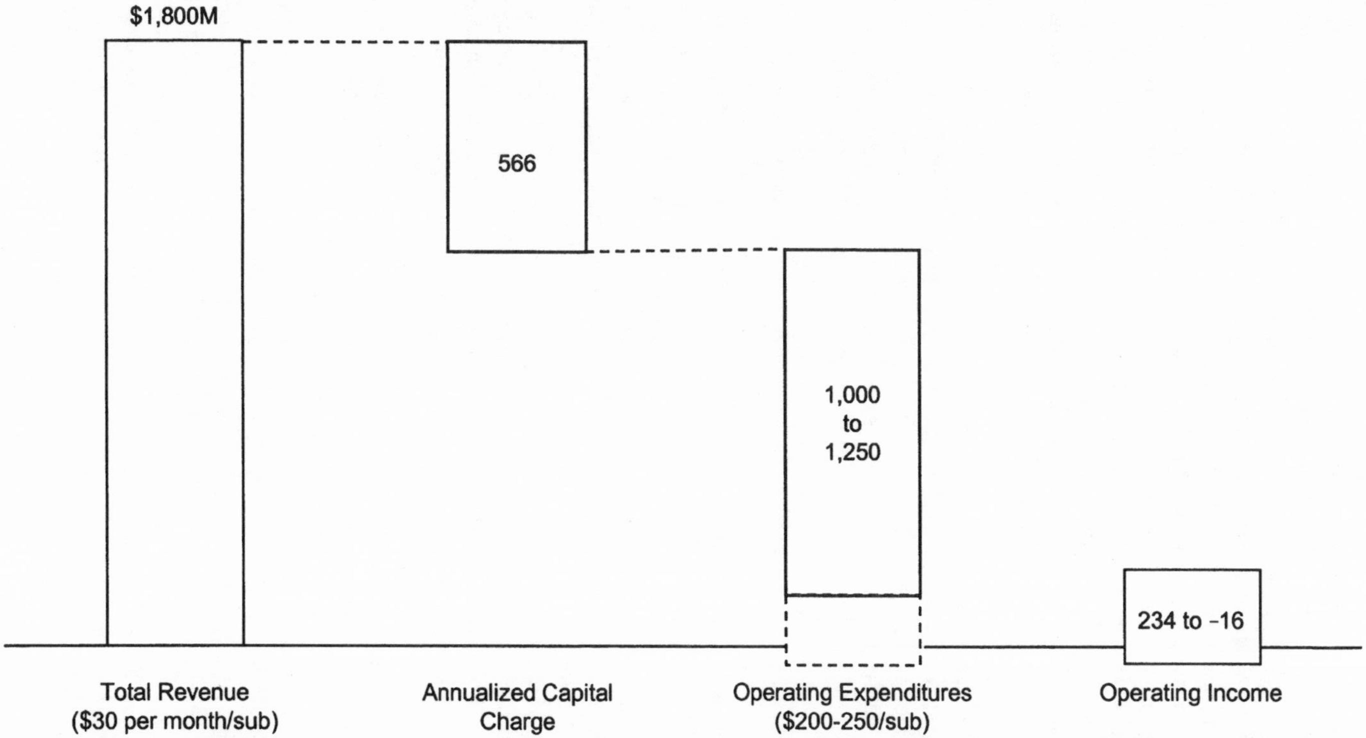

$1,800M

Total Revenue
($30 per month/sub)

566

Annualized Capital
Charge

1,000
to
1,250

Operating Expenditures
($200-250/sub)

234 to -16

Operating Income

THE REAL WORLD

Just because the next era's distribution economics can be modeled on a spreadsheet to look miserable does not mean that they actually will be miserable. Spreadsheet models are only perfect when they model the past. However, in our case, there seems to be some predictive value.

First of all, there seems to be a consensus among all of those who watch the industry that these models are at least directionally correct. The proof is in the stock prices of distributors, particularly the distributors dependent on subscription revenue like cable MSOs and DBS operators. Although there has been recent interest in these companies as investors get excited about the prospect of Internet-related revenue, in general over the end of the Cable Era and the beginning of the Digital Era, investors—analyzing cable MSOs and DBS operators with their own spreadsheets—have not been too eager to hold these stocks, and their performance has suffered compared to the performance of the cable operators and the market as a whole (Exhibit 22).

Furthermore, the spreadsheets built by managers at both telephone companies and cable companies must look like those presented here since their investment plans have progressed much more cautiously than the fanfare of the early 1990s would have suggested.

Most recently, the pendulum of Wall Street opinion has swung back in favor of cable operators. With Microsoft founders Bill Gates and Paul Allen investing in cable, stock prices for cable operators have begun climbing again. Cable's attractiveness is due to the realization of some operating efficiencies and the expectations of increased cash flow from digital services, in particular high-speed Internet access.

Only time will tell how much of this latest wave of enthusiam with cable is hype or reality. Not only does a modeling exercise show how difficult it will be to pay for the cost of the required upgrade, but experience confirms that performance weakens in situations in which two wireline competitors exist in the same market. Some hard data comes from overbuild situations in which profits are virtually wiped out. In a recent study of competition between two cable operators in Paragould, Arkansas, it was demonstrated that both operators were operating at breakeven or a loss.[26]

The data are not limited to overbuild situations. The financial statements of monopolist cable operators have deteriorated in recent years as the reality of competition nears (Exhibit 34). Cash flows have deteriorated as both operating costs and investment levels have increased. These costs have increased as a direct of consequence of cable companies trying to maintain a product edge over the new competition.

The United Kingdom provides an interesting example of the future for the U.S. market because it is a market in which several multichannel

Exhibit 34
Financial Performance of Cable Operators

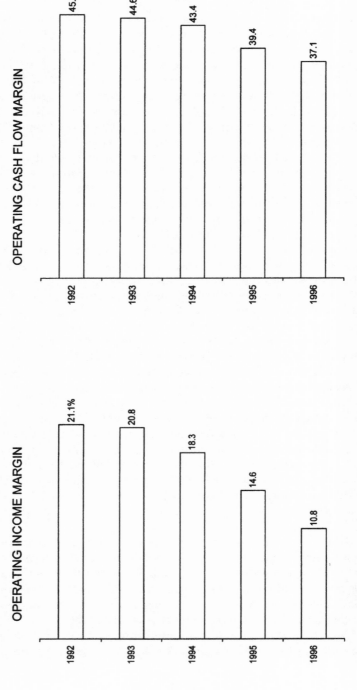

Source: Veronis, Suhler, and Associates, *Communications Industry Report* (New York: Veronis, Suhler, and Associates, Inc., 1998). Reproduced with permission.

competitors vie for subscribers. In the United Kingdom, cable has had to fight for its share of the market. The problem was that a satellite operator already existed before cable got serious about providing service. The cable companies entered the market in force in the early 1990s with deep-pocketed U.S. telephone companies winning licenses. However, despite investing an estimated £6 billion and passing 78 percent of all British households, the penetration rate remains at about one-third or fewer of total households. The systems are still posting losses—losses for Telewest, which is owned by US West and TCI, are expected to be over £220 million in 1997—and their owners' stock prices are in the doldrums.

DBS operator BSkyB, partly owned by Rupert Murdoch, began in the late 1980s with an aggressive campaign to secure quality programming and to sign up households for the service in the United Kingdom. The service was successful because it bought its way into Britain's living rooms with U.K. rights to Hollywood movies and first-run television series. However, it was exclusive rights to English Premier League Football that really put BSkyB on the map.

These moves, however, are a costly and temporary competitive advantage. After their initial refusal, the cable companies have all decided to buy BSkyB's programming. This enriches BSkyB but also decreases the programming advantage that BSkyB had over the competition. Awakened to the importance of programming, it is fair to bet that cable and terrestrial competitors, themselves going digital in 1998 and needing more programming, will not let the next Premier League Football contract go by without a fight. In fact, in a harbinger of times to come, some Hollywood studios have refused BSkyB exclusive PPV (Pay-per-view) rights and done separate deals with cable operators.

The U.K. market has all of the hallmarks of the nightmare for distribution that is on its way to the United States: the presence of more than one provider; heavy spending on product competition—both on programming and advanced services like video-on-demand and interactive services—and intense retail price competition. As an analyst in Britain observed, "In the future, it looks like we will have free television, digital terrestrial television, cable television, satellite television and maybe even a video-on-demand service from British Telecom as well. . . . It is going to be a very crowded market with margins under great pressure."[27]

In the case of local stations, there appear to be no warning signs in the real world of the Great Value Shift. Values for local stations have increased in transactions and stock market prices are high. What is going on? Are the markets blind to the changes that are going on in distribution?

The first thing to be aware of is that local stations are not, strictly speaking, distributors. Both independents and affiliates are also packagers and producers of programming with an attractive mix of local programming and larger-budget national programming. Some of this local programming, the evening news, for example, is quite highly rated. To the extent that local stations can become more than simply transmitters for content providers, they can insulate themselves from the effects of the Great Value Shift.

Buyers of local stations have had other things on their mind than the long-term strategic implications of the Great Value Shift. Prices are being bid up for local stations because three new developments have occurred that favor local stations in the short term. The first is that the Telecommunications Act of 1996 relaxed the media concentration rules and now allow single entities to control up to 35 percent of the national market for terrestrial television. For networks, this means that they can expand their holdings in this still-lucrative business to eliminate the need for several affiliates; and for independents, it means that the formation of groups of stations that can gain greater leverage with program syndicators in acquiring programming is possible.

A second development is the emergence of the mini-networks, first Warner Brothers and United-Paramount and later, networks headed by Barry Diller of Home Shopping Network and infomercial king Bud Paxson. This increased demand for affiliates set off a bidding war.[28] Fox, in particular, has been aggressive in attracting stations: in 1994 Fox got longtime CBS affiliates in large cities—Atlanta, Cleveland, Detroit, and Milwaukee—to defect.

The third development is the DTV rules promulgated by the FCC that give the local stations spectrum to use for either HDTV, multiple stations of conventional television, some of which could be subscriber based, or new data services. This government giveaway could, in theory, give broadcasters new revenue streams.

While responsible for an increase in the value of stations in the short term, these developments do not signal a reversal in the fundamental downward spiral in which distribution will find itself in the long term. As the installed base of satellite dishes grows and the number of homes linked to a wireline provider increases, the stations will lose their unique position of offering ubiquitous coverage. They may even have to pay for their spectrum if Congress decides it needs money. The best position over the next few years is as a seller of local stations.

In the real world, of course, profitable distribution will remain. But, without the bottleneck strategy, the game will not be as easy. Distributors will look for advantages wherever they can find them. Wireline players generally will have an advantage in densely populated areas in which unit costs fall. Wherever cable companies have long histories, they will seek to keep their customers and wherever possible to leverage their existing relationships into new ones with new products, like telephone service. Satellite providers, on the other hand, have an advantage in sparsely populated areas and, for now at least, with viewers who appreciate the immense bouquet of channels offered.

Distribution is becoming a commodity game. Whatever shape the industry takes in the Digital Era, it will be a tougher place for distributors.

Throughout most of the history of television, the conduit was king. First local broadcasters and then cable operators were protected by barriers to entry created by technology, economics, and policy makers. Behind these barriers, they achieved phenomenal returns to capital through the use of the distribution bottleneck strategy. Put simply, when you own the only means of access to viewers—the distribution bottleneck—profits come fairly easily.

Driven by technology, this era is coming to an end. Competition has arrived in the form of telephone companies, satellites, utilities, the Internet, prepackaged video on cassettes and CD-ROMs, and even a reinvented broadcast industry. These alternatives will destroy the distribution bottleneck strategy. Distributors will have to lower retail prices and improve their product. Despite these moves, distributors will be unable to differentiate their services: They all will have clean pictures, good quality sound, and easy-to-understand bills. Only programming will differentiate them. To get programming, the distributors will have to pay. Distribution is on its way to becoming a commodity, and the returns to a commodity are much lower than the returns to a monopoly.

If all this is true, why does one continuously hear that the three most important success factors for a network are "distribution, distribution, and distribution"? Look carefully at the source of this quote. It is almost always distributors and new or struggling content providers. Distributors say it out of self-interest. For new content providers, it is true: they simply cannot succeed without an outlet. Established content providers are not saying anything. It is the distributors that need them.

The fact is that multichannel video delivery is becoming a fiercely competitive business. Distribution is important, as no viewer will see a program without it, but it is no longer the bottleneck that it once was. Distributors will compete, and to do so they will need programming along with any other edge that they can find. Established programming is in the driver's seat during any negotiation. Distributors will pay to have great programming while trying any new programming idea that may give them an edge.

NOTES

1. Christopher Parkes, "Battle above the Rooftops," *Financial Times*, 27 February 1997, p. 11.
2. Kenneth Thorpe, "The Impact of Competing Technologies on Cable Tele-

vision," in *Video Media Competition: Regulation, Economics, and Technology*, edited by Eli M. Noam (New York: Columbia University Press, 1985), pp. 138–153.

3. Lawrie Mifflin, "Possible Shift on Discounting of Cable Rates," *New York Times*, 14 December 1995, Business section.

4. Joe Estrella, "TCI Shaves Rates vs. Ameritech,"*Multichannel News*, 9 December 1996, p. 16.

5. Provided that the customer signed up for a year's worth of programming.

6. Parkes, "Battle above the Rooftops," p. 11.

7. Elizabeth Lesly Stevens and Ronald Grover, "The Entertainment Glut," *Business Week*, 16 February 1998, p. 91.

8. Steven H. Lustgarten, "The Impact of Buyer Concentration in Manufacturing Industries," *Review of Economics and Statistics* 57 (May 1975): 125–132.

9. Mark Landler, "Cable Operators Losing Ground to Programmers," *New York Times*, 17 March 1997, p. 6.

10. Matt Stump, "TCI Pulls NBC's String on Exclusivity," *Broadcasting*, 25 June 1990, p. 21.

11. Ibid.

12. Kathryn Harris, "Endangered Species," *Forbes*, 3 February 1992, p. 43.

13. Barry R. Litman, *The Vertical Structure of the Television Broadcasting Industry: The Coalescence of Power* (East Lansing, Mich.: MSU Business Studies, 1979), p. 78.

14. J. A. Haldi and S. T. Eastman, "Affiliated station programming." *Broadcast/Cable programming*, edited by S. T. Eastman (Belmont, Calif.: Wadsworth, 1992).

15. Thomas W. Hazlett and Matthew L. Spitzer, "Public Policy toward Cable Television. Volume 1: The Economics of Rate Controls," working paper for the Program on Telecommunications Policy, Institute of Governmental Affairs, University of California, Davis, 1996, p. 49.

16. Harvey Liebenstein, "Allocative Efficiency v. 'X-Efficiency,' " *American Economic Review* 56 (June 1966): 392–415.

17. Programmers will likely gain in bargaining power.

18. Richard Bilotti, Drew Hanson, and Richard J. MacDonald. *The Cable Television Industry: New Technologies, New Opportunities, and New Competition*. Volume 1, *Industry Review and Outlook* (New York: Grantchester Securities and Wasserstein and Perella Securities, 1993), p. 32.

19. David P. Reed, *Residential Fiber Optic Networks: An Engineering and Economic Analysis* (Boston, Mass.: Artech House, 1992), p. 130.

20. In order for costs not to triple, this assumption implies that 50 channels would be programmed with pay-per-view movies.

21. Veronis, Suhler, and Associates, *Communications Industry Report* (New York: Veronis, Suhler, and Associates, Inc., 1994).

22. One title takes up nine channels if shown every 15 minutes from 7:00 P.M. to 9:00 P.M.

23. Interview with Arthur Goodman, *Video Store Magazine*, 3 November 1994.

24. Veronis, Suhler and Associates, *Communications Industry Report*.

25. Mark R. Fratrick and Theresa J. Ottina, *1994 Television Financial Report*, (Washington, D.C.: National Association of Broadcasters, 1994), p. 34.

26. Marianne Barrett, "Direct Competition in Cable Television Delivery: A Case Study of Paragould, Arkansas," *Journal of Media Economics* 8, no. 3 (1995): 77–93.

27. Erik Ipsen, "Race to Cable Britain Getting Nowhere Fast," *International Herald Tribune*, February 1997.

28. Elisabeth Lesly, "A Power Jolt for Station Owners," *Business Week*, 13 June 1994, p. 36.

Chapter 4

Where Is the Value?
The Corporate Response

Faced with the conundrum of the Great Value Shift, it is clear that massive profits can no longer be expected in distribution, but what does a
media firm with billions of dollars do? Two strategies have received a
lot of attention: the attempt to create a bottleneck through domination
of the set-top box and the creation of content/conduit combines. Both
strategies, however, are misguided. They miss the point of the Digital
Era. They are attempts to recreate the glory of the past and are doomed
to failure.

THE HOLY GRAIL OF THE SET-TOP BOX

The next great battle that we hear so often about is the battle between
the titans of the television and PC industries for the set-top box. Just
what is the set-top box and why does everyone seem consumed over the
struggle for it?

The set-top box is a term that has its origins in the Cable Era. When
cable operators were extending cable into homes they faced the problem
that most of the television sets in America were not "cable-ready": They
were not capable of processing the signal sent to them via the coax of
the cable operator. To remedy this situation, the cable operators installed
set-top boxes, essentially tuners, in every subscribing household. Similar
boxes are required for SMATV, MMDS, and DBS systems.

The battle for the set-top box centers on the notion that the set-top box
will be the distribution bottleneck of the Digital Era. In a digital world
with multiple distribution channels of high bandwidth into the home,
the opportunity will arise to standardize and centralize the collection of

content in every household. With the prospect of every household in the country replacing its television in the next decade and many households either replacing or buying powerful new computers, the possibility emerges that a new set-top box could be installed in homes throughout the country. In other words, instead of consumers having separate set-top boxes for their cable, satellite, broadcast, and telephone connections, a single set-top box with increased functionality would be available for everything. Once installed, this box would be a bottleneck: The firm that controls the set-top box would be able to charge a toll for all content that passes through it on its way to consumers.

Is there really an opportunity to control a new bottleneck in the Digital Era? Not likely. The set-top box of the Digital Era will be like the Holy Grail—an elusive, exhaustive, and ultimately futile exercise. The bottleneck simply will not exist.

A bottleneck would create a closed system, a system in which one party controls access and writes and enforces the "rules." Closed systems are not in the interest of every player active in the industry—except, of course, for the firm that controls the system. Since access is controlled, these systems stifle competition, creativity, and organic growth. Closed systems, or monopolies as they might also be called, are also extremely difficult to achieve and maintain. Even if one player manages to establish a closed system, the government usually steps in to dismantle it.

Everything that we have learned about the setting of standards in the Digital Era points to the failure of such closed, proprietary systems. The oft-cited example is that of the computer industry. The industry began with several companies trying to create proprietary systems built around their technology. By the late 1980s, these companies were bankrupt. Today, they are remembered only as footnotes on the way to an open system built around the PC.

Two forces were instrumental in the dominance of an open system. As PC processing power as a function of price doubled every two years according to Moore's Law, power devolved from mainframe computers and mini computers to PCs on individual desktops. A basic property of networks is that their value grows disproportionately with its number of users: a telephone network of just a few is uninteresting, throw in the whole neighborhood and one can start to imagine the potential, and add an entire city and things begin to look interesting. With enormous computing power on desks throughout the world and the looming attractiveness of a large network, an open system flourished. Vendors and users could organically add applications without endangering their ability to function in the system or to add yet more applications. In this environment, proponents for closed and proprietary systems were doomed. They competed for some time, but could never offer the vitality of an open system and eventually lost.

Seekers of the set-top box bottleneck are not heeding this great lesson of the computer industry. They are laboring under the belief that they can create a proprietary system that can stand up to other competing systems. They will pay the price for this flawed strategy. The set-top box strategy is the Holy Grail of television strategies in the Digital Era for the same reasons that proprietary systems failed in the computer industry.

While it may now be one of the dumbest appliances in the home, the television is rapidly gaining improved processing power and functionality. It will be difficult to create a set-top box bottleneck when all of the functionality in the set-top box is built into the television. Making the set-top box strategy even more problematic is the fact that if a proprietary system is without compelling content, it will not be attractive. It would be like a telephone network without a critical mass of users. Compelling content is now spread out among ten or twenty competing networks. The system that wins will embrace all of these content providers and, in so doing, be open.

Nevertheless, this argument has not stopped many players from embracing the set-top box strategy. After all, it represents the same kind of thinking that was effective in the previous eras in television. It is an attempt to recreate the bottleneck control that the broadcasters enjoyed during the Broadcast Era and the cable industry enjoyed during the Cable Era.

To more fully understand both the passion for the quest for the set-top box and its futility requires a historical context. The set-top box paradigm was also a product of the great HDTV debates of the 1980s and 1990s. Recall that the technology of television took a major advance in the 1960s with the advent of color television. In about a decade, the entire installed base of television was replaced with new equipment providing a bonanza to makers of television hardware. During the 1970s, the Japanese began research on what they believed would be the next logical step in the evolution of the technology of television. They proposed a new standard, called Hi-Vision, that would offer viewers improved picture quality and dubbed it high-definition television.

By the late 1980s and early 1990s, the United States and Europe woke up to the Japanese challenge for television's next generation and started to develop standards of their own. In 1991, the FCC decided to give, not auction, 6 MHz of spectrum to broadcasters for HDTV, and the work began on a U.S. standard.

Agreement on a standard was not achieved because while the different groups were at work on the problem, technology was rapidly changing. Despite the merging of many competing groups into a single "Grand Alliance," the broadcasters failed to persuade the FCC to canonize its proposed closed standard. The commission was stumped by the fundamental disagreement between the computer industry and the broadcasters over the choice of standards. At the core of the argument is the esoteric question of whether DTV will use interlaced or progressive scanning. Interlaced scanning is used by the television industry to conserve what has traditionally been scarce bandwidth. It involves decomposing each frame of television (there are 30 frames per second) into two alternating fields of scan lines. Together these lines "interlace" to give viewers a full picture using only half of the bandwidth. Progressive scanning is the favorite of the computer industry. By "progressively" lining the entire screen, the displays achieve greater accuracy—important for well-scrutinized computer screens. Of course, there are also other questions: the size and shape of the screen and the level of resolution, in terms of vertical scanning lines, horizontal pixels, and frame rates per second.

The FCC felt that it simply could not make the decision to adopt any single standard and freeze out the competing interests, thereby creating a closed system. Instead of selecting a standard, the FCC threw the whole issue to the television marketplace for an answer. The FCC voted on April 3, 1997, to allow any one of eighteen possible standards to be used for what is now called Digital Television (DTV) (see Exhibit 26).

Television manufacturers and broadcasters themselves must decide which standards to use. This decision is not an easy one. With technology improving digital compression techniques, the original 6 MHz set aside for broadcasters is now an enormous amount of spectrum. As many have observed, the broadcasters can become their own FCC and allocate their spectrum to high-definition television, multiple channels of standard television, or data transmission as they see fit at any moment, in any market.

Their dream is to use their unique position to control set-top boxes in every household. This would give them the means to tap into that lucrative stream of subscriber revenues that the cable industry now enjoys.

Complicating their plans is the growing computer industry. Several of the eighteen possible standards use the progressive scanning favored by the computer industry. Computer firms are championing this standard because they want computers users to be able to receive television on their monitors. They have started selling computers equipped with digital-TV decoders and even raised the vision of a year 2002 in which there are 40 million video-enabled computers and one million high-definition televisions.[1] Their dream is that the computer becomes the display of choice for television, that they sell millions of computers and software packages to viewers who want to combine their television viewing and computational needs into a single device, and that they control the set-top box and collect a toll for all of the content that passes through.

These dreams should seem familiar to anyone who understands the Cable Era and the control that the cable operators enjoyed. Moreover, the broadcasters' position is understandable given the last ten years of digital television development during which they were led to believe that they could dictate the terms of the new standard.

It should also be clear how unrealistic it is for players in the industry to create a set-top box bottleneck—a closed and proprietary system—in the Digital Era. The computer industry would face the daunting task of attracting viewers to a system without the programming from the television industry. The broadcasters—even if they banded together—would have to champion a system without the most popular cable programming and without true Internet functionality. Cable operators, perhaps with the most realistic chance of all industry players, would still need to overcome the problem that the most desired programming on television is still the programming of the broadcasters. And, viewers and content suppliers would be forced to choose between competing closed systems—a choice altogether distasteful after years of access to all available programming either on-the-air or through cable. Even if an industry player manages to impose a closed system on the industry through the control of a set-top box, it is likely that Congress or the FCC would step in to regulate it.

As the Cable Era transmutes into the Digital Era, these grim facts have begun to enter into the consciousness of the strategy directors at the big media companies. A much easier and more desirable answer for consumers and for the industry as a whole is that the set-top box strategy is abandoned and an open system for television evolves. Cable operators are already catching on to this scenario. As their networks evolve, their subscribers will need new set-top boxes to support next-generation services like digital TV and high-speed Internet access. Having watched the PC–Macintosh wars of the 1980s, the cable industry was determined not to let any single supplier leverage an advantage to create a proprietary standard. With TCI leading the way, the cable industry has designed the set-top box into "layers" of technology—the microprocessor and chip set, the operating system and Internet software, the systems manufacturing, the electronic programming guide, and the service provider—so that each must be interoperable with components of the other layers. While this approach delays the development of the set-top box and decreases the level of control that TCI or any one player has, it ensures that a bottleneck is not recreated in distribution.

However, as the dream of controlling a closed and proprietary digital system fades, it is being replaced by a subtler strategy. Another way to turn the set-top box into an advantage without creating a closed system is to use the set-top box to direct viewers to a starting point in their viewing session. The idea comes from the fascination with Web portals that has turned such sites as Yahoo!, Excite, and Infoseek into the darlings of the investment community. These portals do not necessarily own content of their own; they merely organize it so that users seeking content among the vast reaches of cyberspace can easily find what they are looking for. Since Web users tend to come back often to their preferred portals during on-line sessions, these portals have been able to build advertising revenue faster than other less frequently sites on the Web.

The newest version of the set-top box dream is the notion that the appliance can be leveraged to enable a computer hardware or software maker, a cable company, or a broadcaster to control the starting point from which the viewer of tomorrow begins his viewing session. The idea is that this starting point will become the mother of all portals and emerge as the most coveted piece of real estate in the industry.

Several players are angling for this starting position, so the outcome of this battle is far from over. Microsoft has developed a version of its operating system to run on stripped-down network computers that use the television set to access the Web. TCI has tried to create its version of the grand portal using the concept of a television guide. The company has acquired the high-circulation *TV Guide* publication and is trying to take over a small company called Gemstar, the owner of several key patents needed to build a user-friendly television guide. Even if one company manages to occupy this coveted starting position, how valuable will it be? Is it the next best thing to a proprietary system?

Portal theory has a long way to go before it can come anywhere near the power of the distribution bottleneck in its profit-making potential. Portals have shot up in value on the basis of promised, not delivered, profits. The portal business model is untested and possibly flawed. It rests on the notion that value can be retained by packaging alone. However, portal packagers bring few of the economies or synergies that television networks bring to packaging (see Chapter 5). Nor are portals protected by the high entry barriers that television networks enjoyed. Finally, user flow patterns are not well established enough to determine whether users will continue to visit the portals once they have discovered the content that they are interested in, nor whether users will spend significant time at the portals even if they do return to them.

In the long run, the set-top box will disappear. Already, television sets are finally catching up to the other appliances in the household. They are being built "smarter" all the time. Given rapid advances in digital technology, it would not be surprising to see an affordable television/computer that could recognize all eighteen possible digital formats. The set-top box would become an artifact of the Cable Era, the dream of building the set-top box into a closed system would be abandoned, and the possibility of leveraging the set-top box into a super portal would remain a long shot.

THE MYTH OF THE CONTENT/CONDUIT COMBINE

The 1990s have seen the creation of massive content/conduit combines. Newspaper headlines have featured one spectacular move after another in a television feeding frenzy: News Corporation and MCI, the creation of Time Warner followed by the investment by USWest and the acquisition of Turner Broadcasting by Time Warner, Disney and ABC/Capital Cities, TCI and Liberty Media, and the investment of the Bell Operating Companies in newly created programming entities.

Where will it end? What is driving the activity? Does this second strategic response to the Great Value Shift make sense?

In the crisis atmosphere of the Great Value Shift, the second popular strategic response is to integrate vertically and create content/conduit combines. A content/conduit combine is an entity that both makes content and distributes it. The logic on the part of content firms is to secure access to distribution; while the logic for conduit firms is to get commitments for programming. The trouble is that in the atmosphere of crisis, this logic has not undergone a thorough testing. If it had, it would be found to be flawed, and the content/conduit combine strategy would be exposed as myth.

Content firms will soon realize that there is no shortage of distribution. In fact, there is a glut, and in times of glut, there is no need to secure access through acquisition or any other means. From the perspective of conduit companies, the strategy does not make any better sense. To begin with, it may not be legal for a distributor to own content and withhold it from other competitors. Even if that is eventually allowed, it is well nigh impossible for a distribution company—fundamentally a technology company—to manage a content company—fundamentally a people company.

Before debunking the myth of the content/conduit combine, let us review the economic rationale for vertical integration and examine a bit of the history of vertical integration in the television industry.

The Economic Rationale of Vertical Integration

Large firms in our industry, or in any other, must decide what activities they should perform within the firm and what activities should be performed outside the firm and purchased. These decisions are complex and economic theory is yet to provide an answer as to what amount of integration is best. As a result, firms that deliver the same product make different decisions about how much to integrate. In some countries outside the United States, in Britain and Japan, for example, public broadcasters are fully integrated—producing, packaging, and distributing almost all of their own programming. In America, there tend to be varied and changing patterns of integration.

What are the economic drivers behind vertical integration? The economic rationale can be grouped in two categories: efficiency gains and strategic benefits. It is possible to list the various rationales here, but it is much more difficult to quantify their size, particularly in the case of the television industry. There are several types of efficiency gains that are most often considered to exist in our industry. "Transaction efficiencies" are gains that vertical integration can achieve in the transaction, or contracting process, that occurs between buyers and sellers.[2] Integration can reduce the risk and cost of contracting when opportunistic behavior and changing market conditions between networks and distributors occur, especially when such contracts have to be written repeatedly. It also can solve the "double marginalization" problem that occurs as succeeding suppliers add monopolistic surcharges to downstream distributors so that retailers end up sub-optimizing sales to consumers.[3] Another kind of efficiency gain that can come with vertical integration is the gain from efficient sharing of creative, marketing, and financial resources. These resources of distributors and packagers, such as detailed knowledge of audience preferences, are needed by packagers and program producers to make successful programming; they are difficult to contract with formal sharing procedures.

Apart from these potential gains in efficiency, another economic motive for vertical integration is strategic. One important strategic motive for backward integration is to develop earlier stages in the supply chain. In the early days of the television industry, distributors financed and developed the production and packaging stages because they needed new programming to sell their services to subscribers.

A second strategic motive is to harness horizontal market power, market power at one stage of the supply chain, in order to use it in either upstream or downstream activities.[4] For example, fully integrated steel producers could squeeze rival manufacturers by increasing prices for raw materials that they control. Such a move would hurt steel manufacturers that had to buy raw materials, while integrated firms would be protected by being able to take out profits at the level of their raw material operations. This behavior could be extended to foreclose non-integrated firms trying to compete in the industry and raise entry barriers for those contemplating entrance into the industry. Bandwagon effects get created if a few firms decide to integrate vertically. Such moves would decrease the size of the independent segment of the market and force non-integrated firms to think seriously about whether they want to be dependent on integrated firms for supply.

The existence of these motives is often used by regulators of our industry to impose regulation against integration (Exhibit 35). On the cable

Exhibit 35
Overview of Regulations Addressing Vertical Integration in Television

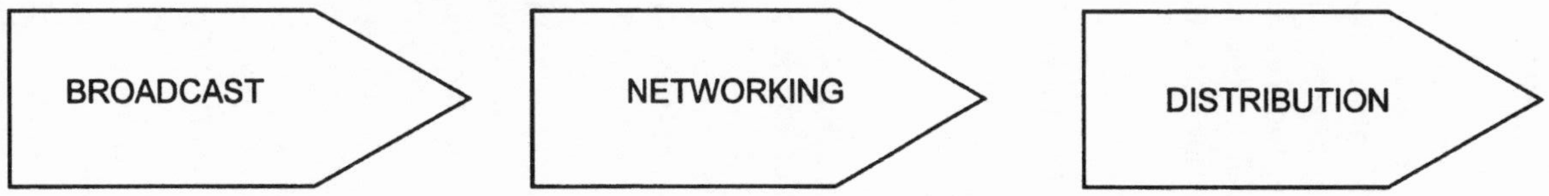

```
  ┌──────────┐      ┌──────────┐      ┌──────────┐
  │          \      │          \      │          \
  │ BROADCAST  >    │NETWORKING  >    │DISTRIBUTION >
  │          /      │          /      │          /
  └──────────┘      └──────────┘      └──────────┘
```

BROADCAST TV
• Fin/Syn Rules lifted in 1955

NETWORKING
• Networks limited to 35% ownership of distribution to national market
• Hours of network programming allowed on affiliate stations limited; other aspects of network/affiliate contracts regulated

CABLE TV
• Program access rules require vertically integrated MSOs to make programming available to all buyers

TELEPHONE COMPANIES
• Subject to cable law if operate as cable system
• Limited to owning interest in 1/3 of programming if "open" system
• Barred from owning programming if common carrier

side, vertically integrated cable operators are thought to be in a position to deny programming at reasonable prices to competing distributors[5] and to deny carriage on their systems to new programmers with which they are not affiliated. Of course, these actions could be taken without vertical integration, but vertical integration facilitates this potential increase in entry barriers. On the broadcast side, the networks were suspected of planning to monopolize upstream production and downstream local station distribution should they be freed from the regulations limiting integration. This was the logic for the Financial Interest and Syndication Rule and the 12-12-12 Rule.

The History of Vertical Integration in the Television Industry

How have these motives for vertical integration and the regulatory environment shaped the pattern of vertical integration in the United States?

The television business, both broadcast and cable, has a long history of vertical integration with sound underlying economic motives. Vertical integration in broadcast television was initially driven by the fundamental scale economics of program distribution. We saw that the FCC's doctrine of localism in assigning spectrum to broadcast stations constrained these stations to a limited local area of signal coverage. At the same time, it is in the interest of local stations to spread their costs over as large an audience as possible in an effort to decrease unit costs. Networking was the industry's response to this problem. By linking local stations together in a network, broadcasters were able to spread the fixed costs of program distribution over a larger audience. Furthermore, by transmitting programming simultaneously to affiliated stations, networks were able to save on distribution costs. Finally, networks can take advantage of transaction economies in advertising and in program distribution. In addition to regulation, the amount of programming that is distributed nationally via the networks is limited by such factors as variations in local tastes and demand for national advertising.

In creating networks, broadcasters formed entities that packaged programming and vertically integrated forward with local stations, or affiliates, that would air their programming. This vertical integration took essentially two forms: direct investment in local stations and vertical contracting. The networks have invested in stations, their O&O's, up to their legal limit. For the remainder of their national coverage, the networks rely on an affiliation agreement with local stations that stipulates the amount and terms of the programming that affiliates receive from the networks. Local stations not affiliating with networks buy programming directly from the syndication market and not through a network. While some of this programming is very popular, affiliated stations are generally more profitable than independents because they can take advantage of scale economies.

Local broadcast stations and networks have always invested upstream in program production. Broadcast networks have always produced their own national news, for example, in order to take advantage of the enormous scale economies of production and distribution.[6] Networks have also invested in sports production and entertainment program production. The rationale is to take advantage of their bottleneck position. Traditionally local stations and networks have held the precious time slots that programmers need to get their programs in front of viewers' eyes. They have wanted to use this bottleneck position to integrate backward into program production and take a share of the "back-end" profits—profits from the sale of programming into the syndication market.

The Prime-Time Access Rules, implemented in 1970, limited the hours that the networks could program on their affiliates and also limited the amount of programming that networks could own and sell in the syndication market. Until recently, the rules have curtailed integration between networks and program producers. Nevertheless, even limited integration has given networks cost information that could be used in negotiations with program producers.

On the cable side of the business, vertical integration dates back to the early years of cable growth in the 1970s.[7] The form that this integration has predominantly taken has been in investment in and ownership of content entities, programming and packaging, on the part of cable operators. The traditional explanation for the early investment was that cable operators were investing in new programming for cable television at a time when little was available and few entrepreneurs were willing to take the risk. In developing new programming, the cable operators were further differentiating their product from broadcast television; without new programming, cable operators could only offer subscribers improved reception. Since Chuck Dolan's pioneering experience with HBO, MSOs have funded numerous other early cable networks in order establish, or preserve, sources of programming.[8]

Investment by cable operators into programming has continued and is now widespread, but not ubiquitous (Exhibit 36). This investment has taken many forms, with no single overriding pattern: Single cable operators have ownership stakes in programmers of varying sizes; multiple cable operators share stakes of varying sizes.

There has also been some integration between networks and program production. One form of this integration is typified by those networks that produce live programming, like CNN, The Weather Channel, or QVC. However, there are also numerous examples of integrated networks and program production companies and film libraries. Of the top

Exhibit 36
Vertical Integration in the Cable Era, 1998

Cable Network (Top 20)	Subscribers (millions)	MSO with Ownership or Equity Interest
ESPN	71.0	None
CNN	71.0	Time Warner
TNT	70.5	Time Warner
TBS	69.9	Time Warner
C-SPAN	69.7	None*
Discovery	69.5	TCI, Newhouse, Cox, others
TNN: The Nashville Network	68.9	None
USA Network	67.7	TCI
Lifetime Television	67.0	None
The Family Channel	66.9	None
A&E	66.9	None
MTV	66.7	None
Nickelodeon/Nick at Nite	66.0	None
The Weather Channel	66.0	None
Headline News	64.2	Time Warner
American Movie Classics	61.5	Cablevision, TCI
CNBC	60.0	None
QVC	58.2	TCI, Comcast, others
VH1	56.3	None
The Learning Channel	55.0	TCI, Newhouse, Cox

*Cable operators provide 95 percent of funding but have no ownership or program control
    interests.

25 cable networks, USA Network, Nickelodeon, Nick at Nite, MTV, and VH1 are linked with Paramount; TBS, TNT, and TCM with Time Warner and with Turner's film libraries; BET with Time Warner; and, Comedy Central with Time Warner and Paramount.

Large investment by networks into film and television production companies is usually explained as an attempt to ensure access to programming and to gain bargaining power over programmers themselves. For example, HBO began to integrate backward into programming in the early 1980s because it needed a larger number of films than Hollywood was producing in order to fill out its schedule. In addition, it became evident that studios were going to try to counter HBO's large buying power by merger and forward integration.[9] By 1983, HBO had purchased part of Orion Pictures, joined with CBS and Columbia in forming Tri-Star Studios, and created Silver Screen Partners. In cases in which programmers have had the size and the inclination to invest forward into packaging, they have been denied entry into programming by the courts on antitrust grounds.[10]

The Pace of Integration Accelerates: The Emergence of the Content/Conduit Combine

The stately historical pace of integration has given way to a feeding frenzy and the emergence of the giant content/conduit combine. Why? Add the Great Value Shift, deregulation, and a strong dose of me-too jealousy to the existing economic motives and a powerful brew is concocted that even the most disciplined managers and boards will have a hard time moderating.

The Digital Era has created tremendous strategic uncertainty for firms throughout the product production and distribution process. Illustrating this uncertainty are the following statements from top executives of two of the top five cable MSOs:

Executive One: I don't think it makes as much sense for us to invest in programming if it's not exclusive. . . .

Executive Two: Nonsense. For years we've invested in programming that's been available to dish owners and the like. The bigger issue is channel capacity, and whether the tiering situation will allow these new services to be economically viable even with ads.[11]

The sexy response by firms in our industry to this new environment has been to vertically integrate, to build the content/conduit combine. Actions by a few firms have had the effect of initiating further moves by other firms as a bandwagon effect is created. Firms want to integrate so as not to be left without a source of supply during a period of perceived shortages.

Deregulation came to the broadcasters in the mid-1990s: the Prime-Time Access Rules ended in November 1995, and the 12-12-12 Rule was extended to 35 percent with the 1996 Telecommunications Act. These dramatic announcements combined with the more subtle technological changes of the digital age to set off a scramble for vertical partners. Program producers Warner and Paramount began efforts in early 1995 to follow Fox and launch broadcast networks that would be integrated with their production companies. The traditional broadcast networks are integrating backward and owning programming as they once did before the rules were imposed in the early 1970s: ABC/Capital Cities initiated several new ventures into program production, for example, with Brillstein-Grey Entertainment and with Dreamworks, before capping them off with the massive sale to Disney in July of 1995.[12] Evidence of just how far the networks are willing to go to become program producers is seen as programming produced by one network is being increasingly seen on a rival network.[13] Not to be left out, groups of local stations are involved in efforts to build networks—Barry Diller, for example—or to buy them—Westinghouse and its CBS purchase.

Activity has not been confined to the broadcast segment. Cable players and telephone companies are also pursuing strategies of integration. Cable operators seem to be divided between investing further in programming and remaining with the status quo. One large player continuing its strategy of backward integration is TCI and its plan for Your Choice Television, a service that offers existing programming taped and transmitted at any time requested by the subscriber. However, the spectacular announcement of Time Warner's investment in Turner Broadcasting topped everything to create a truly massive media company and content/conduit combine. Time Warner already was a content/conduit combine with massive cable plant holdings, a cable network, and program production capabilities. However, the addition of Turner Broadcasting builds up the content side to match the conduit properties.

The telephone companies, in anticipation of their entry into the television business as authorized by the 1996 Telecommunications Act, also integrated backward to form their own version of content/conduit combines. So far, because of the attention that the telephone companies have placed on the coming onslaught of competition in the long-distance and local telephone markets, these ventures have not enjoyed success. They do illustrate the allure of the content/conduit combine. Bell Atlantic, Nynex, and Pacific Telesis formed an alliance to create Tele-TV. This venture had the added feature of using Michael Ovitz of Creative Artists Agency (CAA) in order to bypass traditional program producers and networks and sign up content creators directly. The contract with Ovitz was canceled upon his decision to join Disney, but he was replaced with Robert Kavner and another top CAA executive. The investment by Bell South, Southwestern Bell, Ameritech, and Disney in a new entity, Americast—an investment that Disney is unlikely to remain involved with—was made to do the same thing. While these efforts have so far been unspectacular, the telephone companies often resemble the tortoise in a long race.

The content/conduit combine vision is not confined to the Bell Operating Companies. MCI, the long-distance company, announced in November 1996 the acquisition of a 25 percent stake in News Corporation, the owner of Fox, several DBS ventures, and other publishing operations.

The new entities being formed dwarf any previous efforts of television companies to integrate. They are massive companies with global reach and operations in every aspect of the television production and distribution. They were often expensive to assemble and they are unruly to manage.

What is driving this new round of integration? The logic of the content/conduit combine, once again, is an artifact of the Broadcast and

Cable eras. Unlike the telephone companies, cable operators were not regulated as "common carriers." They were allowed to control what got transmitted on their system and did not have to provide others a right-of-way. Without this burden, the cable companies were free to become gatekeepers, investing in and controlling content on their systems. The hope is that in the Digital Era this winning formula can be recreated.

When one examines the arguments put forth in favor of vertical integration, they are essentially new versions of the same motives previously described above plus a good dose of egoism. Industry players and observers often mention the efficiency argument. The move by programming entities into retailing and merchandising has created a new type of potential efficiency gain. For example, Time Warner argued that its merger with Turner would allow it to boost retail revenues from its cartoon characters by better coordinating its program distribution strategy with its retailing strategy.[14] Another newfangled efficiency gain under discussion comes from recycling content into new delivery forms like CD-ROMs.[15]

While these gains may sound attractive, their size and scope are yet to be determined. Nevertheless, it is hard to believe that efficiency gains could be driving the massive wave of vertical integration that is occurring now. The motivating force is more likely strategic benefits.

The logic on the part of distributors and packagers is to secure access to programming since it is the only way they can ensure that their product is differentiated from their competitors. Extensions of this argument include the use of programming to create new networks that take up valuable shelf space[16] and the creation of networks that can be used to cross-promote programming.[17]

On the other hand, the logic on the part of upstream producers is to secure access to packagers and distribution. As a few firms integrate, the non-integrated portion of the market becomes smaller. Non-integrated firms have become concerned that integrated firms will use control of their bottleneck to squeeze them. It is not surprising that we are observing a scramble for producers, packagers, and large stations.

These two rationales driving the process represent totally divergent views of what is the bottleneck, or critical resource, in the production, packaging, and distribution process. Both cannot be correct. If content is the scarce resource and conduit plentiful, then it makes sense for distributors to scramble for content and for content companies to desire independence and to distribute via as many conduits as possible. If, on the other hand, the conduit is the bottleneck, distributors have no need to seek out producers for special arrangements; the burden is on content to get distribution.

It should be clear by now that the Great Value Shift is characterized by overcapacity in distribution. Distribution will cease being a bottleneck once the barriers to entry are reduced, new distributors emerge, and the capacity of each distributor is expanded. What is worse for the distributors is that with their technology becoming more and more alike, the only way that they will be able to truly distinguish their product from any of their competitors is with programming.

Therefore, distributors will have a strong strategic imperative to secure content, particularly content that is unique and not easily replicated. Content companies have an equally strong strategic imperative to resist overtures from distributors unless the compensation they receive from a tie with a single distributor outweighs the profits that they could earn from the wider coverage brought by relationships with multiple distributors. In other words, there is no reason why a content company should rush into an agreement with a distributor when overcapacity in distribution provides ample opportunity for good content to make its way to viewers.

The rationale is clear from the perspective of companies in the business of providing conduit, like the Bell Operating Companies, MCI, and the cable operators. Their attempts to secure content make strategic sense, but is this enough to justify their massive investments? Likely not.

To start with, the regulators may not allow this strategy to be implemented. Currently, programming owned by certain vertically integrated distributors, vertically integrated cable MSOs, and Regional Bell Operating Companies (RBOCs) must be sold to competitive distributors. Should such rules be extended to all distributors, securing access to programming will not give exclusivity.

But, even if the vertical integration strategy is allowed by regulators, it will not be easy to implement. Marriages between content and conduit are notoriously difficult. Content companies are creative, people-based entities while conduit companies are technology based. Putting them both together in one firm requires unusual management skill. As Sony and Matsushita have found in their experiences with Columbia and MCA, Hollywood has a long history of making money at the expense of owners, who never see a positive return on their investment.

Finally, buying content companies is not cheap. When assets are purchased at a premium, it is that much harder to achieve any synergies or strategic benefits from them. The reason for high prices is that content is the scarce resource: from their perspective, there is no strategic rationale for integrating forward into the conduit business. To do so would be the equivalent of a book publisher buying a book retailer and selling his books through that retailer and not other competing retailers. In a world in which bookstores are plentiful and book buyers shop everywhere looking for their titles, it would make no sense for a particular book to be sold in only one bookstore. Rather, the publisher would want to be in as many stores as possible. The same logic can be applied to content providers in the television business: they should want to be distributed to viewers via local stations, cable, DBS, the telephone companies, and any other distribution channel that emerges.

The premium that is required to buy content companies is hefty. Since content firms give up wide distribution when they agree to be distributed through a single channel, they must be compensated for this exclusive arrangement. MCI paid a significant premium for a non-controlling stake in News Corporation, as did Time Warner in its purchase of Turner Broadcasting. These deals were not cheap, and it is not yet clear that they will ever earn a return.

Vertical integration is not the answer for conduit firms. Even if exclusive use of content is allowed by the regulators, marriages of content and conduit are extremely difficult to manage, particularly given the premiums that content companies require. For content companies, there can be financial rewards of selling out to distributors forming content/conduit combines, but there is no strategic imperative for them to do so. In alliances with distribution, content companies limit their audience and burden their creative processes with unskilled management.

We have not addressed in this discussion the more narrow issue of program production integration with networks. Some of the most significant moves have been between producers of programming and networks: Disney and ABC/Capital Cities and the new broadcast network phenomenon, Fox, Warner Brothers, Paramount, and Barry Diller.

Strictly speaking, these moves constitute integration within the content portion of the supply chain and not between content and conduit. Nevertheless, they are important in the effort to create value in the Digital Era. To address this and other strategies, our analysis must now turn to content itself and the optimal strategies in the Digital Era.

NOTES

1. Robert D. Hof, "Digital TV: What Will It Be?" *Business Week*, 21 April 1997, p. 34.

2. This literature follows from the work of Ronald H. Coase. See Ronald H. Coase, "The Nature of the Firm," *Economica* 4 (1937): 386; Oliver E. Williamson, "The Vertical Integration of Production: Market Failure Considerations," *American Economic Review* 61 (1971): 112; and Oliver E. Williamson, "Transaction Cost Economics: Their Governance of Contractual Relations," *Journal of Law and Economics* 22 (1979): 223.

3. See Joseph J. Spengler, "Vertical Integration and Anti-trust Policy," *Journal of Political Economy* 58 (1950): 347; and Fritz Machlup and M. Taber, "Bilateral Monopoly, Successive Monopoly, and Vertical Integration," *Economica* 27 (1960): 101–123, for a discussion of this dilemma.

4. Walter Adams and Joel Dirlam, "Steel Imports and Vertical Oligopoly

Power," *American Economic Review* 14 (September 1964): 626–655; Alfred Kahn, *The Economics of Regulation*, Vol. 2 (New York: Wiley, 1971).

5. The 1992 reregulation prevents MSOs from withholding programming from their competitors—the Cable Act requires any cable system controlling programming sources to license such programming for a reasonable fee, and on a nondiscriminatory basis, to all buyers, even direct competitors.

6. This is discussed in the chapter on programming.

7. For two good discussions of the history of vertical integration in the cable industry, see Benjamin Klein, "The Competitive Consequences of Vertical Integration in the Cable Industry," paper prepared for the National Cable Television Association, University of California, Los Angeles, 1989; David H. Waterman and Andrew A. Weiss, "Vertical Integration in Cable Television," paper prepared for the American Enterprise Institute for Public Policy Research, Washington, D.C., 17 September 1993.

8. C-Span, Turner's debt bailout, the Discovery channel, for example, in Klein, "Competitive Consequences," pp. 7–10.

9. George Mair, *Inside HBO: The Billion Dollar War between HBO, Hollywood, and the Home Video Revolution* (New York: Macmillan, 1988), p. 73.

10. Premiere and Showtime/The Movie Channel.

11. Michael Burgi and Chuck Ross, "New Cable Nets in Abundance," *Inside Media*, 2 December 1994, p. 28.

12. The merger has endangered, although not completely ended, the relationship with Dreamworks. This relationship may go on in modified form, according to an article entitled "Capital Cities/ABC and Henson Form Family TV Venture," by Elisabeth Jensen in *The Wall Street Journal*, 27 October 1995.

13. *Caroline in the City*, produced by CBS and aired on NBC, and *News Radio*, produced by ABC and Brillstein-Grey Entertainment and aired on NBC.

14. Elizabeth Jensen, " 'What's Up, Doc?' Vertical Integration," *Wall Street Journal*, 16 October 1995.

15. Rita Koselka, "Mergermania in Medialand," *Forbes*, 23 October 1995.

16. Tom Wolzein and John Penney, "Vertical Integration of Media Companies Essential in the Late 1990s," report for Bernstein Research, New York, 1995.

17. Koselka, "Mergermania in Medialand."

Chapter 5

Digital Branding

If the set-top box bottleneck and content/conduit combine strategies are quixotic, what is the winning strategy for the Digital Era? Since distribution is coming to resemble a commodity product, will it be possible to win with content in the Digital Era?

Life for content companies is getting more complicated. Creators and producers correspond roughly to their antecedents in the Broadcast and Cable eras. However, in the Digital Era, television networks may have digital equivalents like program packagers, portals, and intelligent agents. All of these digital creations share the goal of organizing content for the consumer. In the Digital Era, a content provider can choose to compete as a creator, a producer, or a digital organizer of content. Where should the aspiring content provider play?

The trick is to look for the bottleneck—that part of the supply chain that will have the fewest players and the most critical role for users. Since many of the key trends in the industry were already observable during the Cable Era, it is useful to recall that in that era content creators and networks were the bottleneck. They made large profits while program producers were part of an intensely competitive segment garnering smaller profits.

In the Digital Era, these trends will continue: creators will become ever scarcer and more valuable; producers will eke out a living in a crowded, competitive, and unpredictable marketplace; and the Digital Era aggregator and integrator of content will have the opportunity to remain a bottleneck, a valued resource for consumers and quite profitable at the same time.

This function will be important in the Digital Era because users need a filter, or an integrator of content. They will have too little time and patience to do it for themselves. Although the definition of content creators will remain straightforward, the ultimate filter is ambiguous. There are two fundamental visions for the digital filter: the packager or the agent. In the first vision a third party does the job, and in the second vision the user's own intelligent software takes care of organizing and selecting content. What will the winning filter or organizer be? A packager or the intelligent agent?

The winner will be the packager if it can succeed in becoming a "digital brand," the Digital Era equivalent of the broadcast or cable network. Most users will opt for the digital brand of their choice over an agent to select content. Despite the delight that the technology of agents and their many uses brings to the digerati, agents will not be the tool of choice for the average couch potato. Viewers will rely on brands for video content because they trust them, understand them, and like them. Brands will succeed over agents because they can exploit scale economies in production and attract the advertising dollars of Madison Avenue. The companies that succeed will be the ones that rapidly create the strongest brands. Because there will only be room for a handful, the strongest brands will be in a position to dominate viewing and reap financial rewards.

INTRODUCTION: SPORTS

The best way to introduce the concept of winners and losers in the content game is through an example. One of the best examples to study is sports. Sports has already aroused intense interest on the part of competing distributors, networks, and producers as attractive content for viewers and advertisers. Therefore, it provides an early example of what parts of the Digital Era supply chain are likely to emerge as profitable.

In the supply chain of sports programming, the content creators are the sports leagues and the athletes themselves. Understanding the balance of power between them is complicated by many peculiarities—free agency rules and the draft process—of the leagues themselves. As there are very few independent sports producers, most producers and packagers are the networks. As always, the networks use local stations, cable, and other means for distribution.

During the Broadcast Era and in the beginning of the Cable Era, national sports coverage was dominated by the broadcast networks. They split the rights to major sporting events among themselves, paying leagues fees for these rights. The leagues welcomed these rights fees, but did not depend on them. Most teams were owned by individuals who had many other reasons to own teams besides the bottom line. The owners made money on their franchises, but average operating profits were not significant.[1]

While better paid than during the pre-television days of Babe Ruth and Joe DiMaggio, athletes were not highly paid stars. Average salaries in 1970 in the four major sports ranged from a low of $44,205 in hockey to a high of $67,705 in basketball.[2] Compare this to the $15,000 to $20,000 that an engineer earned at that time or the $7,000 that the average production worker in manufacturing took home. Part of the reason for these modest pay levels was that owners maintained strong bargaining power through cartel arrangements like closed leagues, player drafts, and the reserve system. Nevertheless, even in 1980 at the beginning of the Cable Era, when players had won a system of free agency and used it to push up compensation, salaries were still relatively low. Pete Rose, one of the greatest baseball stars of his era, still earned well under a million dollars in 1980, and the average salary for the entire team was $200,000, or thirteen times what the average production worker in manufacturing earned.

As the Cable Era progressed, USSB, ESPN and other cable networks, and the Fox network became interested in sports as an engine to drive growth in viewers and subscribers. They reasoned that sports attracted avid viewer interest and an established advertiser base. Popular sports programming could give them guaranteed viewers that could be converted into audiences for other programming. In the case of ESPN, an entire network could be built around sports and, for USSB, a new satellite-based delivery system could use sports to compete against cable.

In the Cable Era, networks started to bid for the most attractive sports and pay for expanded sporting events that might not have been on television before. Prices for the rights to the Olympic Games shot up with each successive Olympiad. Rights to the four major league sports in the United States—football, baseball, basketball, and hockey—also skyrocketed, increasing by 142 percent in the ten years between 1986 and 1996 (Exhibit 37). By the mid-1990s, spending on sports rights totaled about $2 billion per year and accounted for about 15 percent of all television spending.[3] Who were the beneficiaries of this feeding frenzy?

The beneficiaries were the ultimate creators of content, the star athletes themselves. Athletes are no longer simply decently paid. Stars like Michael Jordan, Evander Holyfield, Tiger Woods, Shaquille O'Neal, and Pete Sampras have joined the ranks of the superrich. We all have heard about the elite players earning multimillion-dollar, multiyear deals that, in turn, lead to even more lucrative sponsorships, but the amounts are staggering. They have increased dramatically in only the last several years (Exhibit 38). These deals have driven up average player costs across all four major U.S. sports leagues. With the average salary in 1995 in the NBA at $2 million, in the NFL at $1 million, in Major League

Exhibit 37
Escalation of National Sports Rights, 1986–1996, in $ Millions

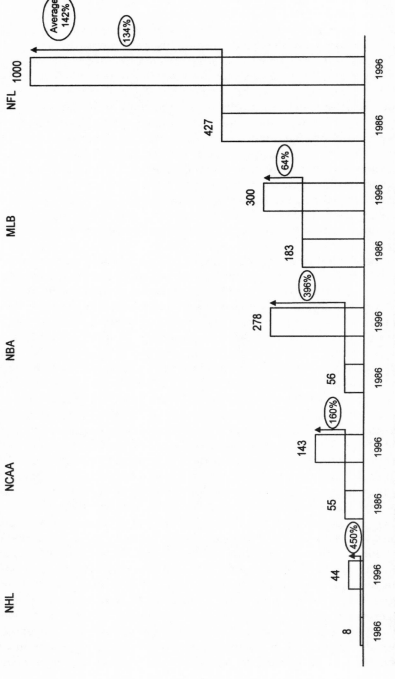

Source: Paul Kagan Associates, *The Economics of TV Programming and Syndication* (Carmel, CA: Paul Kagan Associates, 1996), p. 69. Reproduced with permission.

Exhibit 38
Compensation of Top Athletes

COMPENSATION OF THE TOP 20 ATHLETES, 1996

ATHLETE	SPORT	COMPENSATION ($M)
Mike Tyson	Boxing	75.0
Michael Jordan	Basketball	52.6
Michael Schumacher	Auto Racing	33.0
Shaquille O'Neal	Basketball	24.4
Emmitt Smith	Football	16.5
Evander Holyfield	Boxing	15.5
Andre Agassi	Tennis	15.2
Arnold Palmer	Golf	15.1
Dennis Rodman	Basketball	12.9
Patrick Ewing	Basketball	12.9
Cal Ripken, Jr.	Baseball	12.0
Roy Jones, Jr.	Boxing	12.0
Dan Marino	Football	11.7
Wayne Gretzky	Hockey	11.5
Riddick Bowe	Boxing	11.5
Pete Sampras	Tennis	11.3
Oscar de la Hoya	Boxing	11.3
Grant Hill	Basketball	10.8
Ken Griffey, Jr.	Baseball	10.8
Dale Earnhardt	Auto Racing	10.5

AVERAGE TOP 20 ATHLETE COMPENSATION, 1990-96
$ Millions

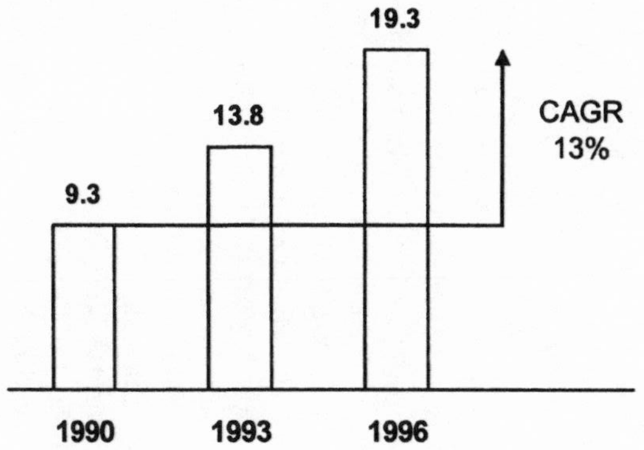

CAGR 13%

1990	1993	1996
9.3	13.8	19.3

Sources: Derived from information in Forbes, "The Top 40," 16 December 1996, pp. 244–259; Forbes, "The Top 40," 19 December 1994, pp. 266–278.

Baseball at $1.3 million, and in the NHL at $500,000, the multiple of these salaries over the wage of the average production worker in manufacturing grew from 8 in 1970 to 44 by 1995.[4]

Even more interesting is the fact that player costs have closely tracked the increase in team revenues (Exhibit 39).[5] The role of sports team owners begins to look like that of the producers for drama and comedy programming. They may be fabulously wealthy, but they are not a scarce resource; they merely assemble the talent necessary to put on a sporting event. It is not surprising that the owners of the leagues, as "assemblers," have given away almost all of their new revenues to the athletes while their own net income margin has remained stagnant (Exhibit 40).

However, the networks cannot be called losers. Clearly they have not experienced the phenomenal increase in their value that the players have, but neither have they simply been sucked dry by their aggressive bidding for sports rights. Networks have been able to extract much of the direct costs of their bidding frenzy from advertisers. Advertisers appreciate the large, predictable, and demographically strong audiences that sports can draw in an era of otherwise fragmenting viewing. As a result, network sports advertising revenue shot up by 76 percent from 1986 to 1995.[6] As advertiser appetite for network sports inevitably weakens, the networks have begun to revolutionize the network-affiliate relationship by turning to their affiliates to chip in dollars for sports programming.

The idea behind such strong interest in sports is the possibility of networks using sports to build their audience and establish their brand. Two cases are instructive.

ESPN has used sports to establish a highly profitable branded cable network. They have used expensive mainstream sports and inexpensive fringe sports to become the dominant all-sports network and are carried on virtually every cable system. Now owned by Disney, they have extended their brand to a second sports network, ESPN II, and a 24-hour sports news channel, ESPNEWS, and are even planning to launch another channel devoted to a single sport. Critics argue that ESPN's success will doom it to failure by drawing in too many competing networks. Clearly, other sports networks have emerged, but most are niche channels, like the Golf Channel, Classic Sports Network, and local or regional sports networks. ESPN has created a powerful brand that is carried on systems around the country and is considered a "must-have" for any alternative distributor.

A second case is Rupert Murdoch's Fox Network. Trying to establish itself as the fourth broadcast network, Fox was desperate for compelling programming that would draw viewers, advertisers, and affiliates. One place that it found such programming was sports. In dramatic fashion, Fox purchased the rights to a conference of the National Football League (NFL) for $1.58 billion for four years, outbidding longtime owner CBS

Exhibit 39
Revenues and Player Costs in Major League Sports,* Per Club Averages, 1992–1996

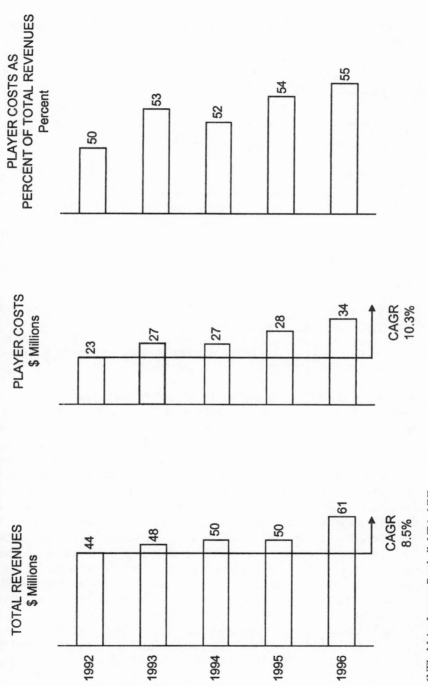

*NFL, Major League Baseball, NBA, NHL.
Sources: Derived from information in *Financial World*, 9 July 1991, pp. 28–43; 7 July 1992, pp. 34–51; 25 May 1993, pp. 26–31; 10 May 1994, pp. 50–64; 9 May 1995, pp. 42–68; and 17 June 1997, pp. 40–59.

Exhibit 40
Operating Income Margin in Major League Sports,* Per Club Average, in Percentage

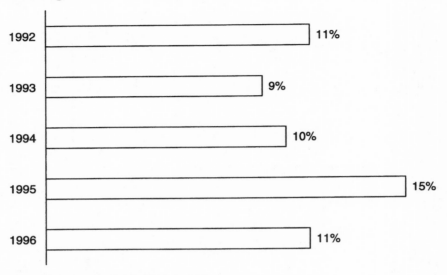

*NFL, Major League Baseball, NBA, NHL.
Sources: Derived from information in *Financial World*, 9 July 1991, pp. 28–43; 7 July 1992, pp. 34–51; 25 May 1993, pp. 26–31; 10 May 1994, pp. 50–64; 9 May 1995, pp. 42–68; and 17 June 1997, pp. 40–59.

and paying over $700 million above what NBC paid for the other NFL conference. The move had its doubters at the time of purchase, but is now regarded as a smart move that helped Fox build its brand among viewers, promote its other programming, devastate counterprogramming on other rival networks, and attract and retain affiliate stations.

This pattern is being repeated in Europe and the rest of the world. Privately owned channels have used sports to attract viewers away from the dominant state-owned television companies. The strategy was used first in France by Canal Plus in the mid-1980s when it outbid the national television channel for the rights for soccer games. Now, in the Digital Era, the stakes have been raised. In Holland in 1997, a new channel, Sport7, has agreed to pay $648 million for soccer, or six times what the previous broadcaster has paid; in Spain, television rights sold for $272 million, or 5.5 times; and, in Britain, $955 million, or four times. As in the United States, salaries for star players have spiked up with the increase in team revenues. Players in Europe, now free to sell their services to the highest bidder after the "Bosman ruling," are taking much of the bonanza with them.[7] The pattern will continue with cricket in India and badminton in China.

The point of this example is to illustrate the changing flow of profits in the television business. Packagers, like sports networks, bid aggressively for content in their effort to build brands that viewers grow familiar with and turn to by habit. Most of the acquisition money goes through the hands of producers into the pockets of content creators, who grow rich beyond the wildest expectations of their predecessors.[8]

The distribution bottleneck is broken, and owners of distribution have little way to differentiate their products. Distributors have no choice but to pay higher prices for carriage to the networks for their brands. Occasionally, a distributor will try to acquire key content rights as Rupert Murdoch did in the United Kingdom when he won the rights to the English Premier League. These moves certainly enrich content creators, but they do not create brands. Sometimes there are legal blocks: In the United States, as has been pointed out, cable companies cannot withhold programming from other distributors. But, most often, the distributor is unable to leverage the content into brand loyalty. If it takes work to get viewers to care about a network, it is almost impossible to get them to care about a distribution channel.

As we move into the Digital Era, we will see this pattern continuing. Some packagers will use expensive programming to create brands. These brands will survive the challenge of intelligent agents and niche programmers to dominate viewing. Despite paying higher prices for programming, their brands will enable them to earn respectable profits. Content creators, ever more valuable to packagers in their struggle, will see their compensation soar.

THE UPSIDE-DOWN BOTTLE

The Digital Era will richly reward those of us who can throw a fastball at 100 miles an hour or tell a funny joke. Not many of us have this gift. Those who do have found that their rare talent is no longer the stuff of family lore: it is big business.

These individuals, the content creators, are the essence of any successful entertainment program. Since the show usually will not go on without them, they are learning how to suck any dollars they can out of business of television. The dramatic increase in compensation toward the end of the Cable Era was only the precursor of what is to come in the Digital Era. In the new era, content creators will amass great fortunes. The money will come from two sources: increasing competition between distributors and packagers for talent and the windfall from new windows through which content can reach viewers.

Take television star Bill Cosby. When Cosby recently announced his intention to air a new program, networks aggressively bid for it. CBS, desperate to turn around its ratings slide, won the series by granting

Cosby an unusually lucrative deal that included a guarantee for a two-year run, or a guarantee of 31 episodes more than the standard.[9] Or consider the supporting cast of *Seinfeld*. In a classic case of the lifecycle of television show economics, the supporting cast of the show, now famous because of the show's popularity, demanded a dramatic and unprecedented increase in their compensation. The phenomenon can be seen in the movie industry as stars now ask for and get multimillion-dollar contracts that allow them to share in all ancillary revenue sources of the film.

In these Digital Era deals, the bottle has been turned upside down: the content creators, the first stage in the supply chain, are the scarce resource. Networks or their descendants will not be able to rein in the spectacle of production. Spending on programming will go higher and higher. This will benefit content creators, especially those lucky enough to be the subject of bidding wars between rival networks not creative enough to imagine what they would do without an established star.

However, content creators cannot get too greedy. Not all competition for viewers in the Digital Era will be good for content creators. Sometimes the best way to get viewers and make money at the same time will be to introduce something completely new or to target a narrow niche. New networks or producers that are daring and creative will not have to compete with others for the services of well-paid content creators. ESPN's X Games, for example, are a showcase for athletes in unusual sports. The athletes are unappreciated distance runners and daredevil skiers who do not compete for compensation with the likes of a Tiger Woods.

Any would-be actor trying to cash in on the Digital Era also has to remember that not all labor that is needed to create content will be rewarded with million-dollar contracts. Since it is sexier to work in Hollywood than in Hartford, most actors, writers, and directors, not to mention hairdressers, makeup artists, or set designers, will be in chronic oversupply. Competing for fewer jobs than they number, they will remain modestly paid.

But, there never has been nor ever will be a glut of content creators that can attract and retain an audience. The bigger audience they draw and the more reliably they draw it, the more lavish their rewards will be. That was one of the first rules of the Cable Era, and it will continue into the Digital Era.

THE PROBLEM OF PRODUCTION, PART II

Program production is much easier than throwing that 100-mph fastball. Ask anyone with a video camera and access to the Web. Program production in the Digital Era will continue to be plagued with too many producers, using too cheap equipment, with too few new ideas. The profits of the Great Value Shift will flow through the production stage without stopping.

If content is king, how can this be true? Isn't demand expected to grow? Won't this benefit producers? Haven't savvy media empires paid hefty prices for libraries of produced product?

All of this is clearly true. The commoditization of distribution means growth in demand for programs. Growth may be slow at first, since new distributors will fill their limited bandwidth with established networks—networks that already have enough programming to fill their schedules. DirecTV easily filled its 150 channels with the big cable networks and some movies and sports. However, as bandwidth expands, new players will enter. As they face the task of filling a schedule, the rush for programming will intensify.

If these new players base their schedules on existing product, the programmers are in luck. Producers of old movies or situation comedies could count on a windfall from new buyers for their programs. As technology advances, even more distribution windows will become available to program producers. Just as cable networks like Nick at Nite or TNT paid unanticipated sums to the owners of the libraries that held nearly forgotten programs like *Mannix* and *Gilligan's Island*, new distribution channels like the CD-ROM and the Web will create additional windows for programmers in the Digital Era. Clearly, programmers will benefit from these windows—just as owners of film libraries profited from the videocassette recorder and cable television and owners of music libraries from the audio compact disc.

Unfortunately for program producers, new demand will not be the answer to chronic lack of profitability. The problem is that there will always be new production companies willing to enter the business to meet any new demand. In fact, there may even be more new players than ever. Technology improvements will allow "mom and pop" producers to tape programming with little more than a video camera. The emergence of distribution alternatives like the Web, in which access is not restricted, will allow these tiny producers to transmit their programming to anyone who wants to see it. The other big problem of production will not disappear either. It will never become easier to predict consumer tastes. Nor will it be easy to keep revenues out of the bank accounts of the key content creators.

What about the windfall from new windows? Won't that be enough to end the problem of production? No. The windfall will go to owners of already produced programming, not to the production industry as a whole, because the phenomenon of windowing also affects the budgets of program producers. Once the potential of a new window is known and anticipated, content creators demand more and program producers figure the extra revenue into their calculations of total revenue and plan budgets accordingly. As soon as cable became a window for films, the average film's budget increased accordingly.[10] For the program production business as a whole, the emergence of a new window will be a wash: Increases in revenues will be offset by increases in costs, and profitability will remain unchanged.

INFORMATION OVERFLOW: THE CASE FOR A FILTER

One of the myths of the Digital Era is that the packaging function will disappear. Cyberpundits argue that the Internet is the great enabler; that it will do away with the usurious media middleman and allow individuals to access whatever information, entertainment, and software that they desire. Without pausing for air, they add that the content production gates will no longer be controlled. Anyone will be able to make content and get distribution, from Warner Brothers to the local kindergarten class. The problem is that the first part of this utopian vision and the second part contradict themselves. It is impossible to do away with middlemen at the same time as content choices are exploding. The reason is that viewers have only so much time and so much patience to deal with media choices. When choices become too numerous, people will gladly use, and even pay for, a middleman.

Clearly the Digital Era has seen an incredible surge in available content. We saw the increase in both broadcast and cable networks in the Cable Era, but this growth is insignificant when compared to the Internet. With a new Web page coming on-line every minute, the content surge on the Internet is mind-boggling (Exhibit 41).

The expanding universe of content is not in dispute. The question is, how will users find the content that they are interested in consuming? Users need some sort of filtering mechanism. Choice in media products becomes overwhelming for two reasons: limited time and limited patience.

Media use is a leisure-time activity. It has to be consumed when we are not working or sleeping. This caps media use at about eight hours per day during the week and sixteen hours per day on the weekends. Studies of media use show that media use is somewhere in the vicinity of nine or ten hours per day, with television taking about one-half of the total time (Exhibit 42).[11] It sounds higher than it actually is because people use media while doing other things, like driving and listening to the radio, and use several media simultaneously. These studies also show that media use in general, and television use in particular, has remained relatively constant throughout the 1980s and 1990s despite the introduction of new media technologies like the VCR, when viewing took a slight and temporary dip.[12]

Exhibit 41
Growth in Internet Domains, in Thousands of Domains*

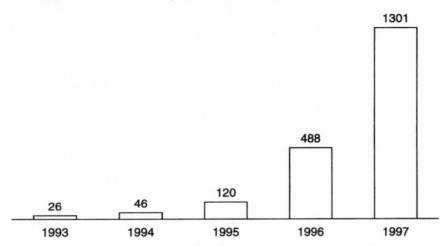

*A domain name is any name representing any record that exists in the Domain name
  system (i.e., com, nw.com, www.nw.com/).
Source: Network Wizards (http://www.nw.com/). Reproduced with permission.

Media consumption falls below its cap since most of us have non-media
leisure time activities, like seeing family and friends or hobbies. It is
actually quite astonishing that media use is as high as it is. With media
use this high already, it is understandable that people simply cannot
afford to take the extra time it takes to select content themselves from the
rapidly expanding content universe. If they were going to take more time
with media, it would probably be spent not in the selection process, but
in consumption. People generally do not seem to have enough time to
want to spend it mulling over choices. The pattern can be clearly seen in
shopping for groceries. The days of going to the market, looking for the
freshest goods, and haggling with the merchant over price are gone. The
magazine *Progressive Grocer* found that the average shopper spends less
than twelve seconds in a product area before making a decision, and 42
percent actually spend five seconds or less making their decision.[13]
   Even if people wanted to give up sleep or their family and friends and
if they thought that picking programs might be fun, they would quickly
give up such notions about content selection in the Digital Era. If they
tried it, they would quickly come up against the frustration threshold.
   Searching through endless programs may be enjoyable for a few people, the cultural anthropologist or the procrastinating student. But, for
most of us, it is a frustrating drain of energy. If all of the programming
in Satellite TV week is considered, about 3,700 programs are available in

Exhibit 42
Media Usage Patterns

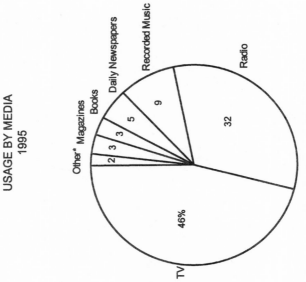

USAGE BY MEDIA
1995

Other* Magazines
Books
Daily Newspapers
Recorded Music
Radio

2 3 3
5
9
32

46%

TV

TOTAL MEDIA USAGE
hours per day

1990	1991	1992	1993	1994	1995
9.0	8.9	9.1	9.0	9.3	9.3

*Includes Home Video, Theatrical Films, Home Video Games, Internet, and Educational Software.
Source: Veronis, Suhler, and Associates, *Communications Industry Report* (New York: Veronis, Suhler, and Associates, Inc., 1998). Reproduced with permission.

a single day.[14] Even the 50 television channels available on most cable systems at any one time is too much for most viewers who, even with a remote control, tend to watch only about seven or eight channels.

The Digital Era will be as far from the Cable Era as the Cable Era was from the Broadcast Era. The World Wide Web can again serve as our model. As anyone who has tried to find something on the Web knows, you cannot simply flip through a few channels until you come to what you are looking for. The answer was supposedly search engines, those database software programs that scour servers on the Web to answer your query. The problem with them seems to be that they do a bit too much scouring. What good does 100,000 hits for "spy classic," or even 20,000 hits for something more specific like "Middlemarch," do at 8:00 P.M. for the worn-out user looking for something to do that night?

Although more technologically savvy than the general public, the latest wave of users of the Internet are not the wizards that the first wave of "initial adopters" were. For them, the Internet experience is proving to be a frustrating one. The latest study on this by Yankelovich Partners reports that many of them are dissatisfied. In fact, users are spending less time using the Web: the average number of hours spent on-line decreased in 1996 from 1995.

Of course, part of the reason lies in the speed of most people's connections to the Internet: people get bored waiting for text and images, not to mention audio and video, to download. Part of the reason also has to be the amazing difficulty in finding good content—especially when you do not know exactly what you are looking for. A search for information about wine might take you to an advertising site for a vineyard, the home page of an oenophile in Schenectady, and a tome about new techniques in cultivating the pesky Pinot Noir grape before it takes you to a decent e-zine about wine. For new users of the Web this may sound like fun, but for a weary couple trying to get an hour of relaxation in after putting the kids to sleep and before going to bed, it is alarmingly close to work.

Even if you do succeed in finding the wine magazine and bookmark it for future reference, you would have to repeat the process again and again to fill out a week's schedule of content. What's more, you could not rest on your first week's work. You would have to continue to search to keep up with noteworthy new content as it becomes available—all the while hoping that your "teleputer" does not crash, losing all of your bookmarks with it.

Since there will be too much content for users to simply do the digital equivalent of channel grazing themselves, only two choices remain. The first is that viewers can harness the increasing computer power at their disposal and "pull" interesting content. They could employ the technological descendants of search engines, intelligent agents, to find and organize an evening's entertainment. Viewers also can continue to have content "pushed" to them; they can turn to digital brands.

THE OPTION OF AGENTS

If the Digital Era makes content available in overwhelming quantities, will it also provide users with tools necessary to sort through this content themselves? Some would argue yes without hesitation. They would describe a vision in which holographic images of English butlers appear on your screen and present you with an evening's viewing on your favorite topics, with your favorite stars, at whatever time you please.

What they are describing are intelligent software agents. What are agents? Software agents are programs that perform tasks for users. The difference between agents and the software programs that we are familiar with today is that agent software does not require users to constantly tell it what to do.

Today's computers run on software that responds to a set of standardized commands that are given by users. I want to read a message from a friend; I key in "check mail" followed by "open letter" and then read my message.

Agents are programs that perform tasks autonomously. With instructions received up-front, agents can, in theory, do anything from monitor incoming mail and retrieve information to organize an agenda and select entertainment.

Agents are already advanced in performing rote functions like e-mail applications. Let us consider something more sophisticated like entertainment selection and its impact on the television industry. Could an autonomous software agent select entertainment for a user, put together this selection into an enjoyable evening's schedule, insert advertising targeted to the particular viewer, and make it available whenever the user wanted it? Would the whole process be easier for the user—not to mention more enjoyable—than the alternative of the user simply choosing a channel or two and seeing what is being presented that evening?

In theory, the answer is yes. There are several ways such an agent might work. The agent could be programmed by the user with specific instructions like "select the hometown team's football matches whenever available." Agents also are being developed that use more sophisticated methods. Such methods include agents being programmed to observe and imitate the user's own selections and agents that are capable of receiving positive and negative feedback from users. Such agents could over time improve their ability to serve as entertainment selectors for users.

One other technique that is under development for entertainment selection agents is called "social filtering." With this technique, one user's agent shares information with other users' agents to make recommendations. For example, my agent, having learned my tastes and preferences, might find another user's agent who has similar tastes and preferences and recommend to me what the other similar person has used and has enjoyed. This technique is already being used in a music recommendation system called Ringo. In this system, user A can get recommendations from user B if user B shares user A's tastes and has already enjoyed a particular piece of music.

Once the agent has been programmed with a method for selecting entertainment, it must then sort through the thousands of hours of programming available that day and the millions of hours in libraries. It does this by examining the "headers" that accompany each program. These headers will be inserted to describe the programming in question with information about the plot, stars, and anything else that viewers might find important. While these headers may have to be written and inserted by people, they will be invaluable to agents in selecting content for their employers.

It is not difficult to imagine a software agent using such techniques, programmed with an individual's tastes for entertainment and capable of creating an evening's schedule of entertainment. Such an agent would rely on this information to find entertainment from all sources and present it to the user. Over time the agent would improve its selections: The user would adjust the agent's programming with explicit instructions, the agent would learn from feedback given it on previous recommendations, and the agent would find other agents and get advice from them. One agent already on the market that offers an early glimpse of the possibilities of the technology is Firefly.[15]

Could this vision actually work? It might for some, but it will not for the majority of the entertainment audience. To start with, there are many practical problems with agents. Computer scientists have been trying to develop agents for the last 40 years. Despite an enormous effort, they have not been able to overcome some basic problems.

Actually getting agents to work—that is, to autonomously imitate human behavior—has proven extremely difficult. In fact, it is so difficult that developers have virtually abandoned the task of getting agents to operate for humans in the world at large. Rather, they have focused on narrow tasks such as filtering electronic mail. Even relatively narrow tasks such as entertainment selection systems encounter thorny problems. For example, how do the vaunted social filtering systems actually get started? If everyone relies on everyone else's recommendations, who makes the first recommendation? Does not the whole system rely on some entertainment critic to make the first choices, which brings us right back to square one?

Even if we could get agents to function as planned, will users ever trust agents? As every computer user knows, programs can be notoriously mischievous—without any interference from the outside. Even the most confident supporters of agents admit that agents will never be 100 percent infallible. With thoughts of automated bank tellers eating debit cards, computer hard drives crashing, and telephone answering machines mysteriously deleting messages, getting users to trust entertainment selection agents is no easy task. To make matters worse, imagine if advertisers, their agencies, and content providers that are cut out from viewing schedules by agents figure out how to counter agents.

Proponents of agents argue that users can be made comfortable with agents if they are designed with human interfaces like faces that smile, wink, frown, and talk. They say that trust can be built up as agents learn their user's tastes over time. Finally, they argue that all delegation, even delegation to other humans, involves risk. You delegate tasks that you can afford to have screwed up: if the costs of a mistake are too high, you simply do not delegate. This is why the new direction for the development of agents is for narrow, relatively small tasks like electronic mail handling and electronic news filtering. Agent promoters claim that entertainment selection fits this niche: trust is not as large an issue. If your agent gives you an entertainment selection that you do not like, you just do not consume it.

The problem with these arguments is that computer programs are the last thing most people would ever trust with their entertainment selections. After wasting one hour of their fleeting leisure time on a lousy documentary selected because it happened to be about their brother-in-law's hometown, who would not return and check out a couple of their favorite channels and watch whatever it is that everyone will be talking about at the coffee break the next day? Why should a human—not a nerd who enjoys fiddling with computers—ever delegate the task of selecting entertainment to a computer program when that program cannot be fully trusted and other methods are available?

Even if the problems of competence and trust in agents are overcome by the artificial intelligence community, agents face other business problems. These economic challenges cannot be met by armies of programmers. For agents to become the filter of choice, they will have to defeat their competitor, the digital brand.

THE POWER OF BRANDS

What Is a Brand?

A brand is a product that is differentiated from its competition by means of a design, name, mark, imagery, or a combination of any or all of these. Firms trying to sell their products and build loyalty with their customers in a crowded field of competitors use branding to distinguish their products.

At a minimum, brands identify products as different. But, brands can go further, to identify products with positive attributes. Well-liked brands can give consumers trust and confidence in products. In this way, consumers pressed for time can quickly make difficult choices by selecting a known brand with an established reputation.

Brand equity is that something extra, beyond the value of the physical asset of the product, that gives the product its commercial appeal. The brand equity of Ivory Soap, for example, is the marginal value, beyond the value of the actual soap, of the Ivory name, design, and image. In this case, the brand equity is substantial. Through years of advertising and promotion, Ivory Soap has assumed a trusted place in the daily hygienic routines of many people. In this process, the product is associated with a strong image—an image that springs quickly to mind when the consumer is standing in a grocery store aisle trying to determine which soap to buy.

Creating a successful brand is quite difficult. Branding requires significant and repeated investment. Only a handful of new brands that are launched enter the pantheon of products that become a household fixture. About 5 percent of new brands end up as long-term successes.

Those that are successful have incredible staying power. Winning brands that enter the pantheon seem to guard their image with customers for generation after generation. An analysis of this staying power revealed that "in 19 of 22 consumer categories, the leading brand of the year 1925 was still the leader 60 years later" (Exhibit 43).

While brands are most often associated with repeat-purchase packaged goods, they need not be. Branding can be successfully applied to many other product categories. Think of Mastercard in credit cards, Prudential in insurance, Sony in consumer electronics, AT&T in telephony, and Electrolux in vacuum cleaners. A brand can be built for any product or service as long as it can be functionally differentiated, distributed reasonably widely, and used to create psychological added values through advertising.

Certain products do not meet this test—or meet it with great difficulty. Products like nuts, bolts, string, electrical fixtures, and fresh meat, fish, and vegetables usually are displayed on open shelves and carry no brand names or identification. Often this is because it is difficult to functionally differentiate the product, but sometimes it is because firms have not tried to create brands. Perdue chickens are an interesting example of a brand that was built for a product that up until Frank Perdue's epiphany had been thought of as an unbrandable commodity.

Exhibit 43
The Durability of Leading Brands

Product Category	Leading Brand in 1925	Position in 1985
Bacon	Swift	Leader
Batteries	Eveready	Leader
Biscuits	Nabisco	Leader
Breakfast Food	Kellogg	Leader
Cameras	Kodak	Leader
Canned Fruit	Del Monte	Leader
Chewing Gum	Wrigley	Leader
Chocolates	Hershey	No. 2
Flour	Gold Medal	Leader
Mint Candies	Life Savers	Leader
Paint	Sherwin-Williams	Leader
Pipe Tobacco	Price Albert	Leader
Razors	Gillette	Leader
Sewing Machines	Singer	Leader
Shirts	Manhattan	No. 5
Shortening	Crisco	Leader
Soap	Ivory	Leader
Soft Drinks	Coca-Cola	Leader
Soup	Campbell's	Leader
Tea	Lipton	Leader
Tires	Goodyear	Leader
Toothpaste	Colgate	No. 2

Source: D. John Loden, *MegaBrands: How to Build Them, How to Beat Them* (Homewood, Ill.: Business One Irwin, 1992).

Television and Branding

In the entertainment industry, the concept of brands has been sporadically used. In the print media, newspapers and magazines are named, designed, positioned, and promoted in the same way as packaged branded goods. The *Wall Street Journal*, for example, has a distinct and recognizable masthead with a memorable name. It is positioned as a complete financial newspaper with high-quality journalism and sold to members of the business community around the country. It has the look and feel of a quality brand, and generation after generation of businesspeople have read the paper as part of their daily routine. Consequently, the value of the paper is much more than the value of the printing presses, the editorial staff, and all of the other physical assets.

With other media, however, the concept of branding has not always been used. In the television business, branding is more common in packaging than in production or distribution. The distributors of television, the cable operators and satellite operators, are difficult to brand. Viewers do not consider their cable operator to be anything more than a pipeline for programming, with bad service. In fact, these distributors are invisible to most viewers, who simply pay their cable bills in order to see programs. How many viewers can name their cable company? Of those who can, how many have any association with it?

Furthermore, most television production companies are not branded. While viewers would probably recognize names of studios like Paramount and Warner Brothers, they would be hard put to name a particular program produced by a studio. They simply do not know nor care that *Beverly Hills 90210* is a production of Spelling Entertainment. Disney comes to mind as an exception. It has a strong brand name that is associated with family programming. For years, a program entitled *The Disney Hour* was a fixture on Sunday nights. Disney, of course, was also able to draw on the other parts of its entertainment business, like the theme parks, to build its brand. But, with very few other exceptions, program production is a little like screws sold in hardware stores: it is very difficult to label and package. Any unique identity usually is associated with the stars or theme of the program and not the producer.

Put the programs together into a schedule or a cluster, however, and the situation changes. It becomes possible to name the cluster, create a visual logo and musical theme for it, differentiate it from other clusters, and, in time, create an image around it. In short, to brand it.

If networks are simply schedules of programming, one might ask how it is that networks have created brands while programmers have not. Clearly, to the extent that each program is different, each network is also different. However, in the minds of many viewers, networks are more than just the sum of all of the programming on their schedules. They are separate products that offer a unique experience to viewers—obviously some networks are more successful than others. Networks differentiate themselves by offering different genres of programming at different times to different demographic groups. In addition to its unique blend of programming, each network also has a distinct logo, jingle, style of promotion, and set of on-air personalities that make up what is known as its interstitial programming. Together, carefully blended programming and interstitials give networks a particular "look and feel." Market researchers often test this concept with viewers, who without fail identify networks from images or descriptions.

There are three broad categories of networks, niche networks, general entertainment networks, and premium networks. Niche networks, found almost always in the cable environment, achieve differentiation by filling their entire schedule with programming from a single genre (sports, music, news, financial news, movies, education, etc.). By doing this, they are differentiated not only from the other two categories, but also from each other. As channel capacity is increased, more opportunities will exist for networks to find ever narrower niches.

Premium networks, like HBO, Showtime, and the Disney Channel, offer subscribers theatrical movies, made-for-television movies, and other special programming without commercial interruption. Typically they charge a fee that they share with the cable operators.

Differentiation is more difficult for the general entertainment networks. In the Broadcast Era, the three networks were protected by high barriers to entry and had less reason to be concerned with differentiation. They all scheduled general entertainment programming: a blend of comedy and drama series, movies, sports, news, and special programming. The local stations themselves were branded and used local news, sports, and variety to achieve differentiation. In the Cable Era, cable networks and independent stations were added to the mix.

It has been difficult for the new terrestrial and cable general entertainment entrants to differentiate their products. This is because their overall mix of programming is similar to that of the broadcast networks. While independent stations can offer local programming—and in so doing threaten affiliates—cable networks have little choice but to share much of the same programming mix. Syndicated programming is now being purchased by national cable networks offering a mix of general entertainment programming, like TNT and the USA Network, and older movies are migrating to American Movie Classics and its new rival, Turner Classic Movies.[16] The difficulty in achieving differentiation for a general entertainment cable network is illustrated by the decelerating pace of launches of general entertainment cable networks: Fox's fx was widely considered to be the last broad-based network to be attempted.[17]

However, in contrast to these relative start-ups, the broadcast networks clearly are differentiated from independent stations and national general entertainment cable networks. Only they can afford lavish original dramas, star-driven comedies, and major league sports programming. Probably the biggest source of broadcast network differentiation, at least from the perspective of advertisers, is that broadcast networks are alone in providing virtually total coverage of U.S. households.

The broadcast networks also achieve some differentiation from cable networks and from each other through branding. Some think of their identity as centering on a signature program: "For ABC . . . it's *Home Improvement*. That's what they're about. For NBC, it's *Seinfeld*. . . . We have to have a defining half-hour comedy that says, 'That's CBS,' " said Peter Tortorici, president of CBS Entertainment (in an article entitled "With Ratings Slipping, CBS Reaches for Youth," by Bill Carter in the *New York Times*, 10 January 1995). Others think of differentiation between broadcast networks as coming from the personalities associated with their news coverage or the look and feel of the interstitial programming.

Often an identity is recognizable because their programming tends to be targeted to certain demographics. In the mid-1990s, for example, NBC was identified with hip urban programming and ABC with blue-collar fare.

Many people think of networks as simply a collection of programs, but there is something in the totality of the package. Whatever the source, differentiation does exist and is proven repeatedly in tests in which viewers are given descriptions of programming and asked what network is likely to feature the programming. Not surprisingly, viewers regularly associate certain types of programming with particular networks.[18]

In the face of their decades-old ratings slide, the broadcast networks are now trying to build on their brands to retain and increase viewership. Instead of using their valuable time between programming to sell advertisers' products, they are using it to promote themselves. Each network is now spending on self-promotion about the same as a leading consumer goods advertiser, like Procter and Gamble: $500 million per year in air time.[19] For CBS and NBC, this translated into 4½ minutes per hour of prime time in 1996. The time is used to promote both individual shows and entire evening schedules. NBC began the trend by labeling Thursday night "Must See TV," with the popular comedies *Seinfeld* and *Friends*, and Saturday night "Thrillogy," using adventures like *The Pretender* and *Profiler*.

These efforts are new so it is unclear how effective they will be. It is clear, however, that with so much at stake, the broadcast networks will continue searching until they find just what it is that makes the value of their schedules greater than the sum of its parts. When they do, they will not hesitate to use their considerable financial and marketing muscle promote it.

If critics of the branded broadcaster think that viewers watch programs and not networks, investors disagree. These brands are worth something to investors. Two recent transactions were made in which broadcast networks ABC and CBS changed hands. The price paid by the buyers, Disney and Westinghouse respectively, was far in excess of the value of the people and equipment that came with the companies. Some would say that this amount was an overpayment. Since there were other bidders, it is more reasonable that the amount represented the market value of the brand as expressed in future cash flow.

ENDGAME: A FEW DOMINANT BRANDS

Can the concept of brand be extended to the Digital Era? Absolutely. In an era of overwhelming choice, brands are more important than ever. A successful digital brand would serve as the filter that users need to cope with information overload. It would be that trusted place where users can go to get a particular type of entertainment or information. Just as shoppers facing an aisle of hundreds of packages of dried cereals simply take a package or two of the brand they know and trust, viewers will go the network they like for their entertainment or information needs. They may set favored brands as default positions to which they or their agents can go when in doubt about a particular selection. Brands may even have their own branded agents that can be used by their viewers.

As agents are relegated to the periphery, a few brands will emerge and thrive in the digital environment. These few are probably in existence today. There are three reasons why:

• Viewers prefer brands
• Brands have better economics
• The Madison Avenue premium

Viewers Prefer Brands

Viewers will prefer a few dominant brands to agents because brands fit better into a long-established pattern of product use and selection. What are the advantages of brands over agents? To start with, they are more consumer-friendly. They do not need to be selected, programmed, monitored, or given feedback. They do not malfunction. Brands are trusted friends that you can count on to deliver a familiar product time and time again.

People feel comfortable with the whole process of choosing their entertainment through brands, and this pattern will be difficult to break. Call it "qwertyness": Just because there are better ways to lay out a keyboard does not mean that users will switch. Likewise, people like their brands and may not give them up just because a new robot has come along that is supposed to do a better job at selecting entertainment than they can.

In the end viewers will select a handful of dominant brands for two main reasons: viewers are "couch potatoes" and they graze channels in herds. People are lazy when it comes to media. Media usage is a leisure-time activity and the history of television has shown that users are passive, preferring to lie on the couch and be entertained or informed.

Despite detailed research into why people watch what they do, among the best indicators of a program's popularity is what is on before and after it. Programs on the same channel have been found repeatedly to have large duplicated audiences, indicating that viewers literally "do not touch that dial."[20] Television viewing is fundamentally passive: Viewers tend to watch programs for the sake of viewing itself regardless of content.[21]

Today, about three-quarters of viewers have remote controls: 77 percent in 1990.[22] It is far easier for a subscriber, having chosen a distributor, to switch networks or channels. Nevertheless, while many viewers do use remotes to change channels frequently,[23] the presence of remotes does not significantly increase the number of channels watched,[24] nor do remotes significantly increase the probability that viewers will switch in the middle of an ongoing program; the average figure is about 3 percent.[25] Most viewers still tend to remain tuned to a particular channel: Henry and Rinne found that lead-in and lead-out share were still the second and third best predictors of a program's ratings.[26] Moreover, subscribers tend to watch channels that have low channel numbers and do not as easily change channels to view those positioned with high numbers.[27]

These are called adjacency effects in the television business. Networks know about these adjacency effects and are doing their best to exploit them. A recent NBC innovation known as "seamless programming" is designed to do just that. No longer are programs separated by a showing of the credits and a break for commercials. Rather, as one program ends, the screen is split: credits are shown on one side and previews from the next program on the other. The next program begins immediately after. NBC says that "seamless programming" has kept many viewers from leaving the network between programs.[28]

One reason for this behavior might be promotion. The most important source of information on new programming is on-air promotions. These promotions are made and aired by a packager and inserted in breaks between popular programming. They feature the actors, music, and overall look of the promoted program and are a critical tool to get viewers interested. Packagers using these promotions dovetails with viewer inertia to keep viewers hooked for the duration of a schedule.

If remote control units could not get most viewers to switch channels between programs, how will agents motivate the necessary change in behavior? The use of agents requires much more activity than consumers are used to when consuming media. Viewers must first choose an agent, then program their selected agent, monitor it, and, finally, pick from the available options. Compare this to selecting a few brands and relying on them to sort out the universe of entertainment for you. Which sounds like the kind of activity that couch potatoes would embrace?

Even if consumers did use an agent, the packager might still end up attracting and retaining the viewer. If an agent selected a program from a branded packager's schedule, the viewer might very well be induced— through some yet-to-be determined agent countermeasure—to remain with the packager for more than one program. Since we know viewers are passive and adjacency viewing is high, the viewer would be sorely tempted to default to the schedule of the packager he was watching.

The second reason that viewers will stick to the dominant offerings is a phenomenon known as the *mass audience*. At the dawn of the Cable Era, narrowcasting was considered by many to be the way television would be watched in the future. Chess lovers would tune in to chess channels and food lovers to cooking channels. Viewing would fragment into hundreds of very personal directions, leaving the mainstream networks to wither and fold. Agents are another variation on this theme. They also have an intensely individual psychology about them. Everyone's agent-selected evenings will be different. Either the timing of the selection or the actual content itself will differ from person to person.

But, is the consumption of media this individualistic? No. Not in media nor in most other products either. In the field of marketing, decades of consumer research have shown that in product after product consumers choose from among seven or so brands and ignore however many others are available.[29] In fact, the human mind in general seems unable to analyze too many choices at the same time. In studies of human problem-solving, researchers have shown that the human mind has a functional limit of about seven factors that it can process simultaneously.[30]

Maybe this why many users have trouble processing information from the Web. In the early days of the Web phenomenon, users spent much of their on-line time surfing serendipitously through the thousands of interesting sites created by individuals and organizations. An interesting shift has taken place: as the Web has grown to offer even more information, users have become overwhelmed with choice. To simplify matters, the average user keeps about 40 bookmarks on his browser and repeatedly visits only a handful of these bookmarked sites. Microsoft's Windows 98 will mitigate the need to find sites to bookmark in the first place: It comes with an "active channel bar" that permits the user to click on icons for preselected sites, including Disney and Warner Bros. One study showed that 50 percent of users do not even surf anymore.[31] A few branded sites now dominate their niches: C/NET and Ziff-Davis are the places for technology news, Yahoo! and AOL for search, and AMR/Sabre's Travelocity and Microsoft's Expedia for travel.

This pattern of behavior can be traced to television. Despite the availability of many channels for many years, viewers still tend to concentrate on only a few options. Channel repertoire, or the number of channels viewed, is found to be typically five to eight channels out of universes of 36 to 50 available channels.[32] Moreover, this handful of channels tends to be the same for everyone. After 20 years of the Cable Era, viewing is still focused on the same broadcast networks, the top five or ten cable networks, and the local independent.

Will television remain a mass audience phenomenon? One argument is that new technology will not change viewing patterns. Viewers will continue to watch only a few of the channels that are available to them. A three-tier system seems to have evolved in the 20 years of cable television in which the broadcast networks continue to dominate viewing, with the remainder split between an independent or two and the top eight cable networks. The hundreds of other networks are nothing more than concepts in the minds of entrepreneurs and cash calls for investors.

The other argument is that viewing patterns will indeed change as technology evolves. Proponents suggest that the enduring strength of broadcast networks may yet be diminished over the long term, that it is simply too early to draw any conclusions about the ultimate strength of cable networks. They point to new inroads that cable networks are consistently making against the broadcasters as empirical evidence that the broadcasters' position is far from consolidated in this Digital Era.[33] The theory behind this argument is that with relatively few channels, networks transmit lowest-common-denominator programming in order to attract the most viewers for advertisers.[34] With increasing channel capacity, it becomes possible for networks to attempt to attract smaller audiences. As program choice options increase, viewers will have a better chance to choose the programs that most closely match their interests.[35] As a consequence, while viewers may still watch only a handful of the channels available, they will tend to watch different channels suited to their interests. Further aiding this pattern would be the proliferation of next-generation on-screen guides, like Starsight, that help viewers navigate through a menu of channel options.

This lively debate will continue. A safe bet is that viewers will continue to graze the channels in a herd. It may be that some of today's dominant networks will wane, but they will be replaced by others. The mass audience has been well documented during the Cable Era and will not disappear. Most media products are consumed by large numbers of people. They may be consumed alone in the privacy of the home, but the experience is then shared. The hit show that was on television last night is discussed around the water cooler today; the popular columnist's piece in this morning's paper is debated over lunch in the cafeteria. Top-rated popular content becomes part of the collective experience of a culture: it is shared, discussed, remembered, and loved or hated. People still live in the real world with their families, friends, and work. As long as this world remains real, not virtual, people will want to share the "media consumption" experience. It is easier to share experiences with brands than with an agent that will make a unique and personalized selection of entertainment for each viewer each and every evening.

Perhaps a good model on which to base future television viewing patterns is the book publishing industry, in which barriers to entry are low, but fewer than one hundred titles become very successful each year, several hundred more find profitable niches, and the remaining hundreds of thousands are not bought by more than a handful of readers. Large and well-branded general entertainment networks would correspond to the very successful books, and some of the cable networks would correspond to the successful niche titles. The remaining thousands of channels—the tiny niche networks, the poorly branded general entertainment networks, and new launches of ambitious fourth-grade teachers—would languish in obscurity.

Brands Have Better Economics

Even if some viewers use agents to select their entertainment, the networks that package clusters of programs and brand them will survive and, indeed, flourish. Despite the changing technology of the conduit, the economic logic of the packaging remains robust. The efficiencies in packaging are relentless. And, the handful of packagers that exploit these efficiencies are protected by high barriers to entry against newcomers, agents, or other packagers. Let me explain.

In a world of intelligent agents, agents could select individual programs for viewers from an array of programs offered by producers, or individual viewers could default to branded packagers. Two types of firms would compete: One type would offer a few programs, perhaps as few as one; and a second type would offer an entire schedule of programs. Which type of firm would prosper? The second would have a distinct advantage.

The economics of production force profit-driven producers to make popular programs. Moreover, as we know, programming is extremely expensive. Since the cost of producing a program for an audience of 10 is the same as the cost of producing one for ten million, obviously it is in the interest of the producer to get the largest possible audience to reduce unit costs. Clearly, hit programming for the mass audience will be profitable. So can highly targeted niche programming be, provided that it is widely popular within a niche—preferably a niche that is coveted by advertisers.

One of the first rules of programming is that viewer tastes are unpredictable. Consequently, production companies cannot be certain of making hits despite the size of the investment in the program. We learned that at most one out of every five new series survives long enough to become a "hit," while fewer still survive the screening process to make it onto a network in the first place.

The implications for independent producers are obvious: they have only a small chance of actually developing a hit program. The independent producer has all his eggs in one basket; the risk he takes in developing programs will be great. This is one reason why the top ten list of television production companies changes so dramatically from year to year (Exhibits 8 and 25). In contrast, a packager will be able to spread the risk of program development over an entire schedule of programming. Thus, a packager is more likely to have hits than a small producer. This does not stop a small producer from entering into the fray with his single throw of the dice and his fervent belief that he has a winner. It merely means that there is strong economic pressure for some firms with access to capital to become producers of many shows and for other firms to package even more shows in order to increase the odds.

If packagers have an economic advantage over agents, incumbent packagers have an advantage over new entrants. Put simply, the economics of brands favor the victory of a handful of powerful networks. We discussed how the barriers to entry from limited spectrum and limited channel capacity are being dismantled by technology advances. Other barriers to packaging in general may not be so easy to overcome. These barriers will limit the number of mass branded networks to just a handful.

Clearly, incumbent packagers are protected by barriers based on economies of scale.[36] Attracting large audiences today requires massive spending on programming. We noted earlier that it takes roughly $2 billion in spending on programming per year for a major broad-based network to compete. At this level of scale, how much room is there for other new networks? Unless advertising revenues were to jump up or profit margins were to collapse, the scale required to break through to mass audiences limits the number of large packagers to just a few.

This scale is the main reason why new broadcast and cable networks have had such a hard time breaking in: They simply cannot afford to spend the $1 million per hour that the Big Four networks can spend to get viewers' attention. To see why, one has to push just a few numbers. Broadcasters start with a universe of about 100 million TV households, versus the 65 million of cable networks. They can expect an average prime-time rating of between 5.0 and 10.0 versus a 2.0 or so for a cable network competitor. Compounding this advantage in audience size is the Madison Avenue premium[37]: the established broadcaster can get almost double the $5.00 CPM that the cable network can obtain. Multiply this out by the ten or fifteen minutes of advertising that can be placed on the program during its airings,[38] and it is easy to understand why the cable network will have a hard time springing for more than $200,000 to $300,000 for an hour of programming while the big broadcaster will easily be able to spend $1 million and perpetuate the cycle.

Even if the money were somehow available, it represents a significant absolute number for a new entrant to obtain. The number would be made even higher by the high interest costs that would be incurred given the riskiness of the project and the need to maintain adequate working capital to withstand industry fluctuations.[39] Any new network would also start without the vertical relationships of existing packagers (e.g., affiliation contracts for broadcasters and MSO contracts for cable packagers) and would have to invest considerable time, effort and funds building up these relationships. General consensus in the industry is that a new cable network requires an investment of $100 million to get to breakeven; the investment would be even higher for a broadcast network.

Furthermore, both new cable packagers and new broadcast networks face a barrier that is caused by product differentiation and viewer behavior. The total hours that viewers watch is relatively fixed and beyond the influence of the actions of cable networks. What is more, during their TV hours, viewers are passive and watch only a few of the channels available to them. Therefore, new packagers must break through to get the attention of viewers and displace viewing of an existing network. This is made all more difficult because the number one reason why viewers will try out a show is because they saw it promoted on television. Since on-air promotions are so much more effective than traditional advertising or word of mouth, the networks with large viewing share have a built-in advantage and start-ups face a "Catch-22" situation.

To break out of the pack, new packagers would require a substantial promotional budget as well as desirable programming. Since many packagers have exclusive contracts with program producers, HBO with Warner Brothers or Fox with the NFC of the NFL, for example, new packagers would have to wait for these contracts to expire and then outbid other packagers for them or find new programming. Since all hit programming is under contract until it goes into syndication, new packagers would have to develop their own programming, a risky proposition, or buy syndicated fare, not a route to large audiences.

Incumbents, of course, recognize that these barriers exist, but they also know that they may not be enough to stop entrepreneurs with dreams of becoming media moguls from attempting to get into the business. Therefore, incumbents have actively worked to make entry even more difficult. In the language of the economist, this is called entry-deterring conduct.

An example of this was the price reductions by CNN that had the effect of keeping TCI from granting NBC carriage agreements for its proposed news station. Clearly, TCI's response to SNC signaled to other potential entrants that entry would not be profitable. Programming investments are also made to deter would-be entrants. To take another example from CNN: It was reported that CNN's central tactic in trying to block the BBC from entering is to increase its investment in news programming.[40]

Networks also deter entry by filling any new available capacity themselves. One way to achieve this is to create "spin-off" networks, new networks related to their existing networks.[41] CNN's Headline News (news summaries), HBO's Cinemax, and Viacom's VH1 Country, VH1 Soul, VH1 Smooth, MTV Ritmo, MTV Rocks, and MTV Indie are all examples of this practice. Another method is to "multiplex," to show an existing service, but begin it at intervals throughout the day.[42] Viacom has already done this with M2, a service that transmits regular MTV at different times of the day.

These methods satisfy some viewer needs and, more important, take up slots on cable systems. This practice interacts neatly with the limited channel capacity of cable operators to deter entry: As packagers convince operators to transmit their new channels through incentives like offering them the additional channel at no cost, as Turner did with CNN International, it becomes difficult for new networks to obtain carriage. In fact, the premium services that are currently transmitted on most systems, HBO, Cinemax, Showtime, and Encore, could take up as many as 23 channels alone. In a recent Showtime survey, MSOs responded that in a 123-channel system they would only need seven new services, with 50 slots going to basic services, 25 going to premium services, and 41 being used for pay-per-view.[43]

By creating spin-off networks, incumbents can capture economies of scope. By combining multiple networks in one firm, the cost of any single network falls. For example, programming acquired for one network can be used for additional networks. The other costs of networks—sales, general and administrative expenses, and transponder costs—can also be shared across networks. In fact, network support companies, like TCI's Vision Group, were able to provide lower-cost sales, marketing, and transponder services to unaffiliated start-up networks.

An example of both economies of scope and scale could be seen in the launch of Turner Classic Movies (TCM). Program expenses were reduced since Turner already owned most of the titles that would be shown on TCM; these came from previous acquisitions of MGM, RKO, and the pre-1948 Warner Brothers libraries that had been exhibited on other Turner networks and on independents. TCM could also take advantage of other fixed costs already in place, such as the affiliate sales structure. Once these costs were put in place and the network was launched, TCM could take advantage of scale economies as its subscriber base expanded (Exhibit 44) and scope economies that an independent start-up effort would not enjoy.

Despite these hurdles, it is still possible to launch a new network. Take the example of Fox bootstrapping itself into the ranks of the broadcast networks by exploiting the success of a couple of hit programs. Or Barry Diller's recently announced attempt to build a national network using inexpensive locally produced programming.

Exhibit 44
Scale Economies in Cable Networking: Turner Classic Movies

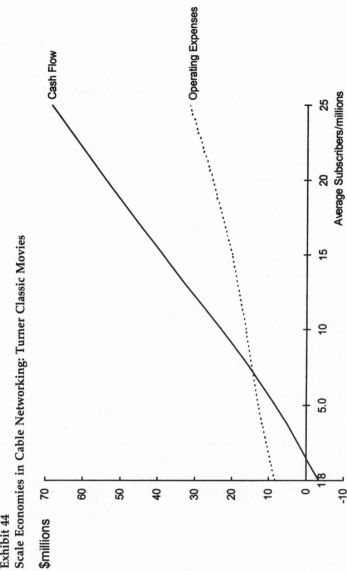

Source: Derived from information in Paul Kagan Associates, *Cable TV Programming* (Carmel, Calif.: Paul Kagan Associates, 30 April 1994), pp. 1–3.

But, remember, these efforts were not made from scratch: both Fox and Barry Diller had the advantage of starting with local stations and cable networks that have distribution and audience. Even if it proves possible to overcome these barriers to entry, advertisers may not permit further audience fragmentation.

The Madison Avenue Premium

With all of the discussion of cable television rates and the hype about pay-per-view events, it is easy to lose sight of the fact that the subscriber market for television barely existed before the 1980s. It was the advertising market that financed the golden age of broadcast television and lured entrepreneurs to develop cable. Even today the advertising market remains dominant: the $34 billion market for advertising is still larger than the $23 billion market for consumer subscriptions. Television stations, whose revenue consists of well over 90 percent in advertising or advertising-related revenues,[44] are still dependent on this stream of revenues, and cable operators, cable networks, and program syndicators increasingly rely on advertising as part of their revenue mix. As long as the television industry remains addicted to advertising revenues, agencies and the large advertisers themselves will play an important role in defining the structure of the television industry.

Advertisers love big networks and mass audiences. Think about the simplicity of reaching almost every adult male between the ages of 18 and 54 through one advertisement during half-time of the Super Bowl or of reaching huge numbers of 18- to 49-year-olds through a series of advertisements on NBC's Thursday night schedule. Obviously there are other ways to reach these people, but no other option is quite so easy. Therefore, for these kinds of advertisements, advertisers are willing to pay a premium over the price they pay for other advertisements: call it the Madison Avenue premium. As long as they are willing, there will be networks trying to build schedules of mass programming.

To understand the Madison Avenue premium, we need to understand more about advertising markets in general. Over the years, the advertising market has evolved and increased in complexity. Today, the advertising market actually consists of several different, but interrelated, submarkets: broadcast network advertising, national and local spot, barter-syndication, national cable networks, and local advertising. These submarkets are distinguished by the type of network and/or programming on which the advertising appears. Broadcast network advertising is inserted into network programming and reaches a national audience; national spot advertising allows national advertisers to reach selective audiences by buying time directly from local stations, either affiliated or independent; barter-syndication consists of program producers selling time directly to national advertisers and then supplying this programming—complete with commercials inserted—to local stations; national cable networks operate similarly to broadcast networks but have much smaller audiences; and local advertising is sold by local stations for local advertisers.[45]

The advertising sold in these submarkets is often unique, but occasionally either a substitute or a complement.[46] Network advertising, for example, is unique in providing national coverage and eliminating the transaction costs associated with buying multiple spot or barter-syndication advertisements. However, since it has disadvantages, like uneven coverage of the country or extra cost for advertisers not interested in the entire country, advertisers will often complement network advertising with spot advertising in a single campaign in order to both cover the entire country and saturate certain key markets.[47] The cable and barter-syndication markets are considered to not be developed enough to function as good substitutes.[48] Yet, it is clear from their growth rates in recent years that they are being increasingly used by national advertisers.

Despite the fragmentation in viewing patterns and the development of new submarkets, Madison Avenue continues to pour money into the big broadcast networks. Even though their share of viewing has decreased, broadcast networks have maintained a disproportionately large share of advertising.[49] In 1996, the four broadcast networks attracted a record $5.8 billion in advertiser commitments in the upfront market despite losing 8 percent of their viewers in prime time.[50]

Advertising agencies are not stupid. They have very good reasons for spending their clients' money the way they do. The large broadcast networks attract the lion's share of the advertising dollars because they provide advertisers with buying and transaction efficiencies. The four leading networks still attract about 60 percent of the prime-time audience. Advertisers can get more exposure to viewers with a buy on CBS, the lowest-ranked broadcast network, than they can with buys of all of the cable networks combined. For most large advertisers, the one-stop shopping provided by the broadcast networks is a value apparently worth paying for. As long as there is such a phenomenal disparity between the top four and the hundred channels that split the remaining 40 percent of the audience, advertisers will continue to pay this premium.

But, the big networks serve another function for agencies: they reduce some of the risks inherent in buying advertising time. Once advertisers decide to buy network time, they usually buy their time in the up-front market, that is, well in advance of the time that advertisement is actually shown. This means that the advertiser is taking a risk that the seller of the advertising time will be able to produce an audience. Big networks that have more programs and larger audiences are likelier to have "hit"

programs at just about any time. Furthermore, since networks have entire schedules of programs, they can spread an advertiser's campaign
across clusters of programming. This way they can reduce risk further
and get all of their needed demographics.

If there is a premium for the broadcast networks generally, there is an
even larger premium for hit programs over average programs. A 30-
second spot on *Seinfeld* cost $550,000 in 1996, while a same-length spot
on *Diagnosis Murder* cost only $60,000. *Seinfeld* commanded a multiple of
almost ten times the competition even though its rating of 20 was only
double that of *Diagnosis Murder*. Agencies often ascribe this multiple to
the "opinion leader" theory of advertising: the theory that hit shows
attract the trendsetters advertisers want to be seen using their products.

Without the Madison Avenue premium, how do the top cable neworks
make money? Recall the new paradigm for network profitability.
Branded niche networks like ESPN and MTV with a small but stable
audience make large profits by airing inexpensive programming and
earning a combination of subscriber fees and advertising revenues.

Whatever the logic of the premium, if Madison Avenue believes it, it
will influence the industry. However, some might argue that the Digital
Era is producing several new trends that threaten the very existence of
the premium as well as all advertising based on mass audiences. There
are four frequently mentioned threats to advertising as the networks
know it: (1) the collapse of the existing measurement methodology; (2)
the trend to performance-based advertising pricing; (3) the trend to targeted advertising; and (4) the pay-per-view model. What is the nature
of these threats and how serious are they?

Since their earliest use, the system of meters that monitor audience
viewing has had its critics. The system is implemented by one firm, Nielsen, and measures the size of audiences by a device attached to the television sets of audiences in a sample. Less popular networks critique the
system and more popular networks defend it. Recently, however, a new,
insidious problem with the system has appeared on the horizon. Digital
VCRs will allow increasing numbers of viewers to record, store, alter,
and retrieve programming at a later date. Can the system survive a situation in which significant numbers of viewers are watching programming at different times?

As long as there is advertising, there will always be a system of measurement. Meters can measure viewing of recorded programming almost
as easily as they measure regularly scheduled programming. The shift
from the old order to the new order, however, may give other firms the
opportunity to challenge Nielsen for dominance. In this scenario, there
would be winners and losers among the networks, since a different standard of measurement might benefit networks differently. But, such a
scenario would not doom the networks since the new measurement firms

would still find that the networks, the good ones at least, registered eyeballs. When industry observers say that the end of Nielsen spells the end of network television, they are usually referring to another trend. This trend is our next threat.

The second threat to network advertising is the trend emerging on the Web of advertising pricing based on performance. Imitating television, early advertising on the Web was priced based on total number of impressions (visitors, or eyeballs in advertising industry parlance) that each advertisement had. In this way, popular sites could charge more than less popular sites because advertisers on their sites received more impressions. However, as the Web began to evolve, this model changed. Since the Web is less dynamic than television and offers fewer opportunities to present details than print, simple exposure to an advertisement on the Web is not as important as whether the viewer of the advertisement actually clicks through to the advertiser's site for further information. In a successful Web advertisement, the viewer gets exposure, goes on to learn more about the product or service advertised, and concludes by making an order. In this world, the advertiser is willing to pay more for viewers that click through, but less for viewers that ignore the advertisement. Moreover, since the advertising regime on the Web is not controlled by Nielsen or any other established player, sellers of advertising were prepared to change the system and offer advertisers pricing based on click-throughs, and even actual orders, in order to compete. Does this trend spell the end for traditional, impression-based advertising?

Clearly, advertisers would rather pay only for the advertisements that are effective. But, that does not mean that they will discontinue brand or image advertising. Brand advertising is considered to be effective as long as it reaches and exposes its target market. Measuring the effectiveness of brand advertising is complex (prompting the famous advertiser's line, "I know that half of my advertising is effective, I just don't know which half"). Nevertheless, advertisers of mass market products and services have reached the consensus over the last 30 years that they cannot do without it.

Of course, even if brand advertising persists, competition from the Web will force television to slowly, but inevitably, move toward performance-based models. This movement is not necessarily a threat to network television. It is only a threat to poor-performing network television. Poorly rated network television always suffered through the loss of advertising, but under the old Nielsen regime it took a long time for advertisers to figure out what was really happening. With performance-based pricing, programming with relatively few viewers will lose advertising more rapidly. Successful television programming, on the other hand, has nothing to lose.

A related threat comes from the trend in advertising away from the quest for mass audiences. For years, direct marketing, including direct mail and telemarketing, has taken increasing share from traditional mass media advertising. The idea is that by focusing on particular target market groups, direct marketing can increase the effectiveness of advertising; instead of using television commercials wasted on the vast majority of the audience, a real estate agent could send direct mail only to those names on a list of people who have already sold or bought real estate.

The Internet can be thought of as a powerful direct marketing tool available to advertisers without the cost of paper, printing, and postage. Advertisers can use it to supply information to their target market. With Web sites that can cost millions of dollars to build and maintain, advertisers can engage potential customers that visit their site with contests, give-aways, or interesting information about their products.

Of course, advertisers must get customers to visit their Web site in the first place. Therein lies the problem for companies with mass products. It is not very easy to generate serious traffic on a Web site. Compare the Web to traditional television. McDonald's budgets about 30,000 gross ratings points in a typical year. This comes out to about 300 impressions per household each year.[51] These impressions are made using the rich format of television, with its luscious mixture of video and audio.

The Web cannot come close to generating this kind of traffic. The most common ways to generate visits to a Web site are advertising in conventional media, putting links to your site on other sites, and advertising your site on other Web sites with a so-called banner advertisement. These methods all have problems. References to Web sites on conventional media require the audience to recall the information at a later date when they are in front of a computer. Advertisements or links on other popular Web sites are more direct for users, but do not offer access to the kind of numbers that traditional mass media do. According to Evan Schwartz, "even if a mass marketer such as McDonald's bought advertising on the most popular 100 sites, it still might miss two-thirds of the audience in a given day.... There are simply too many Web sites, making it impossible to predict where Web surfers will go in any given session."[52] Of course, of the one-third exposed to McDonald's banner ads on those 100 sites, less than 5 percent would actually click on the ad, go to the McDonald's site itself, and experience the flashy world of McDonald's Land in cyberspace; the remaining 95 percent would have to content themselves with a rather flat one-by-four-inch Web banner. Given that only 20 million or so Americans surf the Web in any given month, big advertisers like McDonald's will never be able to reach as many on the Web as they can by using traditional mass media.

Of course, trying to do so really misses the point of the Web. The Web is about providing a rich experience to a handful of prospective customers, not just exposure to the masses. The companies that use the Web effectively are those that can find their target market and use their relatively low-cost site to give a small number of well-qualified leads a unique experience.

However, there will always be products that do not need the kind of experience that the Web can provide. Many products do not require consumers to have much information about them; they are simple and are sold by addressing basic needs or using straightforward images. Hamburgers, toothpaste, razor blades, and soft drinks come to mind. Since people typically do not spend their spare time surfing the Web to check the pH balance of a new shampoo, attracting surfers to a Procter and Gamble site on hair products will never be easy, cost effective, or useful.

Makers of mass consumer products, low-information products, and impulse purchase products, as well as their agencies on Madison Avenue, will always be interested in reaching large audiences with low risk—the very thing that big networks do well.

A final threat is pay-per-view: the system in which the viewer pays for programming that is uninterrupted by advertising. This form of programming has existed for decades. It usually consists of events, movies, or sports and was pioneered by cable companies looking for ways to maximize their stream of subscriber revenues. It has never been considered successful, but recent interest in pay-per-view has been piqued by its use by the satellite operators and its potential applications through digital VCRs (see the section on Videocassettes in Chapter 2). Is pay-per-view the threat that brings down network television?

Media can be supported by advertising, user fees, or a combination of both. Particular business models have emerged for media as a result of regulation, technological constraints, and from business decisions early in the life cycle that were subsequently institutionalized. Inevitably, business models change with time. The telephone, originally conceived as being supported by advertising, became totally supported by user fees, and is now moving to a combination of advertising and user fees (a company in Sweden, called GratisTel, is now offering free long distance telephone service provided that users are willing to be interrupted by advertisements every few minutes).

Given this history, it is not surprising that television will move to some mix of user fees and advertising. Clearly, it already has. Cable subscribers pay fees for basic service and additional fees for premium channels. Pay-per-view for major events, like concerts and boxing title fights, is also a fixture in television. Eventually, other types of programming will also be offered in a commercial-free, fee-based format.

Even if pay-per-view reaches some measure of success, it will not doom packagers of television. There will always be segments of viewers that prefer to watch free television and are willing to put up with the advertisements. Since most of the economies of scale and scope in packaging still apply to fee-based television, successful packagers of television programming will extract just as much value from those viewers electing pay-per-view as from the other segments. In fact, while eliminating some of the value of the Madison Avenue premium, pay-per-view may make up for this loss by giving packagers the opportunity to segment their audiences. For example, new audiences can be found and programming can be windowed. So, the advent of pay-per-view may prove to be a net gain for television packagers.

The habit of viewing, the relentless economies of scale in program production, and the needs of advertisers mean the inevitability of packaging firms—even in a world using agents for entertainment selection. If these packaging firms, with their stables of hit programs, invest properly in building their digital brand, they will maintain their share in the Digital Era.

NOTES

1. Roger Noll in *The Structure of American Industry*, edited by Walter Adams and James W. Brock (Upper Saddle River, N.J.: Prentice-Hall Business Publishing, 1990), p. 368.

2. Ibid., p. 353.

3. "Sport and Television: Swifter, Higher, Stronger, Dearer," *The Economist*, 1996.

4. Kurt Badenhausen and Christopher Nikolos, "Sports Values: More than a Game," *Financial World*, 17 June 1997, p. 40.

5. Expanded ticket sales, corporate sponsorships, and merchandising have also contributed to increased team revenues.

6. Paul Kagan Associates, *The Economics of TV Programming and Syndication* (Carmel, Calif.: Paul Kagan Associates, 1996), p. 70.

7. William Echikson, "Goodbye Hoodlums, Hello Big Money," *Business Week*, 23 September 1996, pp. 66–68; "Golden Goals," *The Economist*, 31 May 1997, pp. 57–58.

8. Every so often, new sports leagues are started with the intent of either siphoning off some of the profits that flow to content or gaining access to content that might otherwise be locked up by long-term deals with networks or distributors. The latest example of this is the announcement of NBC and Turner of a new football league to compete with the NFL. Most of these efforts fail because of lack of audience demand and problems with distribution.

9. Bill Carter, "CBS, Under Its New Owner, Plans a Series with Cosby," *New York Times*, 1 December 1995, Business section.

10. David H. Waterman and August Grant, *Narrowcasting on Cable Television: An Empirical Assessment* (unpublished manuscript, 1989).

11. Veronis, Suhler, and Associates, *Communications Industry Report* (New York: Veronis, Suhler, and Associates, Inc., 1997).

12. Nielsen Media Research, interview with Barry Cook, 12 December 1995.

13. D. John Loden, *Megabrands* (Homewood, Ill.: Business One Irwin, 1992).

14. Nicholas Negroponte, *Being Digital* (New York: Random House, 1995), p. 174.

15. At http://www.firefly.com.

16. Bill Carter, "The Media Business: Television," *New York Times*, 11 April 1995, Business section.

17. Paul Kagan Associates, *Cable TV Programming*, 23 June 1994, p. 1.

18. Interview with David Poltrack, CBS, on 18 June 1997.

19. Kyle Pope, "Networks Sell Themselves as Broadcast Brands," *Wall Street Journal*, 2 April 1997, p. B1.

20. R. Y. Darmon, "Determinants of TV Viewing," *Journal of Advertising Research* 16 (1976): 17–20; G. J. Goodhardt, A. S. C. Ehrenberg, and M. A. Collins, *The Television Audience: Patterns of Viewing* (Westmead, England: D. C. Heath, 1975); V. R. Rao, "Taxonomy of Television Programs Based on Viewing Behavior," *Journal of Marketing Research* 12 (1975): 355–358; and J. Webster and J. Wakshlag, "A Theory of Program Choice," *Communication Research* 10 (1983): 430–446.

21. W. Gantz, "How Uses and Gratifications Affects Recall of Television News," *Journalism Quarterly* 55 (1978): 664–672, 681; A. M. Rubin, "Television Uses and Gratifications: The Interactions of Viewing Patterns and Motivations," *Journal of Broadcasting* 27 (1983): 37–51; A. M. Rubin, "Ritualized and Instrumental Television Viewing," *Journal of Communication* 34, no. 3 (1984): 67–77; and L. W. Jeffres, "Cable TV and Viewer Selectivity," *Journal of Broadcasting* 22 (1978): 167–177.

22. C. Shagrin, "On the Trail of the Elusive 90s Viewer," *Nielsen Newscast* (Spring 1990): 2–3; Douglas A. Ferguson, "Channel Repertoire in the Presence of Remote Control Devices, VCRs, and Cable Television," *Journal of Broadcasting and Electronic Media* 36 (Winter 1992): 237–256.

23. Douglas A. Ferguson, "Measurement of Mundane TV Behaviors: Remote Control Device Flipping Frequency," *Journal of Broadcasting and Electronic Media* 38 (Winter 1994): 35–47.

24. Ferguson, "Channel Repertoire."

25. W. Russell Neuman, *The Future of the Mass Audience* (Cambridge: Cambridge University Press, 1991), p. 112.

26. M. D. Henry and H. J. Rinne, "Predicting Program Shares in New Time Slots," *Journal of Advertising Research* 24, no. 2 (1984): 9–17.

27. While these trends describe the viewing patterns of the average viewer, there are viewer segments—sports viewers and younger viewers—that behave differently. Interview with Brenda Stevens, Director of Research, Continental Cablevision, 14 June 1995.

28. Pope, "Networks Sell Themselves as Broadcast Brands."

29. Research of Andrew Ehrenberg.

30. George Miller, "The Magical Number Seven, Plus or Minus Two: Some Limits on Our Capacity for Processing Information," *Psychology Review* 63: 81–97.

31. Kevin Kelly and Gary Wolf, "Push," *Wired* 5.03, March 1997, pp. 106–238.

32. C. Heeter, "Program Selection with Abundance of Choice: A Process

Model," *Human Communications Research* 12, no. 1 (1985): 126–152; C. Heeter and B. S. Greenberg, "Profiling the Zappers," *Journal of Advertising Research* 25, no. 2 (1985): 15–19; C. Heeter and B. S. Greenberg, *Cableviewing* (Norwood, N.J.: Ablex Publishing Company, 1988); R. H. Lochte and J. Warren, "A Channel Repertoire for TVRO Satellite Viewers," *Journal of Broadcasting and Electronic Media* 33 (1989): 91–95; A. C. Nielsen, "The Outlook for Electronic Media," *Journal of Advertising Research* 22, no. 6 (1982): 9–16; Ferguson, "Channel Repertoire," pp. 83–91.

33. In the fall of 1995, cable's total rating rose by 24 percent over the previous year in large part because of cable efforts to woo children and older viewers, who are not targeted by broadcast network programming, as reported by Lawrie Mifflin, in an article entitled "Cable TV Continues Its Steady Drain of Network Viewers," *New York Times*, 25 October 1995, p. D8.

34. Peter O. Steiner, "Program Patterns and Preferences and the Workability of Competition in Radio Broadcasting," *Quarterly Journal of Economics* 66 (1952): 194; Bruce M. Owen and Steven S. Wildman, *Video Economics* (Cambridge, Mass.: Harvard University Press, 1992).

35. Sug-Min Youn, "Program Type Preference and Program Choice in a Multichannel Situation," *Journal of Broadcasting and Electronic Media* 38 (Fall 1994): 465–475; Jeffres, "Cable TV and Viewer Selectivity," pp. 167–177.

36. Lawrence J. White, "Antitrust and Video Markets: The Merger of Showtime and The Movie Channel," In *Video Media Competition: Regulation, Economics, and Technology*, edited by Eli M. Noam (New York: Columbia University Press, 1985), pp. 188–204.

37. Discussed more fully in the next section.

38. For the incumbent broadcaster: (100,000,000 * .075)/1000 = 7500. 7500 * $10.00 * 30 = $2.25 million in gross advertising revenue. For the cable network or start-up: (65,000,000 * .02)/1000 = 1300. 1300 * $5.00 * 35 = $227,500 in gross advertising revenue.

39. Laurie Thomas and Barry R. Litman, "Fox Broadcasting Company, Why Now? An Economic Study of the Rise of the Fourth Broadcast 'Network,' " *Journal of Broadcasting and Electronic Media* 35 (Spring 1991): 139–157.

40. David H. Waterman and Andrew A. Weiss, "Vertical Integration in Cable Television," paper prepared for the American Enterprise Institute for Public Policy Research, Washington, D.C., 17 September 1993.

41. Clearly these actions are also caused by the variety of consumer tastes, as discussed in the section on structure earlier in this chapter.

42. Multiplexing refers to the transmission of an existing program, a movie for example, at fifteen-minute intervals throughout the evening instead of only once.

43. Showtime Networks, Multichannel Service Operator Tech Survey 1994.

44. Mark R. Fratrik and Theresa J. Ottina, *1994 Television Financial Report* (Washington, D.C.: National Association of Broadcasters, 1994).

45. Television plays a much smaller role in this market; only 16 percent of all local advertising is in television versus 28 percent of all national advertising and 63 percent of all mass media national advertising, according to Robert J. Coen. Robert J. Coen and McCann-Erickson, *Annual U.S. Advertising Expenditures* (New York: Advertising Age, 1997).

46. J. L. Peterman, "Differences between the Levels of Spot and Network Te-

levision Advertising Rates," Working Paper no. 22 (Federal Trade Commission, Bureau of Economics, Washington, D.C., 1979).

47. David Poltrack, *Television Marketing* (New York: McGraw-Hill, 1983).

48. J. Dimmick, S. Patterson, and A. Albarran, "Competition between the Cable and Broadcast Industries: A Niche Analysis," *Journal of Media Economics* 5, no. 1 (1992): 13–30.

49. Michael O. Wirth and Harry Bloch, "The Broadcasters: The Future Role of Local Stations and the Three Networks," in *Video Media Competition: Regulation, Economics, and Technology*, edited by Eli M. Noam (New York: Columbia University Press, 1985), pp. 238–253.

50. Paul Farhi, "Advertisers Find Less Costs More on Network TV," *Washington Post*, 18 September 1996, Business section.

51. Evan I. Schwartz, *Webonomics* (New York: Penguin, 1997), p. 50.

52. Ibid., p. 50.

Epilogue:
The Great Media Free-for-All

The distribution bottleneck is easing and with it memories of one of the most lucrative businesses in the economic history of the United States. For thirty years, firms that transmitted television signals from towers or distributed signals via coaxial cable earned returns that the typical American firm could only dream of. Protected from competition by technological and regulatory barriers, they held the bottleneck through which all content had to pass to get to its audience. By controlling the bottleneck, they could buy their programming cheaply and price it to viewers and advertisers dearly.

Like all good things, this is coming to an end. Deregulation has unleashed technology. Content is being digitized and transmitted through new distribution channels bursting with bandwidth. While this does not make it any easier for a team of writers to write their weekly script for a successful situation comedy, it radically alters the distribution of television. By creating a handful of undistinguishable alternative distributors, technology is breaking the bottleneck and commoditizing the conduit. It is starting a Great Value Shift during which value will migrate from conduit to content.

Creating value in content is not as easy as it might seem. Most people have a difficult time even defining content. Since the content business encompasses so many activities, it makes sense to divide it into three parts, each part with its own economic rules. Content creators are the creative force behind programming, producers actually make the programs, and packagers combine programs into schedules. During the eras of the distribution bottleneck, it was not particularly easy to make money in any part of the content business. It is simply too difficult to predict what will make a viewer laugh or cry, and too many people are willing to try to do it anyway.

After the Great Value Shift, much deserved value will flow back to the content business. But, not all parts of content will benefit equally. Program producers will still struggle against overwhelming odds to make hit programming. Content creators, on the other hand, will reap even bigger rewards for their unique talents.

The real challenge will be for program packagers. Someone will make money helping weary viewers sift through the ever-growing libraries of programs. The question is, who will this be? There are two very stark visions of the future of television. One vision has thousands of producers whose programs are available on video servers around the world. Every night the programs in this expanding universe are filtered and selected by intelligent agents and assembled into personalized schedules. In this vision, we would arrive home, sit back, and watch programs about the country we visited on our last vacation, or perhaps about our favorite hobby. Our agents could find programs about a disease that might concern us or a profession that might interest us. To some, it sounds like utopia. But, when given the chance most people do not really want such personalized evening schedules nor do they trust software to make their selections.

As long the forces of scale economics and Madison Avenue rule, a second vision is likely to predominate. In this vision, viewers sift through programming in the same way they sift through consumer clutter while buying other products: they choose among their favorite brands. Viewers will be happy, advertisers will get their audiences, and packagers will exploit scale economies.

WHY TELEVISION WILL WIN THE RACE TO CREATE DIGITAL BRANDS

If television packagers win the first round of their match for the attention of viewers against the challenge of intelligent agents, they will face a second round in which many more competitors will step into the ring. The Digital Era has eliminated the distinctions among media. It will now be possible for newspaper publishers, magazine publishers, radio broadcasters, and Web-based services to compete against television in a newly created and wide open content business. How will television fare in this Great Media Free-for-All?

Since this is not the first time different forms of media have competed with each other, a lesson from history may be of help in answering this question. With limited time and attention, we have always had to choose among the tremendous volume of available books, newspapers, magazines, radio, packaged music, television, videos, theatrical films, video games, CD-ROMs, and Internet content. So far, television has fared well in this intra-media rivalry. Television killed off the evening papers and has made major inroads against the morning papers, it drastically reduced the size of the threatrical film industry and its place in American life, and it relegated radio from a prime-time medium to a fringe medium that is mostly consumed in automobiles during the morning and evening commute.

Now, however, television faces a new challenge. In the Digital Era, television will move onto equal footing with the other traditional media. In the old world, television offered moving and talking pictures while newspapers offered print and radio offered audio. This was the equivalent of a Maserati competing with horse-drawn carriages. In the new world, all of these content producers will offer digital bit streams. Since these bits can be arranged in any fashion, the playing field is leveled. All of the traditional media can present their content in new ways: newspapers, radio, and television can present video, audio, text, and data in any way they please.

Furthermore, entirely new content producers are emerging on the Web. These new media firms are experimenting with ways to use the properties inherent in digital technology—interactivity, depth of information, combined use of audio, video, and text—to make content more attractive than the traditional media. While no one yet knows what the recipe for success is, or even whether there is one, many firms are investing in the experiment. Some notable examples are ESPN-Sportszone, a Web site that uses depth and timeliness of sports information to create a virtual community of sports fans; Individual news, a site that selects articles of interest to its subscribers and sends them customized news; and Motley Fool, a site that uses financial news and information and the interactive properties of the Internet to build a virtual community. Any player from the established media can combine these new features of the Digital Era with its existing content and create a new space.

Can television compete against this new array of digital rivals?

The battle between media formats has already been fought, and video has won. Television so dominates society that the other media formats, including the Internet, are relegated to virtual niches. The time spent consuming television dwarfs the time spent consuming other media (see Exhibit 42). And, this "share of mind" is finally getting translated into share of revenues. Despite their falling share of consumer "time spend," daily newspapers held the position of having the largest revenues in the media business because advertisers were slow to change their patterns of spending. In 1993, television finally took over with about $34 billion and has never looked back.

Although the Internet represents one of the fastest-growing categories of media time use, its share of the total time devoted to media is minuscule. While Americans spend between five and ten hours per day with television, they average only a few minutes per day on the Internet. Moreover, in recent years, the advent of the Internet has actually corresponded with an increase in the use of television. According to a Discovery Communications study released on September 21, 1998 that was based on data collected from Nielsen Media Research, television use increased by 1.8 percent from a period in 1996 to a corresponding period in 1997 in households that had Internet access, versus an increase of only 1.3 percent for all households in the sample.

There are several reasons for the endurability of television in the face of the Internet challenge. First and foremost, Internet use is most pronounced among the highest educated and highest income group. This is the group that is most likely to have access to computers and modems and, apparently, the group with the most interest in the content available on the Internet. Fortunately for the television industry, this segment of the population happens to watch the least amount of television.

There is also the novelty factor. Once the excitement of a new medium wears off, people usually decrease their use of a new medium and relegate the medium to a niche and return to television. Radio and theatrical films are media that were once dominant and have now found attractive, although relatively small, niches in which they are free from the onslaught of television. Usage of CD-ROMs, VCRs, and portable CD players spiked among users when they were new and different.

Interestingly, television use actually increases with the introduction of new media. This is the effect of multitasking. Multitasking is the media term for walking and chewing gum at the same time. It describes the phenomenon of the contemporary man who comes home and while cooking dinner goes on-line to get e-mail, watches and records a movie on television, and sneaks in glances of the sports page that he missed on the morning commute.

Just as television use increased despite the introduction of the VCR (people recorded shows that they otherwise would have missed) and video games (parents bought second and third television sets), it will also benefit from the introduction of the Internet. Interactive features might enhance the viewing experience rather than replace it.

Television will be the dominant medium for the vast majority of people during the vast majority of their free time, because it is the easiest to consume, the most vivid, and the most familiar. In the Digital Era, television will retain its dominant place and the new challengers eventually will find a nice niche. In fact, the two media are so totally different that there will not even be a contest. Television is a passive medium. It is the technological descendant of the storyteller. It is popular because there is a basic human need to sit back and be entertained or informed. In contrast, the Internet is an active medium. Think of the actual physical circumstances. One sits back in a sofa and watches television, whereas one sits up in a chair at a desk and uses the Web. To take advantage of what the Internet or its descendants have to offer—be it interaction with other members of a virtual community or designing content in cooperation with providers—one must be engaged. Even with agents selecting content and communities, a certain level of involvement is required: one cannot simply sit and be presented to.

It is difficult to imagine any active medium displacing a passive one like television. Despite the fantastic array of information that will be available in a variety of exciting formats in the Digital Era, people will still spend most of their evenings sitting in their sofas or armchairs and watching television. The reason is that leisure time is just that. Television has already taken the place of such activities as reading and listening to the radio because it is easier and more entertaining. If history is any guide, the pattern will not reverse itself and replace television with something that is more demanding.

But, there are those who disagree. George Gilder has argued that newspapers have an advantage over television in categories such as news.[1] The idea is that newspapers, with their depth of coverage of current events, are much more suited to the Digital Era than television broadcasters, who simply present talking heads with pictures of guns blazing and starving Africans. The advantage of newspapers, the argument goes, is that they can present detail to readers on any subject that the reader is interested in. In the Digital Era, the newspaper publisher can link encyclopedic information to any story. A story on the European Community would have geography, climate, economic, and cultural links for those wishing to pursue the topic further. That may sound interesting for the reader of this book, but no matter how much depth, statistics, pictures, and sound clips a newspaper publisher is able to provide to the user, how many people will give up the pictures and verbal narrative that the television broadcasters provide? It is sad to say that the average American, eating or digesting his dinner, will prefer the pictures to the depth.

However, the Internet will not remain the brainy desktop medium that it is today. For example, Web-based content will gradually grow more appealing. Obviously, Web designers have not yet learned how to use the properties that the digital world provides. Just as the learning curve for television programming lasted several decades, so will the learning process for the Web take time.

Ultimately, the Internet and the television set will converge into a single medium. Personal computers will never reach the ubiquity of televisions, but they will coexist with smarter televisions. Smaller processors will be built into set-top boxes, and later into television sets themselves. This processing power will convert the television into a device capable of accessing all sorts of information. How will the television industry fare in this environment?

Television will thrive in the Digital Era for two reasons: the primacy of video and the durability of brands. However, for television to exploit its core competency in video and the strength of its brands, it must engage in three strategic imperatives. Television players must build their strategies around the development of "super" content, "push-button" commerce, and portals.

Broadcasters and the major cable networks are the only players with the capital and the skills to create "super" content. "Super" content is the content that is capable of drawing mass audiences. It is expensive and risky to produce. Right now mass audiences are attracted to productions of major events, movies, dramas and situation comedies, well-produced news coverage, and strong, personality-based features. In the Digital Era, this content will take advantage of the production qualities that only digital television can offer: crystal-clear, wide-screen pictures and CD-quality sound—but it will be more expensive to produce than ever. Not surprisingly, experimentation with digital production techniques have been limited to date: ABC is focused on converting some of its theatrical films, CBS broadcast four NFL football games in the 1998–1999 season with digital equipment, and NBC is planning to broadcast *The Tonight Show* digitally. If television can develop "super" content, it will take advantage of the viewer's built-in bias toward video and secure a place for itself in the Digital Era.

However, since there will be more to the Digital Era than video alone, the television industry cannot remain complacent with "super" content. It needs to exploit the other secret weapon that digital technology offers: interactivity.

Television viewers may often act like potatoes, but they do not always just lay on the couch. Television, not the Web, can make us cry. Of more interest to advertisers and retailers, it can also make us buy. While television advertising has been used to build brands for advertisers, it has also been used as a direct marketing vehicle to sell products. Marketers have more recently noticed that television advertising can elicit active responses from viewers. When 1-800 numbers are used to sell products being advertised, viewers call in; when retailers purchase half-hour infomercial slots to push their products, viewers respond; when Oprah Winfrey recommends a book, viewers buy it; and when Monica Lewinsky appears on a talk show, viewers telephone in to find out who makes the lipstick that she is wearing.

In the Digital Era, television will be able to build on this strength. Digital set-top boxes will give viewers the chance to interact with television. Interactive functionality can be used to offer viewers the option of instant replays, different camera angles, and player statistics during a football game. However, it can also be used to evolve television from push advertising to "push-button" commerce.

Instead of having to go out the next day and buy Oprah's recommendation, or even having to place an order by telephone, viewers will only have to click on their remote controls. This is "push-button" commerce. It is powerful and it does not require a revolution in viewing habits. It simply enables viewers to more easily do something that they have always been able to do—make an impulse purchase.

Television already has the mass audience that Web sites can only dream of. With digital functionality, television can leverage its audiences and programming into the world of commerce. It can offer advertisers the opportunity to place products in programming, to sell to impulse buyers, and to target advertising to individual households. With this functionality, television can evolve its position as the king of the living room into the gatekeeper of the entertainment highway.

Parallel to the entertainment highway will run the information highway of the Internet. If television is to defend itself against any merger of the two, it must build a presence on the Web. Portal theory may not yet be as robust as necessary to justify massive investment. Nevertheless, television players need to have a position on the Web today to hedge themselves against the emergence of new players.

Television content companies have two key advantages over Web-based portals. Most successful Web brands reach their position only by promoting themselves heavily in the traditional media. Television networks and stations already have huge audiences. With these television audiences as a base, television content companies can foray into the Internet space and take a strong position as a portal or niche portal almost immediately. The second advantage that television content companies have is that they own significant quantities of content. The established portals exist as packagers of content only because they offer a simple way to organize and access the content of others. If users end up spending more time with their favorite content and less time with the aggregator of this content, the portal value proposition will prove flawed, and the owners of content will thrive.

Once television content companies establish a Web presence, they can compete as a portal and, at the same time, prepare themselves to fall back on the strategy of being a more limited site that directs users to their own or related content. In either case, the value of their audiences can be extracted through the sale of advertising, commissions on transactions, or the sale of their own content.

The big three television networks understand this imperative to varying degrees. ABC, NBC, and CBS can be placed on a continuum of decreasing commitment to a significant Internet strategy. ABC and its parent Disney have plans to create a major consumer portal called

Go.com using their ownership of ESPN-Sportszone and recently purchased stakes in Infoseek and Starwave. While NBC has a significant cable presence, it has a lukewarm commitment to becoming a major portal. NBC has ventures with Microsoft and a stake in Snap!, an Internet portal that it acquired rather cheaply and will build as much as possible. CBS has been the most tentative of this group in its cable and Internet efforts. In 1998, the network finally ventured into the virtual world with a sports site, Sportsline.

In addition to these ambitious efforts to develop portals, broadcasters are also putting video on-line in a more mundane, but perhaps more meaningful, attempt to attract Web users to their content. They are all trying to take advantage of the digital properties of the new distribution networks. Viewers must be able to select from more programming options, access archived material, download detailed information about a program's stars or storyline, participate in simultaneous chat groups, and order related products. To this end, the networks have created news sites that contain footage from their news departments. NBC has set up a site on the Web called Videoseeker, which will offer music clips, entertainment news from its syndicated series *Access Hollywood*, and searchable video clips of NBC entertainment programming.

While this is a review of the high-profile activities of the major broadcast networks, all of the players in television, from local stations to major cable networks and operators, are using their position to establish a foothold in cyberspace.

There are those who say that television companies cannot make the leap into the next generation of technology, that firms simply cannot keep up with rapid technological change, that the Internet will do to the television companies what the automobile companies did to the horse carriage makers. Before too easily acceding to this argument, let us be aware of the past. While there are many examples of established players dying as a major technological transition is made, so far in the history of electronic media, the established players have been able to make these transitions. The two largest radio networks, NBC and CBS, were able to make the transition to become television networks. The film producers, although they first feared television, quickly learned that television would be more important as a source of revenue to their companies than the theater would. They are now the dominant television programming producers.

In the end, it may well be smaller, entrepreneurial ventures that lead the way to new television content. Already today there are independent Web sites that outdraw the "official" network sites in offering live chat groups during popular television programs. It will be a challenge for the television networks to make the transition to the Digital Era. But with a strong brand, mass audiences that are predisposed to video, and a digital interactive platform of its own, it certainly is a long shot to bet against television at this stage in the game.

Of course, the real test is still to come. It is still too early to tell how the broadband future will evolve. The technology has not developed to anywhere near its full potential, and consumers and advertisers have not yet learned how to use it. My guess, though, is that if it does grow to displace or transform other media, the victim will not be television, but rather a competing active medium, the embattled newspaper.

NOTE

1. See "Into the Telecosm" series appearing in *Forbes* Magazine.

Selected Bibliography

Adams, Walter, and Joel Dirlam. "Steel Imports and Vertical Oligopoly Power." *American Economic Review* 14 (September 1964): 626–655.

Andrews, Edmund L. "Betting Big on Small-Dish TV." *New York Times*, 15 December 1993, Business section.

Arthur, W. Brian. "Competing Technologies, Increasing Returns, and Lock-in by Historical Events." *Economic Journal* 99, no. 394 (March 1989): 116–131.

Atkin, D., and Barry Litman. "Network TV Programming: Economics, Audiences and the Ratings Game, 1971–1986." *Journal of Communication* 36, no. 3 (1986): 32–50.

Bailey, Joseph, Lee McKnight, and Paul Bosco. *The Economics of Advanced Services in an Open Communications Infrastructure: Transactions Costs, Production Costs, and Network Externalities*. Cambridge, Mass.: MIT Research Program on Communication Policy, 1995.

Baldwin, Thomas F., Connie L. Ono, and Seema Shrikhande. "Program Exclusivity and Competition in the Cable Television Industry." *Journal of Media Economics* (Fall 1991): 29–43.

Balio, Tino, ed. *Hollywood in the Age of Television*. Cambridge, Mass.: Unwin Hyman, 1990.

Bates, Benjamin J. "Determining Television Advertising Rates." In *Communications Yearbook 7*, edited by Robert Bostrom. Beverly Hills, Calif.: Sage Publications, 1983.

Bates, Benjamin, J. "Breaking the Structural Logjam: The Impact of Cable on Local TV Market Concentration." *Journal of Media Economics* (Fall 1991): 47–57.

Bates, Benjamin, J. "Concentration in Local Television Markets." *Journal of Media Economics* (Fall 1993): 3–21.

Baumol, Hilda, and William J. Baumol. "The Mass Media and the Cost Disease." In *The Economics of Cultural Industries*, edited by William S. Hendon, Nancy

K. Grant, and Douglas V. Shaw. Akron, Ohio: Association for Cultural Economics, 1984.

Baumol, William J. *Performing Arts, the Economic Dilemma: A Study of Problems Common to Theatre, Opera, Music and Dance.* New York: 20th Century Fund, 1966.

Baumol, William J., John C. Panzar, and Robert D. Willig. *Contestable Markets and the Theory of Industry Structure.* Rev. ed. New York: Harcourt Brace Jovanovich, 1988.

Baumol, William J., and J. Gregory Sidak. *Toward Competition in Local Telephony.* Cambridge, Mass.: MIT Press, 1994.

Besen, S. M. "The Value of Television Time." *Southern Economic Journal* 42 (1976): 435–441.

Besen, S. M., and P. D. Hanley. "Market Size, VHF Allocations, and the Viability of Television Stations." *Journal of Industrial Economics* 24, no. 1 (1975): 41–54.

Besen, Stanley M. et al. *Misregulating Television: Network Dominance and the F.C.C.* Chicago: University of Chicago Press, 1984.

Bilotti, Richard, Drew Hanson, and Richard J. MacDonald. *The Cable Television Industry: New Technologies, New Opportunities, and New Competition.* Volume 1, *Industry Review and Outlook.* New York: Grantchester Securities and Wasserstein and Perella Securities, 1993.

Blumenthal, Howard J., and Oliver R. Goodenough. *This Business of Television.* New York: Billboard Books, 1991.

Bradburd, Ralph M. "Price-Cost Margins in Producer Goods Industries and 'The Importance of Being Unimportant.' " *Review of Economics and Statistics* 64 (August 1982): 405–412.

Burgi, Michael, and Chuck Ross. "New Cable Nets in Abundance." *Inside Media*, 2 December 1994.

Cabletelevision Advertising Bureau. *1995 Cable TV Facts.* New York: Cabletelevision Advertising Bureau, 1995.

Calhoun, George. *Wireless Access and the Local Telephone Network.* Norwood, Mass.: Artech House, 1992.

Carey, John. "The Market for New Residential Services." In *Integrated Broadband Networks*, edited by Martin C. J. Elton. Amsterdam: Elsevier, 1991.

Carter, Bill. "With Ratings Slipping, CBS Reaches for Youth." *New York Times*, 10 January 1995, Business section.

Carter, Bill. "The Media Business: Television." *New York Times*, 11 April 1995, Business section.

Carter, Bill. "Cable Plans to Pounce in Networks' Off-Season." *New York Times*, 26 June 1995, Business section.

Carter, Bill. "Not a Laugh Riot: Comedy Writers in Short Supply." *New York Times*, 17 July 1995, Business section.

Carter, Bill. "News Is a Hit on TV's Bottom Line." *New York Times*, 13 September 1995, Business section.

Carter, Bill. "Nostalgia Gets a 2d Chance, Via Cable." *New York Times*, 30 October 1995, Business section.

Carter, Bill. "Westinghouse Visits TV Land: Can It Put Juice into a Lemon?" *New York Times*, 30 October 1995, Business section.

Carter, Bill. "CBS, Under Its New Owner, Plans a Series with Cosby." *New York Times*, 1 December 1995, Business section.

Caves, Richard. *American Industry: Structure, Conduct, Performance*. 6th ed. Englewood Cliffs, N.J.: Prentice-Hall Foundations of Modern Economics Series, 1987.

Chan-Olmsted, Sylvia M. "A Structural Analysis of Market Competition in the U.S. TV Syndication Industry, 1981–1990." *Journal of Media Economics* (Fall 1991): 9–27.

Coase, Ronald H. "The Nature of the Firm." *Economica* 4 (1937): 386.

Coe, Steve. "Warner Brothers Fifth Network." *Broadcasting and Cable*, 4 April 1994, 6.

Coen, Robert J. "Estimated Annual U.S. Advertising Expenditures." Prepared for *Advertising Age*, New York, 1994.

Collins, Richard, Nicholas Garnham, and Gareth Locksley. *The Economics of Television: The UK Case*. London: Sage Publications, 1988.

Communications Satellite Corporation. *1984 Sec Form 10-K*, 1985.

Compaine, Benjamin M. *Anatomy of the Communications Industry: Who Owns the Media?* White Plains, N.Y.: Knowledge Industry Publications, 1982.

Compaine, Benjamin M. *Understanding New Media*. White Plains, N.Y.: Knowledge Industry Publications, 1985.

Competitive Media Reporting. *Advertising Age*, 8 November 1993, p. 26.

Competitive Media Reporting. *Advertising Age*, 13 April 1994, p. 54.

Conant, Michael. *Antitrust in the Motion Picture Industry*. Berkeley: University of California Press, 1960.

Coy, Peter. "Get Ready for the TV Station on Your Desk." *Business Week*, 6 November 1995, p. 149.

Crandall, Robert W. "The Post-War Performance of the Motion Picture Industry." *Anti-Trust Bulletin* 20 (Spring 1975): 49–88.

Crandall, R. W. "Economic Analysis of Market Structure in the Cable Television Business." Appended to TCI Reply Comments in FCC Mass Media Docket 89–600, 1990.

Crandall, R. W. "Elasticity of Demand for Cable Service and the Effect of Broadcast Signals on Cable Prices." Appended to TCI Reply Comments in FCC Mass Media Docket 90–162, 1990.

Darmon, R. Y. "Determinants of TV Viewing." *Journal of Advertising Research* 16 (1976): 17–20.

David, Paul. *Path-Dependence: Putting the Past into the Future of Economics*. I.M.S.S.S. Tech Report No. 553. Palo Alto, Calif.: Stanford University, 1988.

De Jong, Allard Sicco, and Benjamin J. Bates. "Channel Diversity in Cable Television." *Journal of Broadcasting and Electronic Media* 35, no. 2 (1991): 159–166.

Dertouzos, James N., and Steven S. Wildman. "Competitive Effects of Broadcast Signals on Cable." Paper prepared for the National Cable Television Association, 22 February 1990.

Dimmick, J., Patterson, S., and Albarran, A. "Competition between the Cable and Broadcast Industries: A Niche Analysis." *Journal of Media Economics* 5, no. 1 (1992): 13–30.

Draper, Roger. "The Faithless Shepherd." *New York Review of Books*, 26 June 1986, pp. 14–18.

Dunnett, Peter. *The World Television Industry*. New York: Routledge, 1990.

Economists, Inc. *Competitive Policy Considerations in Cable Television Franchising*. Denver: Economists, Inc., 1992.

Eechambadi, Naras V. "Does Advertising Work?" *McKinsey Quarterly* 3 (1994): 117–129.

Egan, Bruce L. *Information Superhighways Revisited*. Boston: Artech House, 1997.

Elliot, Stuart. "Advertising." *New York Times*, 9 June 1995, Business section.

Euromonitor. *Euromonitor, European Marketing Data and Statistics 1996, 31st Edition*. London: Euromonitor, 1996.

Euromonitor. *International Marketing Data and Statistics 1996, 20th Edition*. London: Euromonitor, 1996.

Fabrikant, Geraldine. "Blockbuster Seeks to Flex Its Muscles Abroad." *New York Times*, 24 October 1995, Business section.

Ferguson, Douglas A. "Channel Repertoire in the Presence of Remote Control Devices, VCRs and Cable Television." *Journal of Broadcasting and Electronic Media* 36 (Winter 1992): 83–91.

Ferguson, Douglas A. "Measurement of Mundane TV Behaviors: Remote Control Device Flipping Frequency." *Journal of Broadcasting and Electronic Media* 38 (Winter 1994): 35–47.

Ferguson, Douglas A., and Elizabeth M. Perse. "Media and Audience Influences on Channel Repertoire." *Journal of Broadcasting and Electronic Media* 37 (Winter 1993): 31–47.

Foisie, Geoffrey. "CBS Edges Out NBC in TV Network Revenue." *Broadcasting and Cable*, 10 May 1993.

Foisie, Geoffrey. "ABC, CBS Tie for TV Network 1993 Revenue Honors." *Broadcasting and Cable*, 16 May 1994.

Fournier, Gary M. "The Determination of Economic Rents in Television Broadcasting." *Antitrust Bulletin* 31 (1986): 1045–1066.

Fournier, Gary M., and D. L. Martin. "Does Government Restricted Entry Produce Market Power? New Evidence from the Market for Television Advertising." *Bell Journal of Economics* 14 (1983): 44–56.

Fratrik, Mark R., and Ottina, Theresa J. *1994 Television Financial Report*. Washington, D.C.: National Association of Broadcasters, 1994.

French, W. A., and McBrayer, J. T. "Arriving at Television Advertising Rates." *Journal of Advertising* 8 (1979): 15–18.

Gantz, W. "How Uses and Gratifications Affects Recall of Television News." *Journalism Quarterly* 55 (1978): 664–672, 681.

Gilder, George. *Life after Television*. New York: W. W. Norton and Co., 1992.

Goodhardt, G. J., Ehrenberg, A. S. C., and Collins, M. A. *The Television Audience: Patterns of Viewing*. Westmead, England: D. C. Heath, 1975.

Graham, Ellen. "Changing Channels." *Wall Street Journal*, 9 September 1994.

Graham, Jefferson. "The Market for Films." *Hollywood Reporter*, 14 February 1983.

Grant, August E. "The Promise Fulfilled? An Empirical Analysis of Program Diversity on Television." *Journal of Media Economics* 7, no. 1 (1994): 51–64.

Haldi, J. A., and Eastman, S. T. "Affiliated Station Programming." In *Broadcast/*

Cable Programming, edited by S. T. Eastman. Belmont, Calif.: Wadsworth, 1992.

Hanania, Joseph. "Media." *New York Times*, 18 December 1995, Business section.

Harris, Kathryn. "Endangered Species." *Forbes*, 3 February 1992, p. 43.

Hazlett, Thomas W. "Three Essays on Monopoly." Ph.D. dissertation. University of California, Los Angeles, 1984.

Hazlett, Thomas W. "Duopolistic Competition in Cable Television: Implications for Public Policy." *Yale Journal on Regulation* 65 (1990): 7–34.

Hazlett, Thomas W., and Matthew L. Spitzer. "Public Policy toward Cable Television. Volume 1: The Economics of Rate Controls." Working paper for the Program on Telecommunications Policy, Institute of Governmental Affairs, University of California, Davis, 1996.

Heeter, C. "Program Selection with Abundance of Choice: A Process Model." *Human Communications Research* 12, no. 1 (1985): 126–152.

Heeter, C., and B. S. Greenberg. "Profiling the Zappers." *Journal of Advertising Research* 25, no. 2 (1985): 15–19.

Heeter, C., and Greenberg, B. S. *Cableviewing*. Norwood, N.J.: Ablex Publishing Company, 1988.

Heflebower, Richard B. "Toward a Theory of Industrial Markets and Prices." *American Economic Review* 44 (May 1954): 128–129.

Henry, M. D., and H. J. Rinne. "Predicting Program Shares in New Time Slots." *Journal of Advertising Research* 24, no. 2 (1984): 9–17.

Holton, Richard H. "The Distinctions between Convenience Goods, Shopping Goods, and Specialty Goods." *Journal of Marketing* 23 (July 1958): 53–56.

Hoskins, C., and R. Mirus. "Reasons for the U.S. Dominance of the International Trade in Television Programs." *Media, Culture, and Society* 10 (1988): 499–515.

Hull, B. B. "An Economics Perspective Ten Years after the NAB Case." *Journal of Media Economics* 3, no. 1 (1990): 19–36.

Internal Revenue Service. *Statistics of Income, 1991: Corporation Income Tax Returns*. Publication 16. Washington, D.C., 1994.

Ipsen, Erik. "Race to Cable Britain Getting Nowhere Fast." *International Herald Tribune*, 12 February 1997.

Jacoby, Jacob, and Wayne D. Hoyer. "Viewer Miscomprehension of Televised Communication: Selected Findings." *Journal of Marketing* 46, no. 4 (1982): 12–26.

Jeffres, L. W. "Cable TV and Viewer Selectivity." *Journal of Broadcasting* 22 (1978): 167–177.

Jensen, Elizabeth. "World's Fare." *Wall Street Journal*, 9 September 1994.

Jensen, Elizabeth. " 'What's Up, Doc?' Vertical Integration." *Wall Street Journal*, 16 October 1995.

Jensen, Elizabeth. "Capital Cities/ABC and Henson Form Family TV Venture." *Wall Street Journal*, 27 November 1995.

Johnson, Leland L. *Toward Competition in Cable Television*. Cambridge, Mass.: MIT Press, 1994.

Johnson, Leland L., and David P. Reed. *Residential Broadband Services by Telephone Companies*. Santa Monica, Calif.: Rand, 1990.

Johnson, Leland L., and Deborah R. Castleman. *Direct Broadcast Satellites: A Competitive Alternative to Cable Television?* Santa Monica, Calif.: Rand, 1991.

Jowett, Garth, and Linton, James M. *Movies as Mass Communication.* 2nd ed. Newbury Park, Calif.: Sage Publications, 1989.

Kahn, Alfred. *The Economics of Regulation,* vol. 2. New York: Wiley, 1971.

Kaldor, N. "The Economics of Advertising." *Review of Economic Studies* (June 1950): 87.

Kapadia, Reshma. "Carriers Wade Slowly into Video Waters." *Telephony,* 27 November 1995.

Kelley, W. J. "How Television Stations Price Their Service." *Journal of Broadcasting* 11 (1967): 313–323.

Klein, Benjamin. "The Competitive Consequences of Vertical Integration in the Cable Industry." Paper prepared for the National Cable Television Association, University of California, Los Angeles, 1989.

King, Thomas. "Zap!" *Wall Street Journal,* 9 September 1994.

King, Thomas. "Entertainment and Technology: What's Intertainment?" *Wall Street Journal,* 15 September 1995.

Koselka, Rita. "Mergermania in Medialand." *Forbes,* 23 October 1995.

Koutsoyiannis, A. *Non-price Decisions.* London: Macmillan, 1982.

Lacy, Stephen, Tony Atwater, and Xinmin Qin. "Competition and the Allocation of Resources for Local Television News." *Journal of Media Economics* 2 (Spring 1989): 3–13.

LaFrance, Vincent A. "The Impact of Buyer Concentration: An Extension." *Review of Economics and Statistics* 61 (August 1979): 475–476.

Landler, Mark, and Ronald Grover. "Media Mania." *Business Week,* 12 July 1993, pp. 110–119.

Landler, Mark. "In a Video Rush, Phone Groups Aren't Waiting for Fiber Optics." *New York Times,* 18 April 1995, Business section.

Landler, Mark. "The Dishes Are Coming: Satellites Go Suburban." *New York Times,* 29 May 1995, Business section.

Landro, Laura. "Rising Star." *Wall Street Journal,* 9 September 1994.

Lazarus, William, and Lee McKnight. *The Design and Forecasting of the New Media.* Cambridge, Mass.: The Future of the Mass Audience Project, MIT, 1984.

Lesly, Elisabeth. "A Power Jolt for Station Owners." *Business Week,* 13 June 1994, p. 36.

Levin, Stanford L., and John B. Meisel. "Cable Television and Competition: Theory, Evidence and Policy." *Telecommunications Policy* (December 1991): 519–528.

Lewis, Peter H. "Technology." *New York Times,* 30 October 1995, Business section.

Liebenstein, Harvey. "Allocative Efficiency v. 'X-Efficiency.' " *American Economic Review* 56 (June 1966): 392–415.

Lin, Carolyn A., "Changing Network-Affiliate Relations amidst a Competitive Video Marketplace." *Journal of Media Economics* 7, no. 1 (1994): 1–12.

Litman, Barry R. *The Vertical Structure of the Television Broadcasting Industry: The Coalescence of Power.* East Lansing, Mich.: MSU Business Studies, 1979.

Litman, Barry R. "The Television Networks, Competition and Program Diversity." *Journal of Broadcasting* 23 (Fall 1979): 393–409.

Litman, Barry R., and Jan LeBlanc Wicks. "The Changing Advertising Market for the U.S. Television Networks." Pp. RC 27–33 in *The Proceedings of the 1988 Conference of the American Academy of Advertising*, edited by J. D. Leckenby. Austin, Tex.: University of Texas, 1988.

Lochte, R. H., and Warren, J. "A Channel Repertoire for TVRO Satellite Viewers." *Journal of Broadcasting and Electronic Media* 33 (1989): 91–95.

Lustgarten, Steven H. "The Impact of Buyer Concentration in Manufacturing Industries." *Review of Economics and Statistics* 57 (May 1975): 125–132.

Machlup, Fritz, and M. Taber. "Bilateral Monopoly, Successive Monopoly, and Vertical Integration." *Economica* 27 (1960): 101–123.

Mair, George. *Inside HBO: The Billion Dollar War between HBO, Hollywood, and the Home Video Revolution*. New York: Macmillan, 1988.

Markoff, John. "Discovery of Internet Flaws Is Setback for On-Line Trade." *New York Times*, 11 November 1995, Business section.

Martin, Stephen. "Vertical Relationships and Industrial Performance." *Quarterly Review of Economics and Business* 23 (Spring 1983): 6–18.

Mason, Edward S. "Price and Production Policies of Large-Scale Enterprise." *American Economic Review* 29 (March 1939): 61–74.

Mason, Edward S. "The Current State of the Monopoly Problem in the United States." *Harvard Law Review* 62 (June 1949): 1265–1285.

McClellan, Steve. "ABC Takes Top Network Profit Honors." *Broadcasting and Cable*, 3 April 1995.

McFayden, S., C. Hoskins, and D. Gillen. *Canadian Broadcasting: Market Structure and Economic Performance*. Montreal: Institute for Research on Public Policy, 1980.

Mifflin, Lawrie. "Cable TV Continues Its Steady Drain of Network Viewers." *New York Times*, 25 October 1995, Business section.

Mifflin, Lawrie. "Possible Shift on Discounting of Cable Rates." *New York Times*, 14 December 1995, Business section.

Mitchell, Kim, and Rod Granger. "Operators Call New Contracts Obscene." *Multichannel News*, 29 March 1993, p. 1.

Mord, M. S., and E. Gilson. "Shorter Units: Risk-Responsibility-Reward." *Journal of Advertising Research* 25 (1985): 9–19.

National Cable Television Association (NCTA). *How to Apply for or Renew Your NCTA Seal of Good Customer Service*. Washington, D.C.: NCTA, 1991.

National Cable Television Association. *Cable Television Developments*. Washington, D.C.: NCTA, 1997.

National Telecommunications Information Administration. *Video Program Distribution and Cable Television: Current Policy Issues and Recommendations*. NTIA Report No. 83–233. Washington, D.C.: NTIA, 1988.

Negroponte, Nicholas. *Being Digital*. New York: Vintage Books, 1995.

Neuman, W. Russell. *The Future of the Mass Audience*. Cambridge: Cambridge University Press, 1991.

Nielsen, A. C. "The Outlook for Electronic Media." *Journal of Advertising Research* 22, no. 6 (1982): 9–16.

Niman, Neil B., and Manley R. Irwin. "Computers." In *The Structure of American Industry*, 9th ed., edited by Walter Adams and James Brock. Englewood Cliffs, N.J.: Prentice-Hall, 1995.

Noam, Eli M. "Economies of Scale in Cable Television: A Multiproduct Analysis."

In *Video Media Competition: Regulation, Economics, and Technology*, edited by Eli M. Noam. New York: Columbia University Press, 1985.

Noll, R. G., M. J. Peck, and J. J. McGowan. *Economic Aspects of Television Regulation*. Washington, D.C.: Brookings Institution, 1973.

Owen, B. M., J. H. Beebe, and W. G. Manning, Jr. *Television Economics*. Lexington, Mass.: Lexington Books, D. C. Heath, 1974.

Owen, Bruce M., and Peter R. Greenhalgh. "Competitive Considerations in Cable Television Franchising." *Contemporary Policy Issues* 4 (1986): 69–79.

Owen, Bruce M., and Steven S. Wildman. *Video Economics*. Cambridge, Mass.: Harvard University Press, 1992.

Park, Rolla Edward. *New Television Networks: An Update*. Santa Monica, Calif.: Rand, 1980.

Paskowski, Marianne, and Richard Katz. "New Networks Square Off." *Multichannel News*, 20 November 1995.

Paul Kagan Associates. *Kagan Media Index*. Carmel, Calif.: Paul Kagan Associates, 30 March 1993, p. 10.

Paul Kagan Associates. *Cable TV Programming*. Carmel, Calif.: Paul Kagan Associates, 31 March 1994, p. 1.

Paul Kagan Associates. *Cable TV Programming*. Carmel, Calif.: Paul Kagan Associates, 23 May 1994, p. 2.

Paul Kagan Associates. *Marketing New Media*. Carmel, Calif.: Paul Kagan Associates, 20 June 1994, p. 4.

Paul Kagan Associates. *Cable TV Programming*. Carmel, Calif.: Paul Kagan Associates, 23 June 1994, p. 1.

Paul Kagan Associates. *Marketing New Media*. Carmel, Calif.: Paul Kagan Associates, 15 August 1994.

Paul Kagan Associates. *Cable & Pay TV Census*. Carmel, Calif.: Paul Kagan Associates, 22 August 1994.

Peterman, J. L. "Differences between the Levels of Spot and Network Television Advertising Rates." Working Paper No. 22. Federal Trade Commission, Bureau of Economics, Washington, D.C., 1979.

Picard, Robert G. *Media Economics: Concepts and Issues*. Newbury Park, Calif.: Sage Publications, 1989.

Poltrack, David. *Television Marketing*. New York: McGraw-Hill, 1983.

Pool, Ithiel de Sola. *Technologies of Freedom*. Cambridge, Mass.: Belknap Press of Harvard University Press, 1983.

Porter, Michael E. *Interbrand Choice, Strategy, and Bilateral Market Power*. Cambridge, Mass.: Harvard University Press, 1976.

Porter, Michael E. *Competitive Strategy*. New York: Free Press, 1980.

Porter, Michael E. *Competitive Advantage: Creating and Sustaining Superior Performance*. New York: Free Press, 1985.

Powers, Angela. "Competition, Conduct, and Ratings in Local Television News: Applying the Industrial Organization Model." *Journal of Media Economics* (Summer 1993): 39–44.

Prag, Jay, and James Casavant. "An Empirical Study of the Determinants of Revenues and Marketing Expenditures in the Motion Picture Industry." *Journal of Cultural Economics* 18, no. 3 (1994): 217–235.

Pruvot, M. J. "On the Promotion of Film Making in the Community." Working

Document 1–504/83. Report to the European Parliament on Behalf of the Committee on Youth, Culture, Education, Information, and Sport, 15 July 1983.

Rao, V. R. "Taxonomy of Television Programs Based on Viewing Behavior." *Journal of Marketing Research* 12 (1975): 355–358.

Reed, David P. *Residential Fiber Optic Networks: An Engineering and Economic Analysis*. Boston, Mass.: Artech House, 1992.

Rees, Albert. *The Economics of Work and Pay*. New York: Harper and Row, 1979.

Renaud, J. L., and Barry Litman. "Changing Dynamics of the Overseas Market Place for Television Programming." *Telecommunications Policy* 9 (1985): 245–261.

Robert Morris Associates. *Annual Statement Studies 1995*. Philadelphia: Robert Morris Associates, Inc., 1995.

Rosen, Sherwin. "The Economics of Superstars." *American Economic Review* 71 (December 1981): 845–858.

Rosenthal, Sharon. "Movies on TV." *TV Guide*, 3 March 1984, pp. 29–36.

Rubin, A. M. "Television Uses and Gratifications: The Interactions of Viewing Patterns and Motivations." *Journal of Broadcasting* 27 (1983): 37–51.

Rubin, A. M. "Ritualized and Instrumental Television Viewing." *Journal of Communication* 34, no. 3 (1984): 67–77.

Samuelson, P. A. "The Pure Theory of Public Expenditure." *Review of Economics and Statistics* 36 (1954): 387.

Scherer, F. M. "The Welfare Economics of Product Variety: An Application to the Ready-to-Eat Cereals Industry." *Journal of Industrial Economics* 28 (December 1979): 113–134.

Schiller, H. I. *Mass Communications and American Empire*. New York: A. M. Kelley, 1969.

Schofield, Lemuel B., and Paul D. Driscoll. "Effects of Television Network Affiliation Changes: A Miami Case Study." *Journal of Broadcasting and Electronic Media* 35 (Summer 1991): 367–374.

Schwartz, Evan I. *Webonomics*. New York: Penguin, 1997.

Shagrin, C. "On the Trail of the Elusive 90's Viewer." *Nielsen Newscast* (Spring 1990): 2–3.

Shepard, William G. *The Economics of Industrial Organization*. Englewood Cliffs, N.J.: Prentice-Hall, 1979.

Showtime Networks, Multichannel Service Operator Tech Survey. Showtime, January 1994.

Smith, R. *The Wired Nation*. New York: Harper and Row, 1972.

Spengler, Joseph J. "Vertical Integration and Anti-trust Policy." *Journal of Political Economy* 58 (1950): 347.

"Stations Prepare for 500-Channel Future; Advertisers Syndicated Television Association." *Mediaweek*, 7 June 1993, p. 23.

Steiner, Peter O. "Program Patterns and Preferences and the Workability of Competition in Radio Broadcasting." *Quarterly Journal of Economics* 66 (1952): 194.

Sterling, Christopher H., and Timothy R. Haight. *The Mass Media: Aspen Institute Guide to Communication Industry Trends*. New York: Praeger, 1978.

Stigler, George. *The Organization of Industry*. Chicago: University of Chicago Press, 1983.

Stump, Matt. "TCI Pulls NBC's String on Exclusivity." *Broadcasting*, 25 June 1990, p. 21.

SVP. *Interactive Consumers: Insights into Demand for Digital Content, Products, and Services*. New York: SVP, 1994.

Television and Cable Factbook, No. 61. New York: Warren Publishing, Inc., 1993.

Thomas, Laurie, and Barry R. Litman. "Fox Broadcasting Company: Why Now? An Economic Study of the Rise of the Fourth Broadcast 'Network.' " *Journal of Broadcasting and Electronic Media* 35 (Spring 1991): 139–157.

Thorpe, Kenneth. "The Impact of Competing Technologies on Cable Television." In *Video Media Competition: Regulation, Economics, and Technology*, edited by Eli M. Noam. New York: Columbia University Press, 1985.

Times Mirror. *The Role of Technology in American Life: Technology in the American Household*. Washington, D.C.: Times Mirror Center for the People and the Press, 1994.

Touche Ross. *Financial and Economic Analysis of the Cable Television Permit Policy of the City and County of Denver*. Portland, Ore.: Touche Ross, 1984.

"TV Buying and Planning." *Competitive Media Planning*, 13 June 1994, p. 30.

U.S. Bureau of the Census. "Current Business Reports, BC/92." *Annual Survey of Communications Services: 1992*. Washington, D.C.: U.S. Government Printing Office, 1994.

U.S. Bureau of the Census. *Statistical Abstract of the United States: 1994*. 114th edition. Washington, D.C.: U.S. Government Printing Office, 1994.

U.S. Bureau of Economic Analysis. *Survey of Current Business*. Washington, D.C.: U.S. Government Printing Office, August 1993.

U.S. Bureau of Economic Analysis. *National Income and Product Accounts, volume 2, 1959–1988*. Washington, D.C.: U.S. Government Printing Office, 1994.

U.S. Federal Communications Commission, Network Inquiry Special Staff. *The Market for Television Advertising*. Preliminary Report. Washington, D.C.: U.S. Government Printing Office, 1980.

U.S. Federal Communications Commission. *New Television Networks: Entry, Jurisdiction, Ownership, and Regulation*. 2 vols. Washington, D.C.: U.S. Government Printing Office, 1980.

U.S. Federal Communications Commission. *Competition, Rate Deregulation and the Commission's Policies Relating to the Provision of Cable Television Service*. Report, MM Dkt. No. 89–600, FCC Doc. No. 90–276, 67 Rad. Reg. 2d (P&F) 1771 ¶ 128. Washington, D.C.: U.S. Government Printing Office, 1990.

U.S. Federal Communications Commission. *First Report in the Matter of Implementation of Section 19 of the Cable Television Consumer Protection and Competition Act of 1992: Annual Assessment of the Status of Competition in the Market for the Delivery of Video Programming*. CS Docket No. 94–48. Washington, D.C.: U.S. Government Printing Office, 1994.

Varis, Tapio. *International Flow of Television Programmes*. Paris: UNESCO, 1985.

Veronis, Suhler, and Associates. *Communications Industry Report*. New York: Veronis, Suhler, and Associates, Inc., 1998.

"Video on the Internet: Webbed." *The Economist*, 20 January 1996, pp. 82–83.

Vogel, Harold L. *Entertainment Industry Economics*. 3rd ed. Cambridge: Cambridge University Press, 1994.

Wakshlag, J. J., D. E. Agostino, H. A. Terry, P. D. Driscoll, and B. Ramsey. "Television News Viewing and Network Affiliation Changes." *Journal of Broadcasting* 27 (1983): 53–68.

Wasko, Janet. *Movies and Money: Financing the American Film Industry*. Norwood, N.J.: Ablex Publishing, 1982.

Waterman, David H. "The Structural Development of the Motion Picture Industry." *American Economist* (Spring 1982): 16–27.

Waterman, David H. "World Television Trade: The Economic Effects of Privatization and New Technology." *Telecommunications Policy* 141 (June 1988).

Waterman, David H. "A New Look at Media Chains and Groups: 1977–1989." *Journal of Broadcasting and Electronic Media* 35 (Spring 1991): 167–178.

Waterman, David H., and Andrew A. Weiss. "Vertical Integration in Cable Television." Paper prepared for the American Enterprise Institute for Public Policy Research, Washington, D.C., 17 September 1993.

Waterman, David H., and August Grant. *Narrowcasting on Cable Television: An Empirical Assessment*. Unpublished manuscript, 1989.

Webb, J. K. *The Economics of Cable Television*. Lexington, Mass.: Lexington Books, 1983.

Webb, P. H., and M. L. Ray. "Effects of TV Clutter." *Journal of Advertising Research* 19 (1979): 7–12.

Webbink, D. W. "Regulation, Profits, and Entry in the Television Broadcasting Industry." *Journal of Industrial Economics* 21 (1973): 167–176.

Webster, J., and J. Wakshlag. "A Theory of Program Choice." *Communication Research* 10 (1983): 430–446.

Weinraub, Bernard. " 'Gump,' a Huge Hit, Still Isn't Raking in the Profits? Hmm." *New York Times*, 25 May 1995, Leisure section.

Weller, Timothy, and Seema Hingorani. *Information Superhighway: Putting the Pieces Together*. New York: Donaldson, Lufkin, and Jenrette, 1994.

Wetli, Patty. "Getting There with Wireless Cable." *America's Network*, 15 July 1995.

White, Lawrence J. "Antitrust and Video Markets: The Merger of Showtime and The Movie Channel." In *Video Media Competition: Regulation, Economics, and Technology*, edited by Eli M. Noam. New York: Columbia University Press, 1985.

Wicks, Jan LeBlanc. "Varying Commercialization and Clutter Levels to Enhance Television Airtime Attractiveness in Early Fringe." *Journal of Media Economics* (Summer 1991): 3–18.

Wildman, Steven, and Siwak, Steven E. "The Privatization of European Television: Effects on International Markets for Programs." *Columbia Journal of World Business* 22 (1987): 71–76.

Williamson, Oliver E. "The Vertical Integration of Production: Market Failure Considerations." *American Economic Review* 61 (1971): 112.

Williamson, Oliver E. *Markets and Hierarchies, Analysis and Antitrust Implications: A Study in the Economics of Internal Organisation*. New York: Free Press, 1975.

Williamson, Oliver E. "Transaction Cost Economics: Their Governance of Contractual Relations." *Journal of Law and Economics* 22 (1979): 223.

Wirth, Michael O. "Cable's Economic Impact on Over-the-Air Broadcasting." *Journal of Media Economics* (Fall 1990): 39–53.

Wirth, Michael O., and Harry Bloch. "The Broadcasters: The Future Role of Local Stations and the Three Networks." In *Video Media Competition: Regulation, Economics, and Technology*, edited by Eli M. Noam. New York: Columbia University Press, 1985.

Wirth, Michael O., and James A. Wollert. "The Effects of Market Structure on Television News Pricing." *Journal of Broadcasting* 28 (Spring 1984): 215–224.

Wolzein, Tom, and John Penney. "Vertical Integration of Media Companies Essential in the Late 1990's." Report for Bernstein Research, New York, 1995.

Woodbury, John R., Stanley M. Besen, and Gary M. Fournier. "The Determinants of Network Television Program Prices: Implicit Contracts, Regulation, and Bargaining Power."*Bell Journal of Economics* 14 (1983): 351–365.

Youn, Sug-Min. "Program Type Preference and Program Choice in a Multichannel Situation." *Journal of Broadcasting and Electronic Media* 38 (Fall 1994): 465–475.

Index

About the Author

TIMOTHY M. TODREAS is an independent consultant to the television industry and to the media industry in general. He has worked with media giants and entrepreneurial start-ups in an effort to capture shareholder value in the Digital Era. Dr. Todreas has also seen the industry from the perspective of a regulator, as Senator John F. Kerry's legislative assistant.